ODD BOY OUT

A MEMOIR

PAUL ASHFORD HARRIS

First published in 2018 by Ventura Press
PO Box 780, Edgecliff NSW 2027 Australia
www.venturapress.com.au

10 9 8 7 6 5 4 3 2 1

Copyright © Paul Ashford Harris 2018

All rights reserved. No part of this book may be reproduced or transmitted in any form or by any means, electronic or mechanical, including photocopying, recording or by any other information storage retrieval system, without prior permission in writing from the publisher.

National Library of Australia Cataloguing-in-Publication entry:
Harris, Paul Ashford, author.
Odd Boy Out / Paul Ashford Harris.
ISBN: 9781925384284 (paperback)
ISBN: 9781925384307 (ebook)

Biography.
Australian and New Zealand history.

Cover and internal design: Kate vandeStadt
Cover illustration: Lady Harris (Frieda), 'The Hierophant', Thoth Tarot deck. Used with permission from Ordo Templi Orientis and the Warburg Institute.

The paper in this book is FSC® certified. FSC® promotes environmentally responsible, socially beneficial and economically viable management of the world's forests.

Dedicated to my children Mark, Sophie, Nicholas and Sam, and my eleven (for now) grandchildren and with especial thanks to my wife Gail for her forbearance.

Acknowledgements

Thanks to my endlessly patient editor Catherine McCredie and all the staff at Ventura Press for bearing with me.

Thanks also to photographers Glenn Thomas and Jack Penman.

CONTENTS

Family tree *ix*

1 The fire   *1*

2 Breaking the news   *7*

3 Jack   *15*

4 Jack in New Zealand   *25*

5 Waikanae: early days   *45*

6 Te Rama   *53*

7 Modern Waikanae   *61*

8 The neighbours   *77*

9 School   *85*

10 Maggie   *101*

11 Christopher   *109*

12 Cambridge   *115*

13 The US of A   *121*

14 Wolf   *133*

15 The Nathans   *141*

16 Bing Harris   *151*

17 Sir Percy   *163*

18 The Bloxams   *187*

19 Frieda   *191*

20 Crowley   *201*

21 Crowley's tarot (as explained by 'lightofisis')   *211*

22 Maggie and Matthew   *227*

23 The aftermath   *235*

24 The end   *243*

Appendix   *249*

Bibliography   *286*

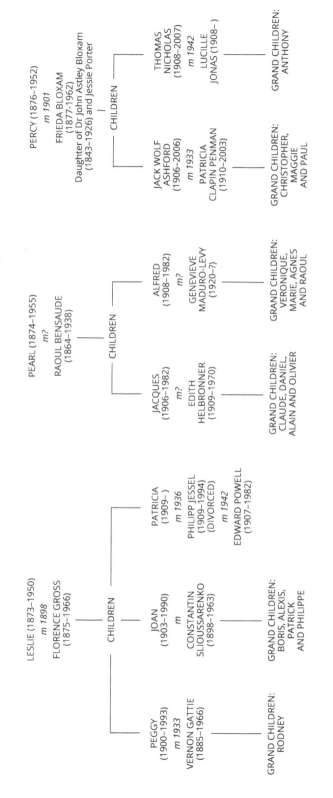

The fan given by Emily Pankhurst, leader of the British suffragette movement, to my grandmother Frieda

1

THE FIRE

Late one July evening in 1996 – the tenth, the newspaper clippings now remind me, I was opening the back door to our Sydney house, sweating from a just completed squash match, when my wife Gail called to me.

'Quickly! Joan is on the phone, from New Zealand. Te Rama's on fire.' She passed me the phone.

'Te Rama's burning. Te Rama's burning.' Joan was crying and out of breath.

Joan and her husband Brian lived in the cottage next to my parents and looked after the homestead known as Te Rama and the spacious gardens that surrounded the house.

She calmed down enough so I could establish this was no minor blaze soon extinguished. From one end of the house to the other the flames were roaring into the night sky, feeding on the century-old timbers and the bone-dry flax that had been packed between the walls for insulation.

Joan left me holding the phone and rushed off to see what she could do; not much, I sensed. I put down the phone and stood for a moment in shock.

My wife tried to console me. After all, the family was dispersed, my parents in Australia and Singapore and my brother and sister elsewhere in New Zealand. But the realisation was dawning on me; everything that meant anything to the history of the family, the story of our lives, was crammed into that house standing alone in the middle of forty acres, just over the river from the tiny town of Waikanae. It was as if someone in the family had died.

It was hard to order my thoughts. What had I not asked? How would I tell my parents? They had invested their lives in the house and it held all their precious treasures. What about the pets who were family? Had the Great Dane and the pug escaped? The cats would be safe – cats are survivors – but Papeeto the cockatiel would most certainly be gone. Locked in his cage in the kitchen there would have been no escape.

After a night pretending to be asleep I was up at 5.30 am (7.30 am New Zealand time) and called Joan.

As I had imagined, the 93-year-old timber homestead had been ablaze from end to end; the house had been exterminated. Even the towering redwood, at fifty metres from the cottage, was badly singed. Joan was confronting nothing but a smouldering heap of ashes and blackened timbers. Only the remains of the brick chimney and some charred walls stood over the wreckage.

The local fire brigade had rattled up the bush-flanked gravel driveway but their efforts to put out the fire were frustrated when water from the pool and reservoir ran out. One firefighter fell through the staircase. A rescue helicopter was called, and a beacon was placed in the main paddock to help the pilot land between the tall surrounding trees. At least the firefighter was rescued.

I quickly realised I must give up any idea that anything would have survived. I knew every inch of that house and it also came to me that there probably had never existed a structure so flammable.

I rang my sister Maggie, six years older and living in Waikanae, where she ran the local riding school. She was distressed but emitted a sort of horsey practicality. Next, I rang my brother Christopher, ten years my senior, in Wellington. He hated the house and my parents anyway and was mostly concerned that I should find out if they had bothered with boring stuff like insurance. He reminded me of just what the house contained.

After putting the phone down, I took stock from memory as best I could. There were my grandmother Frieda's Thoth Tarot card paintings, at least a dozen, the main ones hanging in the corridor that ran down the centre of the house. There was the Adam's chandelier, the Sheraton chairs, the mahogany dining room table, the red Venetian glass, a dozen Hepplewhite chairs, the fan given to my grandmother by Emily Pankhurst when they were striving to secure women's suffrage, and two special pieces: the Chippendale mantelpiece and the King George VI 'Coronation' chairs.

The mantelpiece had escaped from an old house in Wellington, under demolition, when an architect friend of my mother's stopped the builder, who had destroyed one mantelpiece and was about to take an axe to the second. The architect called my mother. Would she like to buy it? Twenty quid would do it. The fireplace arrived a few weeks later. It was blackened by years of smoke and inattention, but after being polished and polished again, it revealed its beautifully inlaid and intricate wood patterns. It was made for Te Rama.

The Coronation chairs were two elegant upright chairs of simple design, covered in a striking, rich, moss-coloured velvet, and decorated in one corner with a large gold-and-crimson embroidered crown. I often used to climb on one of them to reach high places. These chairs had been produced for the Coronation of King George VI, which my grandfather Percy attended. He was graciously allowed to buy them, presumably as acknowledgement of his long and loyal service to Parliament. My father ensured they were not lost after Percy's death by promptly shipping them to the other side of the world, thus sealing their fate. The chairs would have quickly been a victim of the flames.

I tried to make some sort of inventory of the paintings in the house. Apart from a dozen or so of Grandmother Frieda's tarot card paintings, I managed to conjure up the Braque, two Miros, a Dali, and the painting of the seated dancer my father thought was an early Picasso. There were more I could see in my mind's eye but I could not remember or maybe never knew who had painted them. The picture I regretted most was the Braque. I had not seen it for years but remembered every detail. It was a very simple picture, paper on paper. It was called the 'Blind leading the blind', with a nod to Bruegel, and showed a blue figure leaning forward with his hand out to another, smaller figure who was following in his footsteps. Both seemed to be leaning forward as if into a gale.

Gone too was the picture Frieda had painted of the house in Tottenham Court Road where she had lived for a while, away from Percy, with her artist friends. Where its roof had been blown off in the war by a bomb a huge canvas lay in its place. Frieda had painted the house in purple, grey and shades of brown and, with the canvas draped over it, the house had a wonderful air of dissipation.

I had never really known which of the paintings were originals and which were limited edition signed prints and had never bothered about it. Now I would never know.

The worst was the loss of the contents of the window seat – letters, newspaper articles, ancient and modern photographs, paintings, albums – all the collected memorabilia of an eccentric family and its relationship to New Zealand from the beginning of colonisation. All of it would be gone.

The more I thought about telling my parents the more anxious I became. How could I best break the news? Where and when? They could well collapse, have a stroke. My father was arriving in Sydney by air from Singapore just in time to celebrate his ninetieth birthday. My mother was in Hopewood, a health farm on the outskirts of Sydney.

THE FIRE

A few days after the fire my sister Maggie was poking disconsolately through the rubble when she uncovered a charred metal box. Opening it, she discovered the decorated Chinese fan, mercifully undamaged, that Emily Pankhurst had given my grandmother.

Bust of Lady Harris (Frieda) by Edward Bainbridge Copnall MBE

BREAKING THE NEWS

The day after the Te Rama fire I picked my father up from the airport in Sydney. I could not bring myself to say anything until safely in the privacy of the car. I didn't want to look him in the eye and I wanted him seated. We were halfway to the city before I managed to broach the subject.

'Dad, bad news I'm afraid. Joan rang last night to tell me Te Rama has burned to the ground.'

My father, who had listened attentively, gave a sigh and went quiet for a few minutes.

I had moved overnight from feeling sad for him and my mother to feeling angry with him. It was unfair of me but it was not just his life that had gone. It was a lot of mine. Why had they been so careless with our heritage? It would have been easy to fireproof the window box. Surely, they must have given some thought to the fact that the place was a potential fire bomb. But I felt guilty for my anger. Whatever I was feeling would be nothing compared to how he would feel.

Finally, he muttered, 'Oh well,' and asked what my wife Gail might be preparing for his breakfast. Bacon and eggs he thought might be good.

There was some talk about what had happened and why but, as usual in our exchanges, we did not discuss the family's finances. I had no idea what the financial effects of this catastrophe would be.

The previous day my mother had also received the news of the fire with surprising equanimity.

'We'll stay in Australia,' she announced, perhaps feeling that at last here was an opportunity to return to her birthplace.

As I chewed this over it seemed like an extremely whimsical choice. She had left Australia in 1933, sixty-six years ago. Protestations that she knew Sydney and had plenty of friends here were patently ridiculous. Her visits to Australia had been brief and infrequent excursions, mainly to the Wentworth Hotel in Phillip Street. All their support systems revolved around Waikanae. Not only that, Sydney is an expensive place to live, especially if you like the better things of life. It would not be like Waikanae. I decided to leave it to her to break this piece of news to my father. Anyway, I knew my parents; my opinion would not be required. It wasn't until much later that it dawned on me: both my parents thought the subject of 'money' was vulgar. They assumed they had more than enough of it and that was all they or anybody else needed to know. Their decision would not be based on any financial considerations.

Later my father confirmed my suspicion that they had not insured any of the contents of the house, which gave one more twist of the knife as far as I was concerned. The unamusing truth was, in fact, their financial resources turned out, as time passed, to be far from adequate. My father eventually managed to expire like the French aristocrat, with the proverbial one bottle of Chateau Lafite left in the cellar.

It was a few weeks before I could organise myself to fly to Wellington and drive to Waikanae to survey the damage. It was challenging because among the memories were not only my own life there but also those of our own children roaming in the garden, chasing eels in the creek or attending my sister's eccentric riding school. Perhaps our children would never come back.

I arrived on a typical Wellington day. The southerly howled across Cook Strait and the plane bounced and wobbled across the harbour, dropping quickly towards the white encrusted waves. Passengers fell silent and clutched their arm rests. Looking down at the spume blowing off the top of the waves, I thought about happy times spent rollicking across the harbour in my brother's yacht *Wanderer*.

The pilot banged the aircraft down on the runway that poked out into the Strait and after a pause there was a relieved smatter of applause from the passengers.

I picked up my hire car and headed for Waikanae, forty miles up the coast. The road was comfortably familiar. Nothing had changed since I had driven up and down to Wellington all those years ago.

Finally, I reached the turn-off to Te Rama and steeled myself for what I would find at the top of the drive. The press had reported the flames could be seen from nearly twenty kilometres away. As I left the shelter of the half kilometre or so of gravel driveway, protected as ever by a canopy of bush, I was confronted by not much more than a sodden pile of ash-coloured rubble and a few blackened beams.

I walked about, disconsolately kicking at the wreckage in the vain hope that some intact remnant might emerge. Then I just stood.

The ash covered my shoes and I sank a few centimetres into it. A soft wind stirred a few flakes, and a burnt smell was still in the air.

In the bushy area across the lawn, a white-breasted wood pigeon sat in the puriri tree. Soon the tuis would arrive to feast among the red berries. The tennis court and dairy were untouched but the big redwood would take a few seasons to recover.

I took a few paces and my foot touched something solid. I bent down and waved away some ash. A head emerged. I brushed away more ash until there sat the bronze bust of my grandmother, Lady Frieda Harris – artist, suffragette, friend of Emmeline (Emily) Pankhurst, friend also of the infamous occultist Aleister Crowley, for whom she had painted a famous deck of tarot cards, and wife, most of the time, of my grandfather Percy, who had been an eminent member of the House of Commons. The bust was in one piece, with only the timber base destroyed. I wondered if this was a tribute to Frieda's magical powers or the skill of the sculptor, Edward Bainbridge Copnall MBE, one-time President of the Royal Society of Sculptors.

There was little else to salvage.

At least one unique item, I knew, had not been destroyed by the fire. My visits had become much less frequent as our children had grown up but my Sydney family had visited Te Rama only a month before the fire. In the chest under a seat in the dining room, one of my sons, Mark, had come across a faded clay-coloured manuscript entitled 'Souffle with Ganesha', written by Grandmother Frieda, and when my father noted Mark's interest in it he gave it to him.

Of all our children, Mark, being the eldest, had the most intimate connection to Waikanae. As a boy of nine he used to go to my sister's riding school, Ferndale, which was on a back road on the way to the beach.

Maggie, like most Kiwis, believed in everyone, including children, looking out for themselves. One morning, Mark wandered into the stables and decided to investigate a chaff-cutter in action by sticking his index finger in the gears. With the finger reduced to a mushy scrap of bloody tissue he was rushed to Wellington

Hospital. They could do little and so, with the help and advice of our surgeon neighbour in Sydney, we flew him to the Sydney Hospital in Macquarie Street, where they had a specialist hand surgery unit. They tried their best but they could not save the finger. As they said, the gears missed his thumb by a whisker.

Mark laughs about it now. He claims it ruined his ambition to play the trumpet, but he has a lifelong reminder of time in Waikanae.

At first, I had ignored Frieda's diary but eventually, prodded by Mark, I picked it up. There was something mesmerising about this recently widowed, upper-class English lady's account of perambulating around Ceylon in 1953 in pursuit of the famous Indian dancer Ram Gopal and some yearned-for spiritual awakening during the making of the Hollywood movie *Elephant Walk*. It was hard to take seriously, but then maybe she was carrying a lot of baggage as a result of becoming a disciple of someone as weird, not to mention dangerous, as Aleister Crowley.

As I discovered much later, Frieda was an occultist, or a believer and student of hidden supernatural powers – something as a teenager in rural New Zealand I had definitely never encountered or even heard of. My father was not about to enlighten me.

She was my father's mother, and she only once came for a brief visit to Te Rama. I have very skimpy memories of her, except as a gnarled old lady dressed in volumes of some flimsy material, which I presume must have been silk. She gave me an Indian pocketknife, brought from the houseboat on which she lived in Kashmir. I was told pocketknives brought good luck but since I promptly lost it I doubt this accrued to me.

My other grandmother, Dodo, was staying with us at the time. Just as Frieda was about to arrive with my parents, Jellicle the cat deposited a small white intestinal worm on the kitchen bench and when Dodo saw it she blanched and took to the bench with a scrubbing brush and foul-smelling disinfectant, something of course everyone was bound to notice when they came inside.

Later I thought the jet black Jellicle, with green eyes, was obviously a witch's cat, and had done it on purpose as a form of welcome.

Frieda had in part come to New Zealand to see her cousin by marriage, Florence, who lived in Wellington. Their meeting did not go well. Frieda accused Florence of being a drunk and Florence accused Frieda of being mad. I imagine Frieda regarded New Zealand in the 1950s as somewhere to leave without delay. She would certainly not be delayed by the pull of family.

Sir Jack, my father

JACK

My father Jack was born in 1906 in the Paddington suburb of London, a brief stroll from Hyde Park.

In his childhood Jack knew the London of a handful of cars, steam buses and even the very rare aeroplane. Smog ruined the health of Londoners and Charlie Chaplin's black-and-white movies were an exciting new art form. Britannia ruled the waves and Englishmen and a few women strutted with the assurance of people who knew they ruled over an Empire on which the sun never set. It was the best of times to be an Englishman. Although Paddington is a central London suburb it is far from the East End so Jack's lifelong claim to be a Cockney was more than a bit dubious. His justification was, 'to be a Cockney you are supposed to be born within the sound of Bow Bells.' As in those days noise came mostly from horses' hooves, it might just have been possible for him to have heard the bells of St Paul's, but Bow Bells is a stretch.

In my father's memoirs, written in uncharacteristically shaky longhand when he was well into his nineties, he describes his upbringing in detail. As I read his words I can picture him sitting at his desk in the Parkwood Retirement Home in Waikanae jotting down a series of thought bubbles nearly eighty years after events happened and, thanks to the fire, with no records to check against. Plus he had no one to talk to about it, and was coming from the point of view of an upper-class Englishman trying to resuscitate his 'rite of passage'. For instance, was he really that naive about his sexuality and why does he even mention it? Just because he writes about something doesn't necessarily mean he has remembered correctly. When his book came out Christopher wrote to the publishers protesting in the strongest possible terms about its accuracy. They replied that the book was a 'memoir' not a history.

How I would like to know what his actual views and actions were. Accurate or not, his words still have the flavour of an 'on the spot' commentary – a view from the frontline of life before our time.

In accordance with Victorian customs we were left in the care of nannies. They always preferred my brother, who was better behaved; perhaps my behaviour was caused by my being poisoned by my tonsils. We moved around a good deal but before the war we lived at Hampstead in a house known as the Admiral's house. It was built by one of Nelson's Admirals. The roof was constructed like a quarter deck and the Admiral would fire his guns to celebrate Nelson's victories. The family were living in this house but left mainly because my father, as a Member of Parliament, had to live near the Houses of Parliament.

We moved to Queen Ann's Mansions just close to Victoria Station and my mother and the children went to live on a poultry farm on Westerham Hill, which gave me an early experience of country life. During the period of hard rationing the farm was a treat as there was [sic] plenty of eggs and poultry and we made butter from cream in a large bowl.

I was sent to prep school when I was eight. I remember crying all night. I hated prep school and remembered it chiefly for the number of times my bottom was beaten. Before I went to Shrewsbury I was at a school in West Gate called Street Court. Uncontroversially, the Headmaster also enjoyed beating the boys.

I had to struggle a little but passed the common entrance exam and landed in the third form at Shrewsbury School. Our Housemaster did not believe in beating the boys. I admired our Housemaster, who was a very elderly bachelor. He had a passion for books and he would attend the school library on Sundays to talk about the School's unique collection. I spent too much of my time there and neglected my studies.

Some of the Masters were men who had been appointed to fill in during the War, and mine was one. Riots would break out in form and the Headmaster had to intervene. I showed no ability at games but loved rowing on the Severn, which is a beautiful river, and I particularly enjoyed sculling up the upper reaches where one could also swim. The School was completely segregated and sisters only appeared with parents and, as I had no sister, I was frightened of girls. Under these circumstances there was I believe some homosexuality but Masters were too innocent to find out, indeed the word was unmentionable. New boys were subjected to being called out by the prefects who shouted 'scum.' The last boy out was usually me, so I had to do the odd jobs.

It was usual for one of the younger boys to be elected for a year as Hall Cryer and I had the honour or dishonour. I had to get to my feet and announce anything that was lost in the House and say, 'Oh, yes, oh yes – this is to say God save the Tories and down with the Radicals.' I was the obvious choice as the son of a Liberal MP. There were no Labour MPs in those days. I succeeded in making a joke of the whole thing and made quite a lot of friends at school. I did not like school; but did not dislike it.

I noticed eerie similarities to life in boarding schools in New Zealand some fifty years later. New Zealand prided itself on its symbiotic relationship with what was fondly described as the 'old country' so what could be more natural than to try to recreate its educational facilities?

I made some little effort and managed to pass my University entrance and went to Trinity Hall. When I was a boy, my grandfather gave my mother a cottage in Winchelsea, which was one of the Cinque Ports. It has a huge unfinished Church in which are buried some Crusaders. Winchelsea was abandoned as a port when the seabed rose leaving nearly two miles of marshes between the sea and the old port. In the middle of the marshes is Camber Castle, now quite derelict. I think it was built as a possible defence against a Napoleonic invasion.

You enter Winchelsea up a steep hill through some ancient gates and from the lookout you can see the shores of France, particularly at night. It was all very romantic and a suitable home for retired artists and writers.

Ellen Terry (a famous actress at the time) lived there and would organise performances by the locals of A Mid-Summer Night's Dream. *I think it was the first time I saw Shakespeare performed.*

Arnold Bennett, who wrote the book about the Staffordshire Fire Towns, lived there. My grandfather took me to see him. I remember him as a nice old gentleman with a broad accent.

Just after the war Percy took his young son Jack to Normandy for a holiday. One can picture them in their three-piece tweed suits, each walking with hands clasped behind their back, peering at the castles along the Seine and communicating with the locals in schoolboy French with a strong English accent. Jack had not then acquired a taste for wine and complained of the lack of water closets and ginger beer.

Jack returned to take up a place at Cambridge, attending his father's old college of Trinity Hall. Founded in 1345, Trinity is the fifth-oldest surviving college of the University. It was founded by Bishop Bateman for the study of civil law and the canon of Scripture. It may have owed its existence to the Black Death, which led to a shortage of clergymen, among other things. It was one of very few university entities to use the name 'Hall', and after Henry VIII's foundation of Trinity College, it became impossible, even had it been desirable, to change.

My father clearly enjoyed his time at the 'Hall', attending the numerous black-tie dinners and May Balls, rowing on the Cam, and becoming at one stage president of the literary society. He met poet Walter de la Mare, novelist Philip Guedala and actress Edith Sitwell, whom he remembered as 'a very strange person'. Frieda and Edith Sitwell later lived at the Ladies Club in London, until the former, so Jack reports, was expelled for threatening the staff with her stick and otherwise abusing them, and the latter for episodes of drunkenness.

The General Strike of 1926 occurred during Jack's second year at university. He and his fellow undergraduates enlisted as Special Constables and went to London, where they drove around in a convoy. They were given free seats at the theatre and were entertained everywhere. It is hard not to see this as much more than a typical undergraduate romp at the expense of many men who were unable to feed their families. It must have caused embarrassment when they landed at his father's electorate, more especially since Percy's brand of liberalism would have had him in sympathy with the strikers. Showing solidarity, Jack demonstrated in the strikers' favour by reading the *Workers Weekly* in the police station. Politically he clearly supported his father, but with no great passion. Less predictably he was an ardent pacifist until the rise of Hitler forced him, as it did many of his contemporaries, to review his opinion.

Upon returning to Cambridge, he finished his degree in history and economics. More than seventy years afterwards he remembered his university years with great affection and portrayed a romantic England of the 1920s, writing:

> *Before motor cars became so common the country was beautiful in the Spring with its flowers. The hedges were full of sweet-smelling flowers such as violets and primroses, there were bluebells in all the woods and cowslips in the fields.*

But, he added:

> *The fumes from motor cars have now poisoned all the flowers along even Country Roads. In the summer, the meadows were a glory of poppies and cornflowers. These have been destroyed by chemical sprays.*

He contrasted at some length his idyllic memories of England in the 1920s with the nasty brutish place he felt much of it had become, other, of course, than in the haunts of the privileged, of whom in any event he disapproved, having been 'corrupted' over half a century, by the 'socialists' down under.

After graduating from university he decided that New Zealand offered both an opportunity to rescue the neglected family business and adventure. He was drawn to 'the open spaces and the mountains and volcanoes' of New Zealand.

At the time, boys leaving school were expected to go into the services, or one of the professions, or 'lead the life of the idle rich'. Businessmen were looked down upon, and there were no courses where you could study business. Jack tells of his first meeting with his future father-in-law, on board ship:

> *He drew me aside and said with a twinkle in his eyes, 'You can hardly believe this, I was talking with someone aboard ship who said, "You cannot be associated with that man, he is a business walla."'*

However, Percy convinced Jack working with a French couturier might be of benefit, on the flimsy grounds that the family business 'had something to do with women's clothes'.

I found myself in a women's fashion establishment in the heart of Paris. Fortunately, I had learned a little French when vacationing with a French family. I was absolutely terrified at being with all these strange women. I was put in a corner and left to take cuttings from a fashion magazine. I had a romantic idea that it would be wonderful to have a beautiful French mistress but this did not eventuate. I was far too shy to approach any of the girls at work and was also a bit of a snob about any who might have obliged. I think my father paid the owner to pay me a small salary but I was really quite useless. Paris was a very stimulating place to be at that time. All the great French artists were around, some of whom I met. I developed a taste for French modern art and also French food, and found home very English. Roast beef, Yorkshire pudding and plenty of stodgy puddings.

After Jack's six-month stint in France, Percy apparently decided his son would be better off in Germany.

To learn a little German, he sent me to Berlin with an introduction to a bank with which he had some connection. He had no idea that Berlin had the reputation for being the most immoral city in the world. The Bank Manager recommended to me a German Count by the name of Von Becker. The spectacle I saw there was an eye opener to me. Von Becker and his male friend were busy arguing about the boyfriend they both shared and what clothes they should buy for him. Fortunately for me I have no homosexual inclinations and found their activities funny. I collected the granddaughters of Johann Strauss. One of them, the younger, I found very attractive. I was so unsophisticated I thought I had to ask both of them out, and my courtship did not get very far, although they did notice and remark that I was not a homosexual. Practically all the nightclubs were homosexual and it was very embarrassing to go there by oneself. Fortunately, there was also marvellous opera and concerts. There was the beginning of the German movie industry with stars such as Marlene Dietrich.

> *There was also great art developed by such as Marc Chagall, Max Ernst and Kandinsky. All were later driven out of Germany or killed by Hitler.*

But Jack remembers Germany as a lonely period.

> *The winter was bitterly cold and on Christmas day everything was closed and a freezing wind blew snow down the wide streets. It was cold enough to turn the snow into dust.*

After about three months he transferred to Hamburg.

> *...which was not as forbidding a city as Berlin and I collected a young man called Sir Richard Powell with whom I used to visit the nightclubs. Fortunately, I was too shy to approach the tarts. It was still freezing and I would walk across to the small office owned by the Company's shipping agent. I don't know what I was supposed to do there except learn German from the newspapers.*

Of course, it didn't take long for Jack to become more and more aware of the power of Hitler and his growing mob of violent supporters.

> *They wore brown shirts and the Communists red. The British Government was so terrified of the Communists that they backed the Nazis, including the time they invaded Czechoslovakia, and up until the time they invaded Poland.*
>
> *I saw the beginning of the anti-Jewish campaign. My friend Powell and I had a friend who was an Austrian Count but also Jewish. The owner of a shop spotted he was Jewish and tried to throw him out and Powell and I came to his rescue and did some minor damage. We went back to apologise to the owner who was very pleasant and had not spotted my possible taint. The quick success of the Nazis was due to a number of circumstances, starting with the*

signing of the Treaty of Versailles by the Reich Chancellor who was a Jew, instead of the real villains Hindenburg and Lindendorf. Also, the vindictiveness of the French, which destroyed the German economy, as well as the extreme wealth and ostentation of some German Jews. Of course, there was also latent anti-Jewish feeling but that was also present in France. Everyone tried to forget that Jesus was a Jew.

Sensing as he did that German belligerence was increasing, and would end in violent confrontation, he was happy to return to England. He spent a brief time in the London offices of Bing Harris, mostly decoding buyers' cables, which were sent in a coded message system called pantelegraphy, and accompanying the buyers on visits to the various suppliers around Britain.

Lady Harris (Patricia), my mother

4

JACK IN NEW ZEALAND

In 1929 Percy booked Jack a first-class ticket to Australia on the Orient Liner *Orantes*. As the son of a British MP, Jack was invited to sit at the Captain's table. Each night his steward would lay out his dinner suit and he would dress for a five-course banquet replete with the best of French wine. Removed from the unpleasant concerns of the world, Jack enjoyed the romance of shipboard life and fell in love with a pretty and vivacious nineteen-year-old Australian, Patricia Penman, who was returning with her parents from the 'coming out' season in London.

The ship called in at Colombo, still a peaceful outpost of the British Empire, and he recalled an idyllic interlude with Patricia, dining in the tropical moonlight and swimming in the tepid waters of the Indian Ocean. Three years later they married and were to remain together for seventy years. He claimed he never had a cross word with her but we children all knew very well that he had learned it would make for a more comfortable existence if he let her have her own way.

Father remembered Sydney as a smallish town of around a million, with life centred around the Rocks and the Domain. The bridge was not yet built and he crossed the harbour on the little ferries to visit his bride's family in the upper North Shore suburb of Wahroonga. There his future father-in-law, a successful geologist, not to mention sportsman, kept a comfortable Malayan-style bungalow in capacious gardens, including tennis court and swimming pool. It must have seemed all very appealing to this young Englishman on his first visit to the colonies.

The Penman family story is another matter but the other 'Percy' deserves much more than a mention.

Arthur Percy Penman, was a larger than life character in Sydney. He graduated from Sydney University as a mining engineer and first moved to Cobar in remote New South Wales, where Pat was born in 1910, way out where the outback really begins, 700 kilometres from Sydney.

Percy was a mining engineer with the Great Cobar Copper Mining Company Limited, which had been formed in 1878 when some major discoveries in the area instigated a copper (and zinc, lead and gold) rush. The shire is two thirds the size of Tasmania and apart from the town itself it is pretty much devoid of people, even today. In 1910 though, things were booming and the population swelled to 10,000. Its prosperity was reflected in the opening of the stately Mine Administration building, today a museum. It must have been a very different place to spend your early childhood from anywhere else Pat subsequently lived. To my regret, she never talked or wrote about her childhood there but perhaps she had little memory of the town since the mining boom was over by the end of the World War I and her family, along with most of the inhabitants, had moved on. Maybe she was even embarrassed about it.

Percy was a fine sportsman, distinguishing himself by playing cricket for New South Wales and bowling Victor Trumper for a duck, much to the disgust of a large group of cricket fans who had come to see Trumper's legendary batting skills. Percy also played one Rugby Test match for Australia against New Zealand in 1905 in Dunedin, playing fullback in conditions described as 'extremely wet and windy'. The score was 3–3 at half-time and 14–3 to New Zealand at full-time and if there is one position on a rugby field you would not want to play in a first test, in horrible weather and against the All Blacks, it is fullback. There is no record of him playing a second test. The crowd was a measly 3000 so the conditions must have been dire even by Dunedin's extravagant standards for foul weather. He was also a natural golfer and a founding member of the Elanora Golf Club on the northern peninsula in Sydney. My mother worshipped him mostly from afar since he spent a considerable part of his life overseas. I never heard her say a critical word about him, which considering she had a sharp tongue was surprising.

Percy ended up moving to Malaysia to explore for tin, where he had a spacious mansion in the centre of Kuala Lumpur from which he undoubtedly enjoyed the colonial good life. He left his wife, daughter and son in a large house on Water Street, Wahroonga, and returned only intermittently. Percy spent a good deal of his time at the Royal Selangor Club in Kuala Lumpur, home since its inception in 1884 to the colonial hierarchy in Malaya and also to cricket, rugby and other colonial pastimes. The 'old' building, built in mock Tudor style, shows a photograph of Percy captaining the Malayan cricket team against a combined Oxford and Cambridge University cricket team.

Before Pat and Jack's marriage, Percy hosted a grand dinner for the groom in the University Club. Most of the Australian cricket team attended and the guests included Jimmy Bancks, the cartoonist who drew the original Ginger Meggs cartoons. They all drew on or signed the menu, which we now have in our home in Sydney. Percy died on 11 September 1944.

After experiencing the sunshine and sparkling waters of Sydney, travelling to New Zealand was a return to reality for Jack. In contrast to his trip on the *Orontes*, he battled across the hostile waters of the Tasman in an ancient and rusty tub called the *Makura*, owned by the Union Steamship company, which he wrote 'rolled and pitched for four days, finally arriving in Wellington in a howling nor-wester.' He described Wellington as a depressing place.

> *Ancient trams crawled down Lambton Quay. You could not get a drink after six p.m. except with dinner in one of the few hotels. The food was English style, served by forbidding waitresses dressed like hospital nurses. There were no restaurants and only one modern building, the D.I.C., which was shown off with great pride by the locals.*
>
> *The buildings were generally tatty, mostly of wood and corrugated iron interspersed by a few larger Victorian brick constructions. The Great Depression was about to unfold and however downtrodden Wellington might have appeared it was not about to improve.*

Jack recalled that on his arrival in 1929 there were no diplomatic representatives and nor did New Zealand's members of parliament often visit Europe. Eventually representation from various countries arrived and Wellington became less isolated, but Jack recounts a diplomat friend of his being asked by the Prime Minister, 'Where is Czechoslovakia and what is it?'

If much of Wellington was in disrepair when Jack arrived, the Bing Harris warehouse was more dilapidated than most, staffed by old gentlemen, with no connection to the family and no apparent interest in growing a business or even preserving it and, incidentally, their own jobs. The Bing Harris warehouse was a large square building. Originally decorated with concrete balls along the roof line these had fallen off during an earthquake and the building badly needed a coat of paint. Inside, it was dimly lit by bare light bulbs and merchandise was piled everywhere. The manager, noting the arrival of 'family', had set off for an extended tour to Europe leaving the 24-year-old Jack in charge but with no formal title or experience.

Help from England was not available. It was a shock for Jack to realise how isolated New Zealand was. Letters took five weeks to reach England; the only other communication was by cable. There was no radio or television. Entertainment was provided by JC Williamson's travelling musical shows, the then leading theatrical company in Sydney, whose name still exists today. Things might have been easier for Jack if he had been a sporting type, but he had little time for team pastimes, and preferred hiking, often taking long walks by himself.

Fortunately, it had been the custom for the local gentry to send their sons to either Trinity College or Trinity Hall Cambridge and there was therefore a community in Wellington with whom Jack shared a common experience, although many of these men had not actually graduated. Jack was particularly impressed with Alfred de Bathe Brandon, (the third Alfred de Bathe Brandon) MC, DSO, who was credited with shooting down the first Zeppelin of World War I. Jack was put up at the Wellington Club by Alfred, whose father had been its president, and lived there until he found his own accommodation.

The Bing Harris board eventually decided that Jack should proceed to Dunedin where Gerald Benson presided over what life there was in the old firm. At least, unlike the Wellington manager, Benson was usually present at work and frequently sober. Business was hardly vigorous though. He describes arriving to find a Mr Portman, replete with large walrus moustache, seated on a high chair in the office writing out the accounts in longhand. Father commented about the move that:

If Wellington was a dump Dunedin was something worse. Presided over by the Presbyterian Church, Sunday was reserved for religious services; I think you were allowed to play golf in the afternoons. Beach guardians made sure that men's bathing costumes were not turned down and lipstick was frowned on for women. Subjects suitable for conversation consisted of, for men, rugby football, of which I knew nothing, and the price of wool. For women discussing the children and, very important, who did she marry?

Under the long-serving Benson Dunedin was marginally better run than Wellington so to Wellington Jack soon returned. He was not at first given any particular authority, but by 1932, just before he became managing director he received a stipend of some 400 pounds per annum. Around this time Jack's younger cousin George Milne arrived from England. George proved to be a shrewd businessman and he and Jack continued to work together until long after the end of World War II.

My father returned to Sydney in 1933 to marry Pat and they returned almost immediately to New Zealand for my father to resume the task of trying to salvage the family business. For some reason, the board decided he should go to Dunedin. Jack was well aware that the transition to New Zealand and particularly Dunedin would be a challenge for his new young bride.

Pat had married my father not exactly appreciating what Dunedin might be like after the gaiety of Sydney. Back in the 1930s Dunedin had progressed from being the centre of New Zealand's gold rush, and saucy to go with it, to a dour Scottish outpost set in a very chilly southern sea and chock-full of stern Presbyterians all called Mc-something or other. Jack was well aware the move would not be easy for her:

> *Before our marriage, she had quite a successful career in Sydney. She played the Chinese girl in 'On the Spot' and was one of the first broadcasters. She left her lovely home to come to New Zealand, where I had nowhere to live. We went first to Dunedin where we lived for a while in a Hotel, which actually had a fireplace. There was no central heating. She would sit in the Botanical Gardens Greenhouse to try to keep warm. We went to Queenstown and the Hermitage where it snowed heavily. I don't think she had seen snow before. She must have loved me dearly to join me in New Zealand where I was running a half-bankrupt business.*

Despite his reservations about Dunedin, Jack managed to find society that appealed to him.

> *Parents had a way of going off to England and then the parties really started. One of the Sargoods [a family also involved in the wholesale trade and whose business Bing Harris was finally to acquire in the 1970s, to its lasting detriment] had married a man called Mills and they named their home Piccadilly and it was the centre of much social life.*

After a relatively short stint in Dunedin they decided to move with the headquarters of the business to Wellington. Pat must have supposed this would have been an improvement. But nowhere was probably much fun in the depressing economic circumstances that followed the 1929 Wall Street crash, and Wellington with 6 pm closing times and a climate only rivalled by Tierra del Fuego for howling southerly gales strait out of the Antarctic would scarcely have been better. How she must have missed the gaiety of her friends from JC Williamson's, the reigning theatrical production company in Sydney, and the excitement of being on stage. After all, she had been friends with Errol Flynn, a Johnny Depp character who went on to a highly successful Hollywood career, and Bobby Helpmann, acclaimed ballet dancer and actor and subsequently co-director of the Australian ballet. So, as Jack wrote, she must have truly loved my father. For Pat it would have been hard to trump a shipboard romance with the son of a baronet and distinguished English Member of the House of Commons and even more intriguing, whose mother was an occultist? In Sydney society in the 1920s this must have been quite a marital *coup de théâtre*.

Fate however decided to play a nasty card, the joker in the pack. Not only did she end up in Wellington, she ended up in Lower Hutt. For those who don't know, which will be practically everybody, Lower Hutt is a sleepy suburb on the other side of

Wellington's fabled harbour. It was close enough to the city for my father to drive to and from work but there would not have been much in Lower Hutt to engage Pat's attention. She would have needed the dogs for company.

Jack continued with his rescue efforts on the business and bit by bit with the help of cousin George and the guidance of Jack Griffin profitability began to return. In 1936 Pat and Jack's first child, Christopher, was born and by this stage they had enough money to build the new home in Woburn Road, Lower Hutt, half an hour around the harbour foreshore from the Bing Harris office and warehouse. My father added an enormous front wall behind which grew some huge poplars. Pat was left to do her thing behind the wall while he drove off to his Wellington office.

Given Jack's background, he probably had a better idea than most of his New Zealand contemporaries of the rising tensions in Europe and growing belligerence of the Nazis. Letters from family and old contacts would have kept him better informed than did the local paper and radio news. Nevertheless when war broke out in September 1939 it must have been a cataclysmic shock. Anyone his age remembered the carnage of World War I. Britain declared war against Germany on 1 September; New Zealand followed suit two days later, on the third.

I suppose most people like to have a war hero somewhere in the family tree but Father was not to fall into that category. Unmilitary in bearing and personality, Jack became a sergeant in the Volunteer Reserve or Home Guard, a sort of New Zealand Dad's Army. How he was not initially called up is hard to know. He would have been only thirty-four in 1940, and though by this stage he was the father of two, plenty of enlisted men had two children. Perhaps someone had seen him march. More likely it was because he had a business to run.

He was at first a private and his section commander, a returned serviceman, was his near neighbour Jack Riddiford's under-gardener. Most of their time was spent sitting on the beach or in shallow trenches armed with their ancient weapons and ammunition marked 'practice only'. To escape the boredom of sentry duty he joined the Security Bureau, which suited him since he could slip across the road to what remained of the office. Most of his male staff were off at the front.

There were odd moments of excitement and he enjoyed keeping the local Italian fishermen company as they took their trawlers out into Cook Strait. He was supposed to watch them for signs of sabotage, or contact with enemy submarines, but they fed him on large bowls of pasta and he would fall asleep in the sun or, in the frequent southerly gales that plagued Cook Strait, vomit over the side to the immense satisfaction of his companions. On one occasion, exhausted by the rigour of his responsibilities, he fell asleep at the wheel on the way home and crashed into the telegraph pole outside the fire station. This set off the air-raid sirens for the whole of Wellington, thus providing the citizens with their only trip to the shelters in the entire war.

To prepare himself for the day ahead Jack would often repair to the Wellington Club for breakfast where he would find himself sharing the milky tea and congealed eggs with New Zealand's deputy prime minister and foreign minister, Gordon Coates. The fact that such an august personage could share his breakfast with a mere sergeant afforded him some amusement until, one morning, Coates complained of the cold. Father swapped seats so that Coates could sit nearer the fire and two hours later Coates was dead. Apart from being saddened by his death, Father missed him as a genuine Kiwi character and remarked mordantly that Fraser (the prime minister) was a 'dour old Scott', Forbes (the finance minister) 'was practically illiterate' and that 'a drearier collection than the rest of the War Cabinet it would be hard to find.'

After the war things slowly returned to normal in New Zealand and my father went back to running the family business. At some time in the 1960s Bing Harris became a publicly listed company, which allowed members of the family not having a stake in running the business to sell their shares if they wished. As in many family companies the ownership of Bing Harris had gradually broadened throughout the family as generation succeeded generation. By the 1960s, the majority of the shareholders had little to do with the affairs of the company. These family members were mainly situated in England. Uncle Nick ran the London office, between collecting Chinese art and lunching at the Garrick Club, and my brother Christopher, newly married, came into the firm in Wellington. Uncle George Milne was also on the board.

In the 1950s, New Zealand was Britain's larder, and the third-richest country in the world. But in the 1970s the economy was devastated by two blows: soaring oil prices and Britain joining the European Economic Community, ending 'Commonwealth Preferences', a trade deal that had provided preferential tariffs. By the 1980s New Zealand's gross domestic product (GDP) had dropped from twenty per cent above to one third below the Organisation for Economic Co-operation and Development (OECD) average.

At the beginning of the 1960s, there arose one of those fads that takes the business world by storm every few years. This was the arrival of the corporate raiders. These entities specialised in buying public companies whose share price traded below the net value of their assets. Especially attractive were companies whose assets included a nice collection of undervalued real estate. These raiders searched the world for opportunities, represented often by old-fashioned family-run businesses.

By the end of the 1960s Bing Harris's wholesale and importing business was being squeezed by poor economic conditions and the competition for margin between the manufacturers and retailers. Bill Sutch was the Permanent Secretary of the Department of Industry and Commerce. He was a highly controversial figure and had been one of the architects of the measure protecting local industry passed between 1935 and 1938 by the Labour Government. Bing's, along with many other New Zealand companies, had as a result built up a network of tiny manufacturing units behind the wall of tariff protection. Sutch was considered extremely left wing, so much so that he was eventually charged with being a KGB agent. The case could not be proven but the suspicion remains to this day. In any event, not even the highest levels of protection could continue to disguise the fact that these businesses were now totally sub-economic. Bing's found itself sliding into loss as its margins were relentlessly attacked. As an owner of some particularly well situated real estate in New Zealand's major cities, Bing Harris was sooner or later going to become a target for the corporate raiders.

Sure enough, a particularly suave Scotsman named Sir Michael Nairn soon arrived in Wellington and, persuaded by the obvious evidence of good character indicated by his title, my father was soon in serious discussions with him. The plan that unfolded was that Bing Harris would acquire Sargood & Ewen, an almost identical business in Wellington, unlisted and owned mainly by the Ewen family. Sir Michael's company, Ralli International, based in London, would acquire a substantial holding in the combined group. My father and brother would run the combined operation and many savings would be made from running the two companies as one. After the usual rather distasteful haggling a deal was struck.

It transpired that Ralli itself had its genesis in one of the most notorious raiders to emerge in the 1960s, Slater Walker. Slater Walker was the corporate vehicle of Jim Slater, an aggressive financial engineer, and Peter Walker, a businessman and later minister in the conservative government in the United Kingdom. Slater at the height of his career was revered, much as internet gurus currently are, but it turned out that most of the hundreds of deals that Slater Walker had participated in failed to hold up to scrutiny. Eventually Jim Slater was forced out of the business, which finally became a minor outpost of the ubiquitous empire of Sir James Goldsmith.

At the time of the Bing Harris discussions, Slater Walker had engineered a merger between Ralli International and the Bowater

Paper Company. A Slater Walker protégé, Malcolm Horsman, became deputy chairman and managing director of the merged company. Sir Michael Nairn worked ultimately for Horsman.

The demise of Slater Walker saw Horsman's star wane at Bowater's, and the result was that Bing Harris found itself with an English paper company, at the time the tenth largest industrial company in the United Kingdom, as its major shareholder. This was precisely at the time it was discovering that the savings out of the Sargoods acquisition and merger were more difficult to find than anyone had expected. Sargoods, it turned out, was no better run than Bing Harris and had almost identical problems.

Bing Harris found itself the owner of the Onehunga Woollen Mills, which it turned out was only capable of manufacturing heavy woollen blankets, a low margin product not particularly in demand. Modernising the factory was expensive and management was, as so often, a problem. At the same time, the Rainster factory, which Bing Harris owned, was finding its children's wear was no longer in demand as school uniforms became a thing of the past. An attempt to switch to manufacturing jeans was opposed by management, conservative in outlook to the last.

Into this unstable situation stepped New Zealand's answer to Jim Slater, the gnomelike Ron (later Sir Ron) Brierley and his company, Brierley Investments Limited. Bowater, anxious to rid itself of a portfolio of investments unrelated in any way to its core activity, promptly sold out to them. At this stage, Bing Harris managed, with impeccable timing, to announce a loss and the suspension of dividends; my father panicked, and this left my brother furiously trying to defend the family citadel. It was tailor-made for Ron to pitch in with an offer that looked like a godsend to panicky shareholders and by the end of 1975 the old family firm had disappeared and my father was retired.

Besides business, my family were active participants after the war in the political arena. Before the war, they had built their substantial timber home in Woburn Road, Lower Hutt, the other side of the harbour from the City of Wellington. Father takes up the tale:

> *Thanks to having a nanny, [my wife] was able to join in a lot of activities. She was first President of the Housewives Association. Some of our local friends were very antagonistic to the number of Labour Party friends we had, which included Walter Nash, a neighbour and local Member of Parliament, Percy Dowse, the Mayor and his wife, who came from Bethnal Green.*

Wellington was a small place, home to not many more than 300,000 people. It was also the seat of government and Father, as the managing director of one of the larger businesses in the town, naturally got to know many of the politicians, and all of the prime ministers, together with the representatives of overseas governments, most notably the British High Commissioner. The British influence remained strong, and each of the New Zealand prime ministers from the war until David Lange in 1984 were knighted, except for Norman Kirk, who died in office. About Sid Holland (New Zealand's prime minister from 1949 to 1957), Father wrote:

> *Sid was an old-fashioned democrat. When we visited him, he would sit in his braces and collarless shirt and say he liked to feel relaxed. He also liked my wife's bread and had one of our geese for Christmas. He was a wonderful public speaker and was at his best with an unruly crowd. He would persuade noisy speakers to come forward, and then deal with them in the nicest way. He was just the man to put National into power after Fraser's oppressive Socialist Government followed by Nash who openly stated that he did not think anyone should earn more than $500 per annum.*

My parents were also friendly with Keith Holyoake (prime minister from 1960 to 1972), who would, according to my father:

... often visit us in Woburn Road when he was Minister of Agriculture. No one had ever survived being Minister of Agriculture but he went on to become Prime Minister. He was a very shrewd politician. When he was PM I became President of the Chamber of Commerce and also the Softgoods Assosciation. I often led delegations to see the PM. He would always ask me what I thought, which was very flattering. I always admired the way he handled the Vietnam War. He did not believe in 'all the way with LBJ' but did not want to offend the Americans. He sent a medical team and allowed some volunteers as well. I was always against the Vietnam War and thought the Americans should never have been involved. The war ended with the utter humiliation of the United States and the weakening of the standing of Europeans in that part of the world. Muldoon [Sir Robert Muldoon, prime minister from 1975 to 1984] later appointed Holyoake Governor General to get rid of him. He could not deal with the role, he was quite unacquainted with the formalities, and there were too many parties. He fell apart and died shortly after retiring.

Father detested 'Piggy' Muldoon and Muldoon returned the opinion. Muldoon was a squat spherical-shaped man, with a belligerent expression and what appeared to be a scar on one side of his face. What he despised most in the world were 'wet' liberals, and Father was a particularly prominent and tiresome member of this breed. Father had campaigned in the 1975 election against Muldoon and for Rowling, the unsuccessful Labour Party candidate. Prior to that he had led the campaign to save Lake Manapouri, one of the most beautiful lakes in New Zealand. *Manapouri* means 'Lake of the Sorrowing Heart' in Maori and was supposedly named after the tears of two daughters of a local Chief. At the end of the 1960s New Zealand needed overseas currencies and Comalco proposed an aluminium smelter at Bluff at the tip of the South Island. Aluminium is canned electricity, so it was proposed to supply the electricity by damming Manapouri to form New Zealand's largest hydroelectric power station. This would require the level of the lake to be raised eleven metres. Muldoon was a strong advocate of the proposal but the environmentalists, led by my father and others, stirred up a powerful coalition of dissent. Eventually the scheme went ahead but with an agreement that the water level remain at the existing point. It was a rare victory, and one Muldoon, who was a good hater, did not forgive.

Father also gained a radical reputation among the business community for his opposition to apartheid in South Africa. It seems hard to credit, but in 1960, at the request of South Africa, New Zealand agreed to leave Maori players out of their touring rugby team. By the time of South Africa's return tour to New Zealand in 1981 great opposition had built up to apartheid and the tour took place against a wall of street marchers and vigorous, in some cases over-vigorous, police intervention. My father marched in protest with many New Zealanders, prominent and ordinary alike, and the tour was a shambles. He was fortunate to escape arrest as the local police took a dim view of this sort of bolshie activity but he had the sense to link arms in the front row of the protestors with Sir Edmund Hillary and Ken Grey, the former being the conqueror of Everest and the latter being a vast All Black prop forward.

By 1985 the protesters prevented the 1986 return tour to South Africa by court action. In the All Blacks' stead a volunteer team called the Cavaliers toured. They were heavily defeated and returned to New Zealand to a hostile reaction and ongoing questions over how much this party of purported amateurs might *actually* have been paid. It was a rare event in New Zealand's history that prompted the people, normally respectful of the law and the government, to take to the streets in such numbers.

My father retired to Te Rama and spent the next twenty years enjoying the house at Waikanae, visiting the Wellington Club and writing copious unpublished letters to *The Economist*. He and my mother also took numerous overseas trips, which is how they were away when the fire of 1996 occurred.

Neither of my parents were disciplinarians. I never remember them smacking me or even raising their voices. I suppose they thought they had a nurse and sent me to boarding school to avoid all that sort of distasteful confrontation. In my late teens a group of friends staying at Te Rama and I were invited to attend a party forty miles away in Wellington. We had no cars so I drove the tiny blue 'farm' Austin 35 and my friend 'Slug' Sutherland drove my mother's Morris station wagon. Halfway into town, and with no other cars in sight, I decided to pull up alongside him on the wrong side of the road to have a little chat. Slug wound down the window, leaned out to hear me and turned the steering wheel. We ran into each other. When I told my mother she just went a little pale and said it was good no one was hurt. 'Slug' was very appreciative and later, to show it was not just words, turned up at the door with a couple of wild ducks he had shot over the local dam, just what my mother wanted.

Pat was a very complicated character. Probably the worst thing that could have happened to her in suburban New Zealand was inheriting the baronetcy. Once she became Lady Harris she would have been quite unbearable to most New Zealanders, especially women. To be fair, she did some great work for women and abortion reform and not for nothing was she awarded the Order of New Zealand but the truth is she had an eggshell-thin ego and anyone who dared to treat her with less than due deference was in for a vitriolic tongue lashing. She travelled extensively, never 'down the back' and developed a particular affection for Turkey, not that she ever ventured much further than first-class hotels or restaurants, but nevertheless she managed to endear herself to the Turks enough to be appointed Honorary Turkish Consul in New Zealand. The purpose of the role is unclear but she much enjoyed it in any event.

Pat had been a brilliant pupil of Abbotsleigh School for Girls, on Sydney's Upper North Shore. Abbotsleigh prided itself on its high scholastic standards and the girls were reminded not to waste their lives in fripperies by the school motto, *tempus celerus radio fugit*, which charmingly means 'time flies faster than a weaver's shuttle'. Notwithstanding the academic focus of school Pat had managed to become an excellent cook. She authored a number of cookbooks, including *Dining in and Dining Out in New Zealand* and a Turkish cookbook entitled *Fit for a Sultan*, with recipes for all the usual Turkish favourites: *imam bayildi* (stuffed aubergines), *börek*, *kofte*, *sis kebabs*, and sweets like *kadin gobegi* or ladies' navels. What New Zealanders made of them in the 1960s I have no idea but as Pat liked to say, *Afiyet olsun* – 'May it bring you health.'

Pat was very conscious of the pecking order in Wellington, cultivated her relationships with politicians and diplomats, and was capable of being quite cruel to people less well connected. My father's poor secretary, a kindly spinster, once turned up at the Bing's Christmas party in a mink coat. Pat let her scorn be known, ruining the poor woman's evening. Although she never really talked about it, I think she had been badly mauled when sent off at only eighteen to 'come out' in London. The English establishment can be very condescending and a young and probably bumptious young Australian, born in Cobar for goodness sake, would have been seen as fair game. One result of these encounters was that she became a stickler for protocol. She was an early adopter of the 1950s idea of 'U' and 'Non-U', made famous by Nancy Mitford or Stephen Spender, by which a single incorrectly used word can relegate someone to the dungeons of class strata in England. She must have been bitterly disappointed by the linguistic ineptitude of the younger generation in New Zealand. There was definitely no 'U' expression for sheep shearing in New Zealand, although a good vocabulary of salty swear words was quite 'U' in New Zealand and among the upper, but not the middle classes, in England.

She had little ability to laugh at herself let alone let anybody else laugh at her, which suggests a level of insecurity protected by a coat of prickly defensiveness that reared up so often that it kept people away from her.

One of her worst experiences was when my brother's father-in-law was appointed New Zealand High Commissioner in India. Pat practically exploded, feeing that she, Jack and the baronetcy were much better suited than that couple of middle-class Auckland nobodies. In terms of knowledge of the world, and India in particular, she may have been right but I suspect no government was going to let Pat loose with a high commissioner's baton to wield. She would have been insufferable and impossible to control.

Sadly, I don't remember Pat ever showing much sign of happiness. Perhaps she really didn't understand the concept. I wonder now if she might have suffered from depression or even been bipolar.

And yet, and yet ... When she was in her eighties she wrote a poem called 'Time'.

TIME
Time is demolishing me slowly but wantonly,
as days go by and I remember less.
Was youth and strength so easily passed on to age?
And memories built so frail that they can crumble in a day,
leaving no trace of youth?
But yet the memories prevail so strong, and still so warm, that life
depends upon their rich recall, into the present, with its needs to
face what must be realised today.
And still the memories prevail, so precious and so real to me, that I
must learn so late in life the strength to recognise, the strength of
memories' rewards and how to take the path that waits.

I think this is a terrific, if scary, poem. It tells me there was a lot about Pat that I never understood and I am certain almost nobody saw. I wonder what she and Jack said to each other when no one else was around. Because I feel like I didn't know them I have no idea.

Who, in the end, did actually know the real Pat? How sad if, underneath the self-damaging bluster, was someone of real value and insight, but that nobody ever knew.

The stables and chook run at Te Rama

5

WAIKANAE: EARLY DAYS

The first settlement of New Zealand is bound up in a number of richly elaborate myths. Among these it is not easy to discern the truth but the most reliable evidence seems to point to the Maori arriving a mere 800 years ago by canoe from Polynesia, after a voyage of epic proportions through waters not only uncharted but perhaps never before visited by humans. Sir Peter Buck, the great Maori anthropologist, called his forbears 'Vikings of the Sunrise'.

As they explored the coast of New Zealand the Maori would have been attracted to Waikanae as a place to live. It had a welcoming climate. The presence of moas, in particular, made it a good place to hunt, and other sources of food were plentiful. The giant moas had no enemy prior to the coming of the Maori. They were slaughtered in their thousands and were the chief source of protein. The birds, like huge gawky ostriches, stood five metres or more with drumsticks the size of a leg of beef.

The name *Waikanae* is claimed to have a number of meanings but *wai* means 'water' and *kanae* means 'mullet', though some locals claim *Waikanae* means 'The River of Glaring Eyes'. The first tribe to settle the area were the Muaūpoko but no tribe was secure for long from the predations of the warlike tribes both north and south, who were constantly on the lookout for plunder.

The Maori mainly favoured the stretch of open country behind the iron-sand beach and the sandhills, and near the Waikanae River and the local streams. The beach provided access to the ocean and to Kapiti Island, a few kilometres offshore. The area had a pleasant climate and abundant food: birdlife, including the moa, eels in the streams and lagoons, and a wide variety of fish in the sea, plus shellfish such as toheroa, tuatua and pipis.

In the 1820s the Ngati Toa arrived, driven out of their northern New Zealand base, and led by the fearsome Te Rauparaha. They came warlike, carrying muskets obtained from the Europeans, and soon dominated. As European ships arrived in nearby Cook Strait, they were quick to take advantage of local flax and food to trade for muskets and other utensils available from the Pakeha (Europeans).

Ngati Toa eventually captured Kapiti Island, just off the coast and abundant in food, fresh water and sea life. In 1824 at the battle of Waiorua at the south end of the island around 200 Ngati Toa defeated nearly 2000 invaders. From then on, they maintained control of the area, keeping Kapiti to themselves, but coming to an arrangement with Te Ati Awa and Ngati Raukawa tribes to share the land around Waikanae. Most Maori battles began with a Maori war dance and in the Ngati Toa's case this was the Ka Mate, composed by Te Rauparaha to celebrate his escape from death in an 1820 battle. This was the basis for the haka of the All Blacks.

Intertribal battles continued and in 1830 another bloody battle was fought at Horowhenua between Te Rauparaha's so-called allies, the Te Ati Awa and Ngati Raukawa. Skirmishing ran on intermittently for years and gradually sucked in other nearby tribes. The Maori were generally quick to take up arms. Sir Percy Buck, in his book *The Coming of the Maori*, records a South Island Chief, saying of Te Rauparaha's military success, 'If he comes my way, I will rip his belly open with a barracuda's tooth.' The statement was regarded as a *casus belli*. Te Rauparaha duly arrived with his forces, captured the fort, and performed an abdominal operation on the boaster, using a barracuda's tooth for a scalpel. Buck writes, 'Maori humour was apt to take a gruesome turn. An inimical act, such as murder by an individual of another tribe, was sufficient cause for an attack against the culprit's tribe, and, so long as some member of that tribe was killed, it did not matter if the real culprit escaped. Payment (*utu*) was procured by the shedding of blood.'

Cannibalism was still common at the time. Eating your victims was considered a good way to destroy their *mana* or supernatural power, and no doubt fear of being eaten would have been an incentive not to surrender.

Among his many exploits, Te Rauparaha arranged to hire the British brig *Elizabeth* to sail to the South Island port of Akaroa, now the port for Christchurch, where he defeated the local tribe and captured their Chief Tamaiharanui and his wife and daughter. On the journey back, Tamaiharanui strangled his own daughter, fearing what would be in store for her. On arriving at Kapiti, he was tortured and, with his wife and all prisoners, killed.

In 1840 Te Rauparaha was persuaded to sign the Treaty of Waitangi, the founding document between the British and the Maori tribes. He was astute enough to come to terms with Governor Grey, and open-minded enough to converse with the arriving missionaries, including Octavius Hadfield, who learned the Maori customs and language, sympathised with their disputes with the settlers and gradually built a close relationship with Te Rauparaha. Influenced by the British missionaries, Te Rauparaha built the first church in New Zealand at Otaki just a few kilometres up the coast from Waikanae and allowed Christianity to be proselytised by the Church. However, disputes continued and finally Te Rauparaha, who was nearly eighty, was lured into a trap, captured and imprisoned by the British. He was kept a prisoner without trial for eighteen months before being released to return to Kapiti. Te Rauparaha's son was converted by the missionaries and eventually sent to England, where in 1852 he met Queen Victoria. However, resentment continued over the 'purchase' by Europeans of land in the area and fighting continued to flare. The first European settlers in Waikanae would not always have slept easy in their beds.

After the railway was completed from Wellington in 1886 Waikanae became more popular with settlers and the European population increased to around two hundred and fifty. By the 1890s, the wars were over but much resentment remained. Surrounded by none too placid Maoris tribes, the Europeans in Waikanae made a sketchy living from timber, farming and public works.

Henry Elder (HRE) bought the land which the original house, 'Waimahoe', was built on, in 1892, most of it coming from the Chief, Wi Parata, who was later a member of parliament and a cabinet minister. The Maori were happy to sell land away from the beach to settlers, believing as they did that the land along the beach was the most valuable. The land was a few kilometres from the coast and looked out over the low-lying coastal land to the forbidding outline of Kapiti Island. The Elders family eventually became significant New Zealand land owners.

Waimahoe was built in 1884, away from the town, on the south-eastern side of the Waikanae River, which formed its northern boundary, and well up the hill from the main road, which was separated from it by dense bush. Nineteen years later it was destroyed by fire. The sepia photographs show a timber, two-storey cream and black farmhouse with a corrugated pitched roof and large ornate brick chimneys. The style could best be described as 'Rimu Tudor' and looks somewhat out of place sprawled among the stumps of trees crudely felled to make a building platform. The internal design had some attractive features but, due to inadequate windows and the oiled timber, it looks uncomfortably dark. It would have been particularly so after sunset with only kerosene lamps or candles to lighten the gloom.

On the evening of 12 September 1903 the house caught fire in a manner eerily similar to the burning of Te Rama, which was vulnerable for the same reasons: dry timber and flax. From a tiny flame, perhaps just a candle, there was an almost immediate conflagration. The family of five, asleep at the time, miraculously escaped without injury. No fire fighting was possible and the next morning, as recorded in the report later lodged in the Turnbull Library, 'tall chimney stacks stood above a pile of smoking ashes and crumpled roofing iron. A solitary kettle remained on the hob of the nursery fireplace.' As the fire raged, some adults arrived and took the children down the mailbag track by the light of matches to Purdie's cottage where they spent the night. Their last sight of the house before they plunged into the bush was of flames bursting out of one of the bedroom's windows, with the glass clattering down. The next morning the children fossicked in the ashes but instead of a bronze bust all they found was a quantity of melted silver, which they gathered and was later reworked. In the months after the fire, while the new house was being built, the family moved out to the sandhills where a small cottage stood. This was a four-roomed building with a lean-to scullery and an earth dunnikin out in the yard. HRE's first move was to add ugly corrugated iron lean-tos on either side, so that they not only had a little elbow room but managed to put up visitors.

After the new house was built the grass court in front of the house was replaced in the winter of 1905 by a superior asphalt one. A stable was built between the home and the long paddocks. This comprised a couple of loose boxes and a harness room below, a hay loft and a storage room, whose main function was to house about 100 feet of track for an elaborate Bassett-Lowke model railway.

By the time we moved in the whole structure had been turned into stables only, which we used either for Maggie's horses or for the cow.

In 1905, one of the most memorable events to occur in Waikanae took place. Wi Parata, the Maori Chief, elected Member of Parliament for the district in 1871, and first Maori cabinet minister, died. A huge *tangi* or funeral was held in Waikanae. In the notes from Henry Elder he describes it.

> *The funeral was heralded by gunfire. His body lay in state surrounded by portraits and emblems of his rank and status in an 8-foot by 10-foot canvas tent to one side of the meeting-house. Along the marae stretched a Hakari, a staging, seven to eight feet high, made of supplejacks on the ledges of which were displayed sacks of flour, of potatoes and other food-stuffs, contributed by visitors. The tops of the supplejacks had been split and in the top of these fluttered bank notes.*
>
> *When the time came for the burial in the Hapu graveyard behind the church, the coffin was placed on a gun carriage, covered with a union jack and hauled across the main road and the railway line. It was preceded by two men with stockwhips, which they played close to the crowd on either side. A vault had been prepared in the cemetery which was sealed and for the next three nights it was guarded against grave robbers until the cement dried. Heirlooms were being buried with the body. The marble bust of Wi was later erected facing north towards the lost homeland of the Atiawa side of his ancestry.*

The funeral was a reaffirmation of the status commanded in contemporary society of the Maori Chiefs and the respect with which they were treated by both Maori and Pakeha alike.

Between the Elders' and our ownership, the property, which under the Elders had been a major rural concern and a substantial employer of local labour, was owned by the Higginson family, whose father was the chief engineer on the railway during its construction. For much of the time Te Rama operated as a small school, run by the Friendly Society. During this period, the property was renamed Te Rama and the farm was whittled away to the forty acres my parents bought.

Te Rama means 'Place of Light', referring possibly to the glow-worms that reside under the leaves of the low-lying foliage along the edge of the stream and the driveway.

Watercolour painting of Te Rama

6

TE RAMA

My parents bought Te Rama and moved there in 1953, when I was eight years old. It must have been a difficult decision for my father. From a short drive around the harbour to his office in Wellington he now had a forty-mile drive along a winding single-lane road.

All the same, Te Rama was a natural choice for my parents. It was really a kind of country estate providing privacy but within comfortable enough reach of Wellington that they could be as much engaged in 'town' as they might want. The fact that it had no entertainment, beyond what nature provided, or friends and neighbours for children would not matter since we would all be off to boarding school. I was the only child to have lived for any time in the Lower Hutt house so we weren't even losing any friends.

My first impressions were not favourable. Te Rama seemed like a great rambling house, forbidding and without the comfort of any neighbouring homes. There was only the bush. Inside the house was sombre, with dark wood-panelled corridors. Somehow, I managed to put my hand through the stained-glass windows surrounding the front door. The entrance to our new home was stained with my blood, but once I had been repaired no harm was done since my mother had determined the windows were to go anyway, as part of the extensive renovations which would be required to bring light and modernity to the house. To a town dweller, the lack of people or sounds of civilisation were at first alarming, but later came the tuis, and the wood pigeons, the possums and the hedgehogs. New friends.

Well before we moved to Waikanae, Nurse had been installed in the house at 105 Woburn Road, Lower Hutt to take care of me. I was her sole charge since my sister and brother, six and ten years older, were beyond requiring a nurse and in any event, they were off at boarding school. By and large Nursey was a kindly old thing. True, she could wield a wooden spoon and on occasion a decent length of cane but most of the time she settled misdemeanours with a little advice. For a five-year-old most of this advice was mysterious. What 'worse things' could happen at sea? There was hardly ever 'spilt milk' about except in a deliberate attempt to curry favour with one of the cats and what exactly would 'manners' make the man into? Still, advice was a good alternative to the spoon or the cane. One proverb that Nursey and my parents alike agreed on was 'Children should be seen and not heard.' In those days, larger houses all had nurseries and they were not there for decoration. Small children stayed in nurseries and grown-ups stayed everywhere else.

One morning I escaped down Woburn Road to one of my favourite places: the Recreation Ground. There were always interesting things to see: rugby training, people walking dogs, flying kites, and sometimes the local pipe band practising with a scary drum major wielding his mace. This day it was very quiet until I spotted Nursey, wheezing and wobbling her way towards me, wielding her cane. Self-preservation set in. I climbed up the nearest lighting tower and peered down at Nursey.

'Come down this minute. You're a very naughty boy.'
Silence followed by, 'Promise not to hit me.'
Negotiation.
Promise extracted, I climbed slowly down.
Whack.

A new lesson learned about life.

We knew Waikanae quite well – not the area where Te Rama was or the village but the beach area where our family, long before we moved to Te Rama, had owned a smallish wooden bach, as New Zealanders call their beach houses. Our beachside house provided us with endless holiday pleasures, racing around the sandhills or netting whitebait in the little stream just before it reached the sea. A few miles across the water stood Kapiti Island. We used to take fishing trips out there but we never went ashore. The beach was dangerous and as far as we knew no one lived there. The fact that Te Rauparaha had made his base there many years before added to the island's mystery and, for me, a faint sense of dread.

My father used to drive us out to Waikanae at the weekends in his bilious green Mercury which rolled around the corners with an elephantine sway that made us all carsick. As there was no reception on the car radio outside Wellington we passed the time, when not vomiting, singing tone-deaf renditions of 'Ten Green Bottles' or 'Incy Wincy Spider'. I would often be crammed in the back with Maggie and Nurse, which was not helpful in the carsick department.

Down at the beach I would be left with Nurse while my parents went back to the house in Woburn Road. I had some friends across the road, Pete and Dorothy, and we would spend all day in the sandhills hiding in the long grass, chasing each other into the water and throwing spears made out of toetoe fronds. My friends' mother baked wondrous apple pies in humungous quantities. These were apple pies to die for. Not sophisticated little tarts that my mother might make but huge piles of crusty pastry covering great chunks of cooked apples freshly picked from the local orchid and smothered in local cream. For a small boy, it was impossible to eat too much apple pie.

Nursey was at the house in Lower Hutt as long as memory existed. She was there at bathtime, there at teatime (boiled eggs and soldiers a speciality) and there to conduct potty training.

'You sit there until you go.' Lifted up by the elbows, bottom of potty and bottom of boy inspected. No pellets or other emissions discovered; replaced until remedied. Squeeze hopefully. Nope. Oh well.

Nursey mostly did bedtime until father, if he was home, came up to read a story. Nursey leaned over, tucking me in, the odour of sour sweat or something more mysterious, finally recognised years later to be gin.

Nursey could best be described as bulky. She bulged in almost all directions. Pink arms extended from her uniform, steel-rimmed glasses gleamed and wispy grey hair tumbled down when not restrained by a posse of hairclips. Did I think she was my mother or didn't the distinction matter to me? Did I really have two mothers, the other one of whom was as different from Nursey as it was possible to be?

Mother probably didn't approve of proverbs, but when I had stuffed myself with whatever food was around and had to say 'no' to whatever was left on the plate she would pronounce that I was 'up to dolly's wax'.

'Waste not, want not,' muttered Nursey.

Small boys never ask questions about old people, at least I didn't, so I hardly knew anything about Nursey's background.

Each weekday I was left in the care of Nurse, an uncommon event in New Zealand in those days, and highly improbable these days. Families in New Zealand by and large never conceived of the idea of going through the trauma and joy of childbirth to then hand responsibility to another person, probably largely unknown to the parents. Mothers tended not to have jobs other than 'family duties' and, in the case of rural families, helping the old man run the farm, but my mother was engaged in important matters and spending quality or any other time with her children certainly wasn't part of her plan of how to spend a rewarding day.

It was not until years later when it was all too late that I pieced together Nurse's story (well, bits of it anyway). Her name was Ida

Nursey, me, Maggie and her friend

Rule and she came from Ashburton near Christchurch. She never married or had children so I became a surrogate baby for her and she loved me dearly except when belting me occasionally with a fair-sized stick. In the 1950s kids got belted when they did something wrong and there were tears but pretty soon we got over it. The exciting thing was finding out that she had a brother Jack, and Jack had the best job in the world. He was a fire spotter in the national forest outside Ashburton on the South Island. That meant he got to sit on a specially built wooden platform with a roof, at the top of the tallest tree in the forest, so he could look out for smoke. Sometimes he could sit up there all night. Imagine that. What a job. I knew about fires. Sometimes at night I could look out of the upstairs window in the Lower Hutt house and see gorse burning on the hills beyond the valley, twinkling and flaring and springing up somewhere new. I would hear a fire engine and hope it would come in our direction. I don't think Jack ever reported a fire since it rained a fair bit of the time around Ashburton. Nursey also said he was a rouseabout but I never was sure what that was.

My parents would have well understood the need for a good education and no doubt found the little public school down the road would not suffice. My only memory of that school was of being hit in the eye by a cricket ball while taking a shortcut across the cricket field, thus preventing a six being hit and incurring the wrath of a very pissed off batsman. In 1951 the family, including Nursey, decamped by ship to England, leaving my brother Christopher to his own devices in the Waikanae beach house. I never knew the main reason for this move but I think my father must have wanted to try running the business from the London end and I'm sure my mother would have been utterly sick of provincial Wellington and yearned for post-war London.

In England, I was sent to Eton House Preparatory School. What a dreadful shock for a six-year-old from Lower Hutt, New Zealand; however, I must have adapted. My school report noted I made 'excellent progress' and was ready for promotion. I did well at sport and also it seems in the classroom and, I note with pride, in music I was reported to have 'acute aural sense and sings very nicely. He enjoys Band, but his rhythmic sense is erratic.' This was sadly to be the pinnacle of my musical achievement.

My parents took my sister Maggie to 'the Continent.' She was eleven, probably a little young for a continental tour but my parents would have seen it as a great opportunity to show her that there was a world beyond the walls of the British Empire. The first stop was Uppsala in Sweden for a Liberal Party conference our grandfather Sir Percy was addressing. Then down through Germany to the Italian Lakes. They rolled along in a huge Humber Super Snipe: my father, mother, grandmothers Frieda and Doris, with Maggie squeezed in a corner. Two people less alike than my two grandmothers it would be hard to imagine but they apparently got along very well. I was sent with Nursey to a hotel somewhere on the south coast of England. All I remember is paddling out what seemed like miles in the freezing seawater before the water even reached my knees.

After nearly a year in London we returned to New Zealand first-class on the *Dominion Monarch*. Nursey must have found first-class interesting but she concentrated on looking after me and I suppose mixing with the other mothers or nannies whose major task was childminding and ensuring their charges didn't fall overboard.

Me with my friend Mopsie

7

MODERN WAIKANAE

At the age of six I don't remember having any real sense of the past or the future. I lived entirely in the present. I had spent virtually no time with my sister and none at all with my brother. There was no play, no chat, no correspondence, no shared experience of any sort. I neither looked forward to their company nor resented them. Since I had no close cousins and my parents seem to eschew close relations with friends, my memories are mainly of just me and Nurse. Oh, and the pets. I don't remember a single childhood friend before boarding school but I do remember the pets, the cats and most of all the dogs: the fat dachshund Adolf, who used to waddle around the garden chasing the chickens; later, the pug Mopsie, the standard poodle Schnapps and the canary; and much later the Great Danes and Dalmatians. They were always there to talk to and they always wanted to play.

The Waikanae town consisted of two parts; the older part lay to the east of the main road and rail link between Auckland and Wellington. Further east the land rose gently for about a mile and then lifted almost vertically into hills that were farmed on the lower slopes and topped by thick native bush, except where scarred by a deep quarry. Running east to west through the town, the Waikanae River flowed gently enough to the sea, unless carrying the sudden bouts of heavy rain or occasional snow melts from the Rimutaka Range behind. To the west, several miles from the main road, the toetoe covered sand dunes and the grey iron-sand beach looked out to Kapiti Island. This western part of Waikanae has developed steadily over the years as the citizens of Wellington have built their holiday 'baches' or retired to lawn bowls or fighting with the sand dunes to build a garden. Kapiti Island is now a bird sanctuary.

The town in the 1950s was unremarkable. For many years it contained no more than the normal requirements for a simple life: a butcher, bank, garage and Four Square store. Recently, like everywhere else, it has added the obligatory shopping centre, pub, betting shop, more garages and so on. Notwithstanding that, little beyond the desire for a quiet life would draw anyone to live there. The principal occupation of the current incumbents is 'retired'.

Te Rama stood almost in the centre of about forty acres, of which a good third was taken up by native rainforest. On the eastern and northern boundaries were substantial sheep properties, the main one only accessible by sharing the driveway. No other dwelling was visible from it, except from the upstairs windows, which also overlooked the distant beach and Kapiti Island.

The design of Te Rama reflected that lessons had been learned from the 1903 fire that had destroyed its predecessor. All chimneys were carried up free of the walls except the one from the drawing room fireplace in the centre of the house, and this was encased in a solid mass of concrete that interrupted the rimu panelling of the main passage. The passage was a gloomy channel running through the centre-line of the house with a right-angled bend to the side door, which was our usual way in and out of the house. All bedrooms were initially on the ground floor, the two upper rooms being known as the 'day room', 'school room' or 'sewing room' at different stages. These were eventually converted into bedrooms. The gable had a wonderful folding set of windows which looked west over the tree tops to Kapiti Island, a few miles out to sea from Waikanae Beach, itself a good four miles from the house site. This room adjoined another bedroom with gabled windows over the garden and these two, with a shared bathroom, became almost a self-contained apartment.

My original bedroom was the small annex at the very end of the main corridor. It had a double bunk and a set of drawers and a lavatory at the end, which opened onto the veranda. I kept some of my pets in there. Tadpoles in jars, waiting to grow legs, lizards in a box of dried leaves, which kept escaping under the bed, worms in a jar of compost. The black cat slept on the end of the bed and kept my feet warm. I didn't like the dark so the light in the corridor had to stay on at night. It was always silent at night except for the wind in the bush and the moreporks calling to each other.

After a few years at boarding school and conquering my fear of the dark I moved upstairs to the self-contained apartment. It was a wonderful space to live in. My Scalextric electric car and other 'stuff' could be strewn across the floor. My mother never came up there so the bed could remain unmade and books, dinky toys and meccano (the precursor to Lego) lay about everywhere. I would watch the sun set behind Kapiti and shine through the bay windows, or listen to the rain beat down on the corrugated iron roof. I luxuriated in breaking every rule that applied at boarding school: stuff lay everywhere, the bed was unmade and instead of being woken by the chapel bell at 6.30 and subjected to a freezing morning walk I could lie in bed as long as I liked, accompanied by a dozing cat.

It was a wonderful, romantic idea for our family to move to Waikanae from the suburban comfort of our family house in Lower Hutt. I suspect my mother was determined to escape suburbia and the beautiful native bush surrounding the farmhouse was anything but suburban. Never mind that my father had to drive the hour into town and back again every day, that they were far from the comforts and convenience of city living – here she could be ruler of all she surveyed.

I am grateful to have grown up in such a landscape and in such a uniquely New Zealand house. Arriving at Te Rama always produced a stirring of excitement. Abruptly the car left the main highway and entered a gravel driveway. The drive plunged into a vault of dark green native trees intertwined with ferns, pungas and nikaus that leaned towards each other. At the top of the drive the old house sat comfortably just where you wanted it. It was as if you had somehow crossed a border into your own kingdom, a place apart from the aggravations of a world run by others.

Te Rama's main veranda ran the whole length of the front of the house and spilled onto a terrace surrounded by garden beds, a pool full of rushes and goldfish, and finally the lawn. On the other side of the lawn lay the bush, which had never been touched. It grew just as it always had before any white man, or even the Maori, had come to the area. It was a wonderful sub-tropical jungle of high trees, which spread a canopy over the underlying growth of pungas and low ferns, sloping steeply up from the lawn and made impassable to most people by a profusion of thick vines. In among the general foliage grew large pururi trees, covered with berries, and home to the huge native wood pigeons, pale grey with white aprons on their chests. The pigeons would gorge on the berries and then scarcely be able to fly as they swooped across the lawn. The tuis, shining blue-black with the white tuft under their chins, would perch somewhere and sing their peal of bell-like chimes in the morning sun. Lower down the smaller birds could be seen in profusion. White-eyes, fantails, grey warblers and some of the introduced birds like thrushes, blackbirds and various finches would nest without fear of any worse predator than a couple of bored cats.

In the evening after dinner I had some interesting choices in those preteen years. There was no television and not much on the radio, except when I was glued to BBC imports: 'The Day of the Triffids', 'Hancock's Half Hour', 'The Goons', 'Journey into Space'; the BBC was keeping a small boy at the other end of the planet from BBC's Broadcasting House transfixed, even though there were many references to things British I hardly understood.

When nothing was on the radio I had other diversions. On a cool clear night, I would take Kichi the Great Dane for a walk the half mile to the letterbox. There were no letters of course but I would crunch across the pebbles on the drive under the overhang of trees. At the halfway point Kichi and I would pause in silence. After a few seconds, I would gently lift the canopy of ferns that hung over the banks that had been dug out when the drive was originally built. There I was mesmerised by a carpet of stars twinkling and glowing like tiny sapphires – the whole bank glittered with glow-worms. I would crouch down and just look until my knees hurt. I could never reconcile myself to the idea that these tiny worms could live in a light silken web and somehow produce a light at the end of their body to attract their prey or for mating purposes. They were vicious little predators. If you touched the web or used a light their glow would disappear, so crouching in the dark was the best way to share this hidden treasure. If you looked up through the canopy of bush, the stars were there, a sky full of glow-worms.

In some ways for me the creek was the heart of Te Rama, neatly bisecting the forty acres that the property covered.

The creek was the dwelling place of my enemy – the eels that lived there, the fat oily predators that fed on the life in the stream. The eels grew thicker than my arm. I hated the eels. Eels are everywhere in New Zealand rivers and streams, big ugly buggers, fat and menacing, the masters of the waterways. We had heard somewhere they came from the Sargosso Sea, wherever that was, and that each year they went back to the sea to breed and then returned. My favourite activity was to slip out of the house at night and down to the stream, where it ran into the pond below the weir. The stream held small native trout, cockabillies and tiny fresh water crayfish but they were all preyed on by the eels. They ate the fish and the crayfish and would attack the ducklings as they were learning to swim in the pool in the chookyard.

I would set off into the night.

I took a shovel handle, shortened it and fixed a couple of feet of Number 8 fencing wire to it, using fencing staples. Then I patiently filed the end of the wire until little by little I had a razor-sharp point with flukes. Preparing for my hunt, I had secreted a couple of chooks eggs in the undergrowth by the stream. After a few days, they were well and truly rotten. On a cloudless black night, I set off from the house, makeshift spear in one hand and torch in the other. I collected the eggs and headed for the pond below the waterfall, where I knew I could scramble down the bank. Once perched on the water's edge I cracked the eggs, ignoring the foul smell, tipped them into the water and waited patiently, scanning the water with the torch. Sure enough, soon there was a disturbance below the surface, a flash of skin and then the wedge-shaped head of an eel, gills slowly fluttering as he warily approached the eggs. Backward and forward cautiously he finally came close enough and I very slowly lowered the spear tip into the water just behind his head so that it was nearly touching his skin. Then I thrusted as hard as I could and the spear went right through him. The eel thrashed and twisted itself around the shovel handle, squirming and writhing in anger at this attack. I scrambled back up the bank and drove the spear into a fallen tree branch so the eel was pinned there writhing, exuding a sticky ooze that covered everything. Satisfied he was not going to escape I headed back to the house. There was no point staying; all of us boys knew that eels never die until midnight.

In the morning, sure enough the eel would be dead and I would need to hack him off the spear with an old scout knife, trying to avoid the slime as best I could. He could be a metre or more long and in an act of revenge I would feed the bits to the geese and ducks, cackling in excitement in the chookyard.

During the day, I liked to go after the young eels further up the creek where the pools and, likewise, the eels were much smaller. I would turn over a large rock in a pool and wait until the mud cleared. Sometimes there was a small freshwater crayfish, a cockabully or a native trout but often there would be a smaller eel. The eel would flee to the end of the pool but then lie still in the shallows. I would creep along the bank, step into the shallows infinitely slowly, pause, slide my fingers under his belly, rub gently until in position and with a flick land him up the bank where I would slam a bucket over him. I would turn the bucket over and off we would go to the geese who would waddle over to meet me, excited at this unexpected delicacy. Sometimes a few sheep would wander over to see what the fuss was about but they soon returned to slowly chomping grass. Eels were of no interest to sheep. The magpies sat on the fence and talked to themselves: a bit of eel might have suited them quite well but the geese had first call.

Whenever I went out at night the bush would be gently disturbed by the sigh of a light breeze and the call of the moreporks, the owls that perched up high surveying the nocturnal goings on and whose name mimicked their call. Always there would be the rustle of possums scrambling through the fruit trees. Introduced from Australia, the possums were busy, without any natural predators, devastating the bush and the gardens alike. Kichi hated them and would rush into the trees barking in furious frustration. We kept the .22 rifle leaned up against the front door, which of course was never locked.

Not that we ever worried about intruders but a Great Dane was a comfort if someone happened to be in the house alone. The bullets for the .22 were kept loose in the desk drawer next to the rifle, which had been in its position for so long the forward sight had scratched a hole in the wallpaper. No one ever worried about gun crime because there had hardly ever been any in New Zealand, at least that we had ever heard of, but the .22 got plenty of use. Kichi's ears would prick up at some sound too low for us to hear and she would be on her feet and at the door. As soon as she was let out she would tear across the lawn and plant herself beneath the tree with the offending possum. I would go after her with the rifle, some bullets and my headlamp. It didn't take long to locate the possum and light it up with the lamp. Then bang, and the possum would tumble out of the tree to land with a crash. Kichi would leap on the unfortunate possum and disappear with her victim, which would be found weeks later half-buried somewhere around the garden. The possums became such a menace in New Zealand the government paid a bounty and many a farmer's son would make some pocket money taking the tail and an ear to a collection point in return for two and sixpence, I seem to remember. Something like eight million possums were shot under this scheme but that hardly made a dent in the numbers.

If, after dark, I went to the back door where mother had put the cat's milk, often I would find a hedgehog or two with their snouts over the edge of the saucer, enjoying a drink. I would very gently slide my hands under the hedgehog and carefully lift him up. He would immediately curl up into a tight ball where his sharp spines could protect him. After a time, he would decide there was no danger, cautiously unwind and sit on my hand sniffing suspiciously, the soft hair of his underside tickling my palm. I would slowly put him down and he would return to his milk. The hedgehogs became quite tame but even though I called one of them Henry I never really knew which was which.

One birthday my parents presented me with an air rifle. It fired little lead pellets not a great distance using a spring action mechanism. I mostly fired at static targets like leaves or tin cans on the top of fence posts. One day I was wandering through the orchard cradling the air rifle when I saw a pair of tiny fantails doing a sort of dance, suggesting the proximity of a nest. One of them stopped at my approach and flew to a branch. I raised the air rifle and fired. The bird toppled over and fluttered to the ground where it did a few slowing circles and then lay dead. Its companion squawked and conducted a frantic flutter above its body. I stood staring. I couldn't believe what I had done. I picked up the small body in a vain hope that it was somehow still alive and then had to put it gently back down. How had I thought this was a good thing to do? I never told anybody and certainly not my parents. Even as I grew older and the event more remote I would find myself full of remorse. I still do.

There were plenty of jobs to occupy a small boy. We had a dairy cow, a Jersey, naturally called Daisy, and she had to be milked. I soon became used to putting a bridle on her and bringing her into the shed. I would sit on a stool and milk her, holding a teat in each hand between thumb and forefinger, and soon fall into a satisfying rhythm until the bucket was nearly full. A surviving amenity, far enough away to miss the fire, was a complete brick dairy, with wide concrete shelves for the milk pans. In the early days of Waimahoe, years before we arrived at Te Rama, the operation of the dairy was described by an unknown writer in a manuscript entitled 'Waimahoe: The Old House' that exists at the Turnbull Library, as follows:

> *The cream was skimmed by shallow perforated discs and drained into earthenware jars till there was enough for making butter. The churn was a solid oaken barrel mounted on trunions on a solid stand. Making butter was one of the chores for a boy and the steady turning in the height of summer could seem interminable till the monotonous gurgle changed to the thrilling slop, slop and the eagerly awaited sight through the glass peep hole of a splodge of yellow. Adults could now be called in to open the churn, and the reward was a drink of fresh butter-milk. Butter was still kept in summertime in the cool tunnel of the creek deviation at the gate of the home paddock.*

In our day, the inside of the dairy was immaculately clean and the milking machine stood on a bench, a Laval model, I remember. I would help the gardener, Joan's husband Brian, separate the milk in the old hand separator. The separator was a work of art. The milk trickled down through a series of inverted funnels from a bowl and as the whole thing revolved the milk and cream separated, the latter to be used to make butter. You had to wind the handle on the side of the churn as quickly as you could or the warning chimes would start ringing to tell you the funnels were clogging up. The whole process took quite a while, what with having to wash all the pieces each time.

On Wednesdays, I would wait for the greengrocers' truck and climb up on it when it arrived rumbling up the drive, and talk the old Chinese man who owned it into an apricot or a peach out of the array of boxes at the back. The truck had a flatbed and he displayed his wares each side of it. All manner of fruit and vegetable was on offer, all of it grown on the rich local soil minus any poison spray or artificial fertiliser. In those days, the countryside seemed to be devoid of pests much beyond caterpillars and a few wasps.

The hens had to be attended to as well. They lived in the stable, which only occasionally held one of my sister's horses, or in the chook shed next door to the milking shed, and it was somehow always a thrill to open the nesting box and find some fine brown eggs sitting there in a nest of straw or even to slip a hand under a protesting hen to feel how many eggs she might be sitting on.

The fruit trees had been at Te Rama, dotted randomly about, long before we arrived. When the fruit ripened, a contest would take place between the possums, the birds and the humans over who would get to them first. Actually, there was always enough to go around. There were a few varieties of apples, but my favourite was russets. They had a hard, olive-coloured skin and a wonderful sweet-and-sour taste. There were apricots, plums and peaches, and lying about under the trees were overripe fruit, birds pecking at them.

Behind the stables was the vegetable patch. It was protected by wire netting but it always had holes in it so rabbits and birds were constantly invading. Weeds would spring up and my father or

Brian would grub them out so the vegetables and fruit could grow up. Cabbages, lettuces, carrots, potatoes, globe artichokes, onions, aubergine (never eggplant) and then the fruit: strawberries and raspberries, blackcurrants and boysenberries, and rhubarb, which was supposed to be planted over the body of a dead animal if you wanted it to grow especially well. Adolf the dachshund was under there somewhere.

I don't think the plants were ever sprayed. In Waikanae's pleasant climate everything grew and there was no shortage of manure around to give them a boost.

The house framed and gave shape to my life. Parents came and went, doing whatever grown-ups did, older brother and sister always seemed to be somewhere else, and boarding school was never more than a week or two away. But the house and the redwood tree near the cottage, and the cats and dogs and birds and eels, were always there. Looking back, my life there was quite solitary. I would disappear all day without telling anyone where I was going, something I never knew until I arrived anyway. No one worried and no one ever asked and somehow, I never seemed to miss the company of other children.

Waikanae Beach also played its role in my life. My father had an open timber clinker-built boat with an inboard engine. It was immensely heavy. He would sit it on a wooden trailer and back it down to the water's edge where it would inevitably get stuck in the sand but there were always a few locals to give us a push. The same procedure occurred to get it out of the water, although even more heaving would be required and usually at the cost of a couple of snapper by way of thanks. We would hop over the side of the boat, cross fingers the engine would start and head out to Kapiti for a bit of fishing. The fishing was really good at Kapiti and mostly we had it to ourselves. There were snapper, terakihi, blue and red cod, moki, John Dory, grouper, gurnard and more. On the way back we would watch out for the white terns and head to them, as underneath would be big schools of kahawai. We would throw a line over the back with a crude lure and straight away we would be hauling them in, as quickly as we could. Kahawai like to jump and fight, which only made it more fun. It was a bit of a waste because in those days no one would eat them. If we wanted fish for eating, the snapper, cod and terakihi were great. Sometimes the waves got up pretty high between the island and the beach, especially if a southerly gale was building up through Cook Strait. Short waves with steep sides would begin to roll in. You needed to keep the nose of the boat headed into them to avoid being swamped. We would be soaked and cold but it was so much fun.

Back on the beach we would unwind the flounder net. It was pretty big, about ten metres long, weighted on the bottom with lead and with cork floats on top. With a grown-up on the deep end and me on the shallow end we would sweep along the beach parallel with the shore, slowly moving through the waves. I would have to jump off the bottom when a big wave came in but also try to keep the net on the sand. When we turned into the shore there would be a couple of beautiful flounder in the bottom.

My other favourite fishing expedition was to take my whitebait net, made of Number 8 fencing wire and a sort of muslin, and head off to the Waimea stream at the other end of the beach from the river. For certain there would be hardly anyone around, maybe an 'old chap', hat pulled down, trousers rolled up, smoking a 'roll-your-own', with his net in the best spot. I would soon find a spot of my own on a bend in the stream, position my net close to the edge and walk a few metres downstream, scattering a few bits of sand into the water to stir up the whitebait. If possible, I would time my expedition for the incoming tide. You could hear the ripples slapping gently on the sand as the incoming sea ran up against the outgoing stream, the perfect time for whitebait netting. Of course, these are real New Zealand whitebait, like no other in the world, not much bigger than a match. I would sit dreamily on the bank of the stream, watching the seabirds and oystercatchers and, using a blade of the spinifex or sedge that grew everywhere among the sand dunes, stir up the little crabs that scuttled importantly about. Along the banks of the stream grew flax bushes with long sword-shaped leaves and rigid flower stalks projecting high above them. Toetoe were everywhere, their soft white fronds fluttering in the breeze. Soon a tui, black and gleaming with a white tuft of feathers under its chin, would come to feed on the nectar, emitting clicks and cries and then the bell-like call. There was always plenty of life to see in and around the stream if you just sat still and quiet, listened to the breakers on the beach and the gulls mewling, and waited. Peace would be upon the Earth. After a while I would stop daydreaming and lift the net and there in the bottom would be a shimmering little ball of tiny white and silver fish. Before long I would fill my billy with my catch, take it home and into the pan with just a little beaten egg and flour to coat them, salt, pepper and lemon and you truly have one of the dishes of the gods. Master chefs, with a thousand ingredients, mixing and mashing and beating and stirring, could never make anything as delicious as whitebait out of the stream and into the pan.

    High on the Kebble farm behind our house the mountain stream fed a pipe that provided our domestic water. From the collection point for the house water, the creek ran steeply downhill, through the Kebbles' lambing paddock and under the barbed wire fence that formed the southern boundary. More slowly it meandered down through the sheep paddock, under the fence behind the stables, through the chook run, then the yard where the ducks and geese squabbled with the hens over the scrap bucket each morning, through a small patch of trees over a weir into a pond and down further behind the orchard, into another deeper pond and into the native bush. From there it ran on, overhung by thick native trees and hanging vines, spilling into one more deep pond and then out of the bush and over a small waterfall before a final long leap into the Waikanae River.

    When it rained hard I would lie in bed listening to the rain pounding on the corrugated iron roof. In the morning, the stream would be up and you could hear it leaping over the waterfall into the pond by the apple trees. The water would quickly turn brown and that would be the end of the stream's activities for a few days.

No one but I ever ventured along the banks of the stream but I knew every pond and waterfall and where all the river life lived. The only way to get through from the house to the Waikanae River was at the last of the ponds, its sides steep and impassable rock faces, to jump in, swim across and scramble out on the rocks on the other side. Who on earth but I would want to do that? The bush in New Zealand has no predators and neither do the rivers so all I needed were a pair of shorts, bare feet and a sixth sense about where you could safely put a foot down or use a low hanging vine as a swing.

Our parents, when they moved to Te Rama, lived in some style, approximating as closely as possible in rural New Zealand the local squire and his wife. Father had inherited a baronetcy when his father died in 1952, and people with a title were not common in rural New Zealand. In those days, New Zealand was still very much an outpost of the Empire, so the title conferred a degree of status that, in these days of growing republicanism, no longer applies. Father always opened the local gymkhana, and handed out prizes for best cake or prettiest pony. Although our parents were well recognised in the tiny village, the two of them had virtually no contact with the surrounding farmers, with whom they had nothing in common, and a strictly working relationship with the tradespeople.

Te Rama became something of a destination for all sorts of visiting dignitaries. My mother was delighted to offer sophisticated entertainment in the bush, with the tuis and wood pigeons providing an exotic backdrop for overseas visitors. Chancellor Willy Brandt of Germany was one such visitor, and Swedish prince Count Carl Johan Bernadotte of Wisborg another, the latter taking a fancy to the two Dalmatians then in residence. On one occasion, most of the officers of a British aircraft carrier HMS *Hermes*, visiting Wellington, made the journey out to Waikanae. I was dazzled by their array of medals. Edward Woodward and Vivien Leigh also visited and there were of course a string of local politicians and diplomats. My parents were friends with the British High Commissioner, Sir George Mallaby, and the Governor General of New Zealand, the 10th Viscount Cobham. The Governor General lived in an appropriately substantial mansion in Wellington next to the Basin Reserve cricket ground. My parents were always attending functions there or at the High Commissioner's house. Viscount Cobham's daughter Katy was part of our group and 'a good fun gal'. The Viscount made the error of inviting us all to celebrate her birthday at the Governor General's residence. The Under-20 Varsity rugby team all dressed up in black tie and off we went. Things predictably deteriorated and I was ashamed, the next day at least, to have been politely reprimanded after an involvement in a food fight in the kitchen.

Pat involved herself with a variety of charities and, in the early days, with politics, until she fell out with the National Party. She thereafter decided she was a socialist, so far as her commitment to socialism didn't prohibit first-class travel, and became a ferocious partisan of the Labour Party.

Te Rama before the fire, mid 1980s

8

THE NEIGHBOURS

Shortly before Christmas each year my mother would hold a party, to which a few locals, the odd potter or artist, and one or two of the neighbouring farmers would be summonsed. The parents of my friend Peter Field ('Young Peter'), who owned 'Tini', the farm up the road, would be included. The Fields were one of the very few old Waikanae families and had, at one time, owned half the surrounding farmland. My friendship with 'Young Peter' was wonderful, giving me friendship and the chance to roam beyond my adventures at Te Rama and into the surrounding farm country, especially Tini.

Tini was one of the Field family farms and had been in the family for many generations. 'Old Peter', a decorated ex-fighter pilot with a strong liking for whisky, would seize the rare opportunity of the Christmas party to swallow as much of my father's liquor as he could. Thus fortified, he would dare to treat my mother with casual familiarity, which she would be forced to tolerate. Old Peter's ruddy complexion, the result of years of sun and wind and whisky, was rutted like the gullies and ravines in the hills of the family farm. My parents were not keen on the telling of jokes, but Peter, to muffled titters, would regale the room with the latest from the saleyards. I was always delighted. Inevitably he would be the last to leave, dragged away puffing his foul-smelling pipe by his wife, Dorothy. Demure and self-effacing, the very picture of a prosperous farmer's wife, she would push him into the passenger's seat and drive very slowly the mile up the road to Tini. As the door closed my mother would explode. 'God, I thought they would never leave. He really is the most ghastly old bore.' But I loved Peter and was especially in awe of his war stories, which had me in a Spitfire over the English Channel with an ME109 on my tail.

During school holidays, I would 'help' on Tini. The Fields' farm fronted the highway, which went the length of the North Island, from Wellington in the south to Auckland in the north. Tini was about 700 acres, which was more than enough to be economic in those days, especially given it had some good arable land and abundant water. 'Help' consisted of me, a couple of years younger than Young Peter, trailing along behind Young Peter and Old Peter. There was always plenty to do. There was lambing when the ewes had to be watched and sometimes helped with a difficult birth, crutching the sheep to remove the dags (wool with matted pellets of manure around the tail), running the sheep through the sheep dip, and castrating and docking. They used rubber rings for castrating but the first time I went Young Peter told me they were going to bite the testicles off with their teeth. I shot away as quick as I could in case they wanted a new recruit. Old Peter had a good laugh and swore it never happened but later I found out sometimes it did. 'Mountain oysters,' he said. 'Bloody tasty on the hotplate.'

Young Peter was my best friend, I suppose, but he was older so even though we both went to Wanganui Collegiate we never spoke to each other at school. Only on the farm could we be friends.

One of the biggest events was when shearing time arrived. The sheep were herded into the pens around the shearing shed with the dogs racing back and forth snapping at their hooves. The shearing gang would arrive, mainly Maori men from up the road in Levin, wearing their shorts and Jackie Howe blue shearing singlets. They were big guys with bulging thighs and biceps. They ruled the shearing shed and everyone else was just there to help push the sheep through the race or sweep up or make endless cups of tea. They could toss a big ewe on her back, grip her under the chin and shear her in nothing flat. The shearing shed had a corrugated iron roof and a slatted floor for the waste to drop through. It smelt great – hot sheep, humans but most of all newly sheared wool. When it was all over Old Peter would throw a massive party with a local band playing country music, beer in kegs, wrestling, shouting and excitement and best of all, girls, or so Young Peter told me.

Sometimes for a change we would hop in the jeep and head out to do a bit of fencing, carrying rolls of Number 8 fencing wire and fixing broken fences or rigging new ones. Then in the spring the hay had to be cut, baled and stacked. I would stagger about with one bale of hay trying to heave it on top of the stack and avoid the Scotch thistles. All the time the farm dogs would be with us, black and white and running everywhere under the control of Old Peter, who would curl his tongue and whistle or yell 'get in behind' at them. I loved the dogs but lived a bit in fear of them. We had been lectured about washing our hands and not letting them lick us. Hydatids was a scary disease. A cyst full of worms that could burst and infect your innards. Young Peter and I believed the worms would crawl through your intestines and out your bottom when you were sleeping, or eat your brain. We reckoned some village kid had had one a foot long but it was probably a tapeworm.

Old Peter decided to build a new milking shed on some flat land the other side of the main road down the hill from his house. Everyone driving past on the newly christened 'State Highway 1' saw this white-painted brick building with a terracotta roof and windows going up, and thought Old Peter was building a new house. It was the best milking shed ever built but nothing was too good for Old Peter's cows.

The seasons changed and pretty often a southerly gale would blow in over Cook Strait. Huge gusts of wind would deposit buckets of rain in a wet blanket over the steep hillsides. The rain would cascade down the gullies, digging them ever deeper. The trees had all been cut down long ago and the sheep had grazed the grass down to nothing so sometimes there would be a landslide. Erosion would cause the whole side of the hill to slip away, leaving a clay scar behind on which nothing could grow. It would take years to repair the damage. The creek would burst its banks and I would stomp around in my gumboots looking for frogs or tadpoles in the isolated pools that formed in the gullies.

When the weather improved, it was time for aerial top dressing. I would go up to the boundary paddock at Te Rama and watch as the Fletcher top-dressing plane would come rumbling in low over the neighbours' paddocks, dropping a ton of fertiliser as it went. The Fletcher was a stubby little plane, specially designed for tough conditions. They could take off anywhere and fly between the hills and trees, just above the ground. Too high and the fertiliser would blow everywhere. If the wind was in the right direction, the pilot would give me a cheeky thumbs up, and Te Rama would receive a free top dressing and so would I. Sometimes I wanted to be a Fletcher pilot and sometimes a shearer but I kept these ambitions to myself.

As a special treat, Old Peter would roar through the Waikanae River in his World War II jeep with Young Peter and me hanging out the sides. The jeep would be in four-wheel drive and lurch over the boulders before struggling up the far bank. The windscreen had long gone so as we charged into the river a tidal wave would come over the bonnet and I would arrive home soaked to the skin. Bliss.

An annual event, looked forward to for months, was the Field cricket match, held in the front paddock at Tini, with a specially mowed pitch and the sheep shit mostly removed. It involved a keenly fought contest between the 'Country Hicks' and the 'City Slickers', who had come out from town for the day. The field was lined by ancient poplars with the shearing shed on one boundary. I was immensely proud to be asked to play for the Hicks, not those city softies. A barbecue was set up in half an old oil drum, sausages cooked, sandwiches eaten and fairy cake with hundreds and thousands served with tea, the canteen overseen by Old Peter's wife, Dorothy. Of course, there was plenty of beer cooling in the chilly bin. Old Peter, who was umpiring, persuaded the Hicks' captain, who had been in the Air Force with him, to have a quick whisky or two before the start to keep the cold out. The captain then trundled uncertainly out to open the batting for the Hicks. He missed the first two deliveries by a wide margin. The third ball, he took a tremendous swing, missed and the ball bounced twice before rolling into the stumps with just enough momentum to dislodge the bails. It was one of the rare balls our 'leggie' bowled straight all day. Young Peter was our bowling strike weapon and soon had four of the Hicks on their way, three of them LBW. Old Peter, who had elected himself a permanent umpire, solemnly raised his finger and waved away any protests.

My parents usually avoided this entertainment and of course as usual my brother and sister were elsewhere so no one from my family was ever there to cheer me on, but since my cricket skills were less than scintillating that was probably for the good.

Sometimes I would do odd jobs around the district but holidays were short and opportunities were few. I do remember helping the village butcher. On one occasion, I helped with the tripe. The texture and the smell put me off tripe forever. Another time, we were making sausages using a sort of churn to push the sausage meat out of a tube that had sheep intestines rolled over it; a quick churn, spin of the wrist to tie off and, hey presto, a string of sausages. The butcher thought this was a particularly all-purpose material since the sheep's intestines could also double as French letters, he told me with a wink. I tried to look knowing.

Old Peter's reputation locally finally reached legend status in the village. He was rumoured to have inoperable stomach cancer, and subjected to constant sympathy and concerned inquiries from the locals. After many much discussed visits to various local medical luminaries, someone decided to X-ray him. It revealed he was walking about with a small half-moon-shaped piece of glass in his stomach. Luckily for him it was lead crystal and showed up on the X-ray machines. Upon further reflection, he recalled that at a particularly long and wet dinner party he had bitten a chunk out of the Stuart crystal. On not finding the missing piece the next day he had forgotten about it. There was collective relief and admiration for anyone who could go about their daily business with a chunk of glass embedded in their stomach.

Young Peter's Uncle Geoff was a recluse who lived in a crumbling timber house halfway to the beach. He wasn't invited to the party at Te Rama, and wouldn't have come if he had been. He was a bachelor and spent his days entering the crossword competition in Wellington's newspaper, *The Dominion*. He always won the very small cash prize that was on offer, and eventually they refused to accept any more entries from him. Geoff was hardly the domestic type; he disliked cooking, making tea being an exception, so each day he would cycle to the shops and buy two pies – one for lunch and one for dinner. What's more, he kept every newspaper he had ever read. When he finally died, the house was filled to the ceiling with old newspapers. Those cleaning up shook the mouse droppings off the papers and spent a happy time looking at faded yellowing headlines covering the end of the Great War, the Depression, Pearl Harbour and the assassination of Kennedy.

His most prized possession was a vintage Lagonda that none of the locals had ever seen. The trees grew up in front of his garage so that he couldn't get it out, until eventually his teeth played up and he chopped down the trees and drove the Lagonda at twenty-five miles an hour to Levin to get a plate fitted. Thereafter this became an annual pilgrimage and, if you wanted to see the Lagonda, you had to find out when the old man was scheduled to have his teeth fixed.

Sometime in the mid 1960s when I was in the UK at university and receiving a letter every couple of months from home I learned that Young Peter had died in a car accident. Apparently, it was Easter, the roads were busy and Pete tried to turn off the main road across the traffic into the gateway of the old Tini, where the annual cricket match was played. He mistimed and turned into the oncoming traffic. It was a head-on and Peter never recovered consciousness. For his parents, it was a total tragedy; their only child was gone and they had no one to pass their beloved farm to. I'm ashamed to say I couldn't think about it so I deliberately put it out of my head and I never wrote. I'm still ashamed; it was important to write. We had been old friends in a special way and it would have mattered. How did I not know that I should have written?

Living in Waikanae sent confusing signals to me about who I was. We lived in two different cultures. On the one hand, we were surrounded at home by books, international art and affairs, and in all our other contacts by local matters, the price of wool and the rugby. We drank coffee, the locals drank tea. We drank French wine, they drank local beer. We had the Miros and they had the Frances Hodgkins landscapes. We were Knightsbridge living in rural New Zealand. My father would be complaining about the number of Etonians in the Tory Government, mother would be describing some unfortunate local dignitary as 'common', while I was in the back paddock kicking a football with a mate and pretending to like the taste of beer. I never talked to my brother or sister about how they felt but it must have been the same, but not quite. How we turned out depended on how strongly the contrary currents pulled at us.

Boys at the swimming pool, St Peter's School, Cambridge, New Zealand

9

SCHOOL

I couldn't spend all my time roaming around Te Rama's forty untouched acres on my own. With no suitable local school, there was no alternative for me but boarding school, even had my parents been minded, which they were not, to keep me closer to home.

In the 1950s, most boarding schools in rural New Zealand were alike, imposing red-brick and tile edifices surrounded by damp lawns and conifers. Each of us three children dutifully attended one of them. Year after year teachers tried with slowly dwindling enthusiasm to instil into uncomprehending children the same curriculum that had dominated the lives of thousands of British children: English, maths, French, geography and history, the latter focusing on William the Conqueror, the perfidious French and how the great Anglo-Saxon alliance won any wars worth mentioning. A smattering of Latin was added for the upper stream and children gazed out of the window or used penknives to redesign their desks as the mysteries of Caesars' Gallic campaigns unfolded. The buildings were designed to remind the children of the 'Old Country', and of course all these boarding schools were single-sex and for that matter single religion, either Catholic or in our case Church of England. Jews were tolerated as long as they didn't practise. I knew nothing about the Jews as either a race or religion, nor did I even know about my Jewish great-grandfather.

My mother was an ardent atheist who had been brought up in Australia, and her grandfather had been a Presbyterian pastor. Years later it occurred to me that she was probably mildly anti-Semitic and I think she must have had some sort of agreement with my father that the Jewish connection would never be mentioned in our house. Jack was hardly Jewish. He had been brought up in Church of England schools and university, and by a mother who was steeped either in faddish new age religions or occultism. When Percy had a Rabbi sent to instruct Jack and Nicholas in Yiddish Frieda refused to let him in the door.

It was probably not until I was well into my forties that I discovered we had cousins in Auckland and that they were Jewish. I have still never been inside a synagogue. Like Jack, the schools we children attended were all strictly Church of England and no nonsense was allowed relating to other branches of the Christian Church let alone, perish the thought, Catholics. Catholics attended the school up on the hill and we didn't know anything about them beyond the fact that their lives were regulated by women dressed as penguins. We certainly didn't compete with them on the sporting field but fortunately no one had thought to rule out sporting contests with nearby Maori schools nor to exclude Maori from attending our school where we were all great friends and ardent in our desire to smash any other school at rugby, whatever their background.

My brother Christopher, ten years older than me, remote and venerated by me from afar, had attended a preparatory school called St George's up the coast a few hundred miles in Wanganui, but unbeknown to me there had occurred a nasty scandal involving the headmaster and 'interference' with the boys. After decades of indifference to widespread claims of grotesque abuse of children by institutions, almost entirely run by men, the last decade has seen the public exposure, particularly in Australia, of the extent of the abuse. But this was 1950s New Zealand and no self-respecting Kiwi was going to stand for that sort of behaviour. All hell broke loose. The headmaster committed suicide as I later discovered and presumably everyone was then satisfied. My parents had to find an alternative to St George's for me and St Peter's was their choice.

St Peter's was something else in 1950s New Zealand. Back in England there had existed for many years a successful textile business called Tootal Broadhurst Lee, with branches or distributors all over the world, including Australia, Canada and New Zealand. It seems Arthur Francis Brooks Broadhurst was at some brief point a director. Arthur Broadhurst monetised, to use a twenty-first-century expression, his share of the family investment and set off across the world to pursue his dream of creating an English public school to engender the virtues of the Empire in some far off and deprived venue. Godliness, Cleanliness, Manners, Truthfulness et cetera were trumpeted, but above all these was his passion for music. Arthur Broadhurst had travelled across Europe, the Middle East, Asia and finally Australia and New Zealand before he came across 100 acres of beautiful rolling countryside on the banks of the Waikato River, New Zealand's longest river, and resembling as closely as possible a part of Kent. The school, designed by the renowned American architect Roy Alston Lippincott, opened in February 1936 with only thirty-five pupils.

By the time I arrived in 1953 the countryside was decidedly English. There were hawthorn hedges along the fence lines, oak trees, silver birches lining the elegant driveway that swept up to the main building from Hamilton to Cambridge Road, chestnuts and a well-developed orchard full of apple, apricot and plum trees.

Dressed in my brand new powder-blue school blazer, short pants, and matching cap emblazoned with the school motto '*Structa Saxo*', my parents dumped me, aged seven, with Nurse on guard, at Paekakariki Station to await the arrival of the overnight express to the Waikato where the school was located, near the small town of Cambridge. '*Structa Saxo*', meaning 'built on a rock', was central to St Peter's ethos. It comes from Matthew 16:18 in which Jesus says to his disciple Peter, 'Thou art Peter and upon this rock I shall build my church and the gates of hell shall not prevail against it.' But initially I had bigger preoccupations than any building assignment, school or church. Nurse was gone and I was on a train and on my own except for a new cabin trunk.

The train chugged along for hour after hour through the pitch-black night, emitting clouds of black smoke and occasional loud hoots. Presumably someone kept an eye on us but I can't remember who and in any event, I was in such trepidation about what was to happen to me that I scarcely moved all night. The next bunch of cowering inmates, we were unloaded early in the morning at Hamilton Station, where St Peter's staff awaited our arrival.

The main part of the school was an elegant two-storey symmetrical building with a pitched roof, facing the drive. It housed administration rooms and dormitories. Two walkways led from the end of this building to two single-storey buildings; one accommodated the classrooms and the other the dining room and kitchen. Between these was a lawn where outdoor assemblies or gatherings of boys took place. A large chapel with belltower stood prominently to one side. The school sat slightly above the local countryside, surrounded by mature trees and stretching out to large playing fields, the school swimming pool and the farm beyond. The Waikato is essentially flat and vegetated by hawthorn hedges and imported trees. The driveway to the school was flanked by silver birches and behind these a dense macrocarpa hedge. Each morning, winter or summer, we walked to the end of the drive and back. A small pond was hidden behind the hedge and later I discovered it was full of tadpoles. The majority of the 100-acre school grounds was farmed with a dairy herd, this being prime Waikato dairy country.

SCHOOL

The names of various parts of the school were inspired by obscure Latin or biblical references. The lavatories were called 'foricas', after the Latin word utilised by Winchester College. The washroom was called 'Moab' and the changing room 'Edom'. ('Moab shall be my wash basin, on Edom I toss my sandal'; Psalm 60:8.) We were seven or eight years old; all seemed perfectly normal. Off we went to chapel each morning and each evening of each day except Saturday for six years. Religious instruction was paramount but somehow, perhaps because religion was of absolutely no interest to my parents, notwithstanding being solemnly confirmed into the Church, I remained stubbornly indifferent.

There were 100 boys at the school, aged between seven and thirteen. We were grouped into houses and placed in dormitories under Sister Grant, who was young and kind. I was grief-stricken by the abrupt separation from Nurse, the family, and especially Mopsie the pug and Kichi the Great Dane, not to mention the cats, Misty, glistening jet black, and Ginger, who was, naturally, ginger. I began wetting the bed in the middle of the night. I would creep out of the dormitory to report this humiliating disaster to Sister Grant who would leave me wrapped in a blanket while she quietly repaired the damage. Sometimes I would solemnly inform her that I needed to telephone my mother and she would tell me she had placed the call and would come and get me from my bed when it came through. There was no such thing as dialling and calls had to be placed through an operator on the local telephone exchange. I was soon fast asleep. I'm sure she never once placed a call.

Breakfast consisted of porridge and cold toast. Afterwards we went to class. How to wriggle through Latin and maths and get to history and art? Afternoon was sport: cricket or rugby.

Three times a year for six long years I left Te Rama with perturbation in my heart to be driven to Paekakariki Station for the overnight train to the Waikato and twelve or thirteen long weeks of school.

Not all boys handled being away from home and every now and then a hush would envelop the school and the word would spread. Some boy, usually young, had escaped and made his way as best he could in the general direction of home. Sometimes he only escaped as far as the road past the gate and was caught trying to hitchhike to Cambridge town, but one or two made it to Auckland or even home. I thought about it, but how would I get myself on the train back to Paekakariki?

Prep school boarding was probably the same the world over and Broady had replicated the English experience as closely as possible. We slept in dormitories in iron beds on masonite, open and airy and bracing in the winter; up at six for our walk to the end of the drive and back, in the winter jumping on the ice in the puddles, in the summer running to the pool with a towel around our waist then dropping the towel and in for a quick swim. These days there would be plenty of snide comments about little boys running about in the nude but probably not until fifty years later did those odd little occurrences seem to have any sinister aspect.

While Broady had perambulated around the world looking for a site for his school he had kept a diary and on Sunday afternoons those boys not out with parents would gather under the largest macrocarpa tree in the garden and listen to tales from his diary. Sometimes for a change and for a little more excitement he would read Sherlock Holmes to us and I found the antics of Holmes and Watson in 'The Hound of the Baskervilles' or 'A Study in Scarlet' pretty ripping yarns. I would listen attentively while two chosen boys took around two trays of assorted sweets. Broady had first choice and we were allowed two each at an offering. Broady liked the toffees or the chocolates or even better the chocolate toffees, called caramel creams, which in hindsight and in keeping with his contempt for any sport except walking, probably accounted for his rotund physique.

He walked in the recommended posture, shoulders back, head up and feet slightly splayed, the posture which an Englishman would naturally adopt in order to convey to the colonials that they were in the presence of a superior culture. He would stride about his domain on his regular walks, inspecting his school and intimidating small boys as he gazed upon us. I suppose it would have been some time since he had looked down at his feet but still his shoes were immaculately polished.

When not in the classroom or on the playing fields the smaller boys used to raid the fruit trees, perching in the branches with plum juice dribbling down our chins, keeping an eye out for masters or the local wasps, which had a particularly vicious sting, or we would entertain ourselves for hours with a sort of dirt city built under a tree. We constructed roads and all kinds of earthworks for our favourite toys, which were called Dinky Toys, made in England and stamped accordingly. We collected all and every sort: cars, trucks, buses, bulldozers, tractors and military vehicles, the tank being our favourite. We lovingly cleaned them and kept them in boxes and they formed a sort of currency, being swapped for each other or outside goods or services – an excellent system involving no issues of depreciation or inflation.

What we boys didn't know until years after leaving, although we would have been highly excited if we had, was that Mr Broadhurst had been a pilot during World War I and was reputed to have once flown a red de Havilland Moth from the school's playing fields.

On one occasion Mr Broadhurst decided sex education was required. He marched into the dormitory and using the index finger on one hand and thumb and forefinger on the other hand he gave a rough demonstration of the process of creation. Small boys were bemused and not much enlightened. One particularly alert young man asked if that was how we had all been created. Faced with the confirmation that it was, there was a round of gagging noises and a secret tryst never to engage in whatever it was that had just been explained.

Headmaster of St Peter's School Arthur Broadhurst demonstrating his athletic prowess

Broady, as he was inevitably known, but never to his face, wanted us all in the orchestra or choir. It appeared, contrary to my Eton House report, I had no musical ability whatsoever – none. I was tried with the violin and put in the second desk of the third violins and asked to play softly. I had one tune, 'Men of Harlech', which I practised in the school holidays until banished to the attic. It was no good. How about the viola? No. The cello? No. The recorder? The piano and finally the choir? Nothing was to any avail.

Well, at least I was good at sport. As it happened, my parents and Mr Broadhurst were the only three people in all of New Zealand to have no interest whatsoever in sport. Many years later it seemed to me a rich irony that my most recognisable talent hardly registered with the three people most important to me. I was captain of rugby at both St Peter's and Wanganui Collegiate, and a member of the crew that first won the New Zealand school rowing championship, the Maadi Cup, for Collegiate. 'Well done, dear,' I think was Mother's contribution when she eventually heard about it.

I had two other interests that were quietly simmering: a love of reading and art, interests potentially fatal to a seven-year-old boy in New Zealand in the 1950s. On holidays from school, my father would arrive home and at bedtime he would read me *Winnie the Pooh, Wind in the Willows, Biggles, The Faraway Tree, Doctor Dolittle, Ferdinand the Bull, Alice in Wonderland* and so on. Most of the stories I liked involved animals. The nearest story to my actual experience in New Zealand was the Norman Lindsay Australian classic which my mother had been brought up on, *The Magic Pudding*, that I dearly loved, the characters being a bit more knockabout and boisterous than those from a northern continent.

At St Peter's we were the easybeats of the local competition. In all my time, eventually in the first eleven and fifteen, I think we only won one cricket match and no rugby matches. But there wasn't a sense of grievous disappointment. We just didn't have the competitive spirit. I remember my friend Jones Minimus (who had two older brothers at school called Jones Maximus and Jones Minor, hence, for him, the 'Minimus') being upbraided for happily daydreaming at square leg as fours and sixes whistled past him.

There was one notable intrusion of a sporting event into our sheltered lives. In 1956, the South African rugby team, the Springboks, conducted a major tour of New Zealand, playing twenty-three games, including three test matches. The entire country, except of course the boys and staff of St Peter's, was in a fever of expectation. The first game of the tour was against Waikato and was played in Hamilton, not far from the school. The whole school was bussed to the match, seated cross-legged between the touchline and the first row of seats, and told not to move.

I was agog. These Springboks were like gods and they had funny names: Van de Merwe, du Preez, van Vollenhoven. The Waikato team managed to win 14 to 10 and the three Clarke brothers who played in the team became instant heroes.

I followed every move of the rest of the tour, helped by my collection of ink blotters, which were oblongs of blotting paper available from garages when you filled up with petrol. They had all sorts of information on the back about the tour: the games, the teams, the players, anything you might conceivably wish to know. We collected them and swapped them. The blotters were also useful because we all used fountain pens. In our case Broady made us write in italic script. This required a fountain pen with a special flat nib. Vertical strokes required the flat face of the nib and horizontal strokes the fine edge. Italic writing looked most elegant when done correctly, but I could never master its intricacies. Dribbling ink everywhere, we were required to write a carefully scripted letter home once a month. Mine usually went something along the lines of 'Dear Mum, I hope you are well. I am well. It is raining. Love etc.' I kept my unsullied blotter collection in a cigar box, where it became another minor casualty of the fire.

We could escape and explore the farm in our spare time and we used to steal the molasses that was supplied for the dairy herd when the farm manager wasn't looking. We had another passion, the memory of which has filled me with shame ever since. We used to collect birds' eggs. We could spot a bird's nest from miles away and thought nothing of climbing to the highest branch and clambering down with the eggs cradled gently on our tongues. We would then bore a hole in each end of the egg with a pin, blow the egg clean and put it in our collection on cottonwool in a cardboard box. Sometimes we wouldn't blow the eggs as clean as we thought and pretty soon there would be a disgusting smell of rotten eggs. We swapped eggs with one another but I hate to think what we did to the local bird population. I've been donating to Birds Australia ever since.

Another occupation that gripped us was playing conkers. Conkers were the seeds of the horse chestnuts that grew in the school grounds alongside the playing fields. We collected the biggest conker we could find and carefully drilled a hole through the middle. Thread the conker with a shoelace, and it was ready for battle. One boy would allow his conker to dangle from its shoelace while the other used the shoelace to swing his conker at it. Contact was often severe and the first conker to shatter its opponent won. We tried all sorts of tricks to harden our conkers: baking them in the oven, soaking them in vinegar, polishing them with boot polish. To have a King Conker, one that had survived at least twenty games, was to earn immense kudos among the boys.

At one point, a few of us started to sneak out of the dormitory at night and, hopping over the barbed wire fences in our viyella pyjamas, find our way to the plantation of trees a mile or so from the school. We never could find anything much to do when we got there so we would soon turn around and head back to bed. We were eventually caught and soundly beaten.

On one mysterious occasion, we were allowed out after dark in our pyjamas. It was in 1957 when Broady marched into our dormitory, switched on the lights and commanded that we rise, put on our dressing gowns and slippers and, without explanation, marched us out into the cool night air, across the grass, under the trees and out into the middle of the sports field, where we gazed without comprehension up at a starlit sky. It was then that Broady explained. If we looked carefully to the low horizon we would see a special star and it would be moving; and so we did and soon were rewarded with the wondrous sight of the Russian satellite *Sputnik I* steadily traversing the night sky.

Looking back, it seems strange to think that none of us boys thought there was anything unusual about our incarceration in boarding school. We just accepted that this was our life and got on with it. We accepted that we were totally within the authority of teachers, parents and whatever other large people chose to exercise their supposed authority over us.

We did have one small avenue of rebellion, one which still amuses and fortifies generations of small boys, one which in its simplicity is a wonderful act of subversion that summed up and provided a response to all the petty humiliations which dogged our lives: we had the freedom to fart whenever we wanted to, and so with pride and the equivalent of two fingers in the air, we did. It was bound to end in disaster.

My particular friend was Danson, a robust lout with a head of tight curls, a turned-up nose and a belligerent expression. As far as we knew he had a mother but no father, which was rare in those days. When his mother came to visit, he would invite me out and we would set off in her ancient car, sitting up in the back seat and firing our homemade shanghais out the car window at the Indian mynahs on the edge of the road and any pedestrians we spied until eventually his mother would screech to a halt and threaten to give us a good belting.

It was at one of our morning assemblies as the headmaster was calling out our names, to which we were supposed to respond 'present', that I, as a precursor to rebellion, emitted a small rebellious squeak. Danson would not be outdone and screwing up his face he emitted a low rumble which reached its final crescendo as those around him burst into delighted giggles.

The headmaster exploded. A particularly noxious odour spread along the row and Danson's expression turned from triumph to dismay. In his efforts to impress, Danson had emitted a residue of semi-solids that was now seeping down his leg. The humiliation was there for all to see as the headmaster, threatening him with a good thrashing, naturally after a change of underpants, banished him to the territory of the matron. Thus were the seeds of revolution sown among us.

Broady was sparing with the use of the cane. I remember being caned by him only once, twice, or maybe three times. One event caused me considerable resentment. We were rolling the cricket pitch and one of the weedier masters, of which there were quite a few, came over to give us instructions. One of the boys farted. We all dissolved into giggles and as I was the senior boy in charge I got the blame even though not being the *fartor*, to use a technical expression. Broady decided to make an example of me, '*pour encourager les autres*' perhaps. I was bent over in his study and with Broady wielding a cane of about five feet in length I received 'four of the best'. Broady was a right-hander and used the conventional left foot forward and forehand grip to get maximum leverage. I left with a sore arse but not much worse. Caning, I was about to discover, was *de rigueur* at Wanganui Collegiate. These days of course this sort of premeditated violence almost exactly fits within the definition of the serious offence of causing 'grievous bodily harm' and can get you a spell in jail.

One treat that I looked forward to each month was the arrival by post of my copy of *Eagle*, the popular English comic printed in colour. I was in a lather of anticipation over PC 49's adventures as a bobby, 'Luck of the Legion', and a strip about a football player called Stanley Matthews, 'the wizard of the dribble', who was the hero of Blackpool Football Club and I thought was made-up. Best of all was 'Dan Dare, Pilot of the Future', a square-jawed British spaceman.

There were precious few highs and lows during the six years and eighteen long terms I spent at St Peter's. The routine varied little so the contents of a day, a term or a year, whether you were a seven-year-old or a twelve-year-old, were much the same.

One enormous source of prestige occurred when just once my older brother Christopher came to visit to introduce me to his fiancée. He roared up the drive in what was probably the one and only silver-blue Austin Healey sports car in the whole of New Zealand. Certainly, none of us had ever seen one. Not only that, the roof was down, the car made a great growling noise and better still my future sister-in-law was called Anna de Malmanche (how exotic) and she looked just like Gina Lollobrigida, or so I thought. Off I went, perched between the two seats, waving nonchalantly at my goggling schoolmates – no seatbelts in those days. Huge credits for me. I went to their wedding in Auckland a few years later but somehow no memories of it remain.

I didn't excel at St Peter's. I don't think Broady liked me and if so the feeling was mutual. Even though I was head prefect in my last year, my school reports were mostly average except for sport and perhaps English and art. In giving me the obligatory Head Prefect's Prize (*The Coming of the Maori* by Sir Peter Buck, clad in blue and gold leather), Broady's only comment was that I was not 'the worst head prefect the school ever had.' Sometimes I wonder wistfully if my life would have been more satisfactory from an educational viewpoint if I had somehow stayed at Eaton House in England.

Maggie and her Great Dane, Hamlet

10

MAGGIE

Maggie, my parents' only daughter, was brought up like my brother and me, by a nurse, and was, I presume, subjected to the same routine. When we were young, we had dinner or, probably more accurately, tea, in the kitchen. As we grew older though, we were allowed to join the dinner table and sample a little watered-down claret, the taste of which we detested.

One night at the dinner table, my father broached the subject of travelling 'home' to England by ship. He dropped in the idea that perhaps it would not be necessary to travel first-class. Pat nearly exploded at the suggestion and when he protested the dispute ended with her labelling him a 'bad-tempered old man'. Maggie and I listened in awe.

First class it was. I think Pat was worried about how steerage would look to the Wellington smart set of whom the most prominent was Frank, later 'Sir Frank', Renouf, a property developer, stockbroker and prominent socialite. A first-class type of guy. He later gained great kudos for marrying Sydney socialite Susan Peacock, ex-wife of both Andrew Peacock, the prominent Australian Liberal politician and then legendary British racehorse owner, Robert Sangster. Sir Frank was her third attempt at connubial bliss. It was reported that when New Zealand prime minister David Lange was invited to the socialite wedding he responded that he would be unable to attend on this occasion but would be happy to be present at the next one.

Most of the time at dinner Maggie and I were daydreaming or feeding Kichi the Great Dane under, and often on top of, the dining table. Her head was exactly at plate level. I loved our two dogs; they were endlessly affectionate and so different from one another. Mopsie was a tiny male pug with a curled-up tail and squashed nose, and used to skitter around on the hard wooden floors. Kichi was a huge female Great Dane, bought from a breeder and friend in Auckland. Mopsie occasionally tried hopelessly to mate with her which irritated her and drove him near to apoplexy. Kichi at one stage had ten puppies. She patiently suckled them and put up with them climbing all over her. As the puppies grew stronger they ran all over the house and garden and piddled and pooed everywhere. There were little fawn Great Dane pups exploring every corner. The cats disdainfully ignored them. We eventually had to give the pups away or back to the breeder one by one. It was huge fun.

Maggie was sent to a small boarding school called Nga Tawa in the middle of nowhere and an especially long way from boys. In fact, the nearest boys were us at Wanganui Collegiate, which was my senior school, probably fifty miles away. It might as well have been Mars.

The girls dressed in woollen uniforms the colour of the cow pats lying around on the local farms. I don't think they ever escaped far outside the school gate. Goodness knows what happened there. Maggie never talked about it or more likely I wasn't listening. I doubt it would have suggested a life much beyond that awaiting most of the girls: wife of the local farmer and mother of many. Her future was something of a problem for our parents. Maggie was out of school and spending most of her time at Te Rama looking after her horses and riding in local gymkhanas. She could hardly enter the workforce, given their probable view of her social position, and in any case what occupation would she find? Like most girls at rural schools in those days, university was considered exotic and for 'blue stockings', and, as far as my parents were concerned, the 'coming out' events in New Zealand were an unsatisfactory and distant parody of the real thing.

They thought they saw in some of her drawings the flickering of her grandmother Frieda's artistic accomplishments so an elegant solution was found to the twin aims of furthering her artistic abilities and brushing off the rough edges, by packing her off to England, to that fine old symbol of the Art Establishment, which her Uncle Nick had attended, the Slade. At this stage, our roles reversed. I was at boarding school and she was just out of school. Her horse was still in the top paddock but where was Maggie? As usual I had only the vaguest idea.

The Slade was set up in 1871 from a bequest from a Felix Slade, a generous benefactor and art patron. Slade believed in the then radical concept of placing fine art within a university structure. The Slade was in a splendid old building in the West End of London, and was part of the University of London, where it remains to this day. If I quote the current description from the website you will get the general idea: 'From its radical beginnings, the Slade continues to foster an approach to the study and practice of art which is enquiring, investigative, experimental and research minded, not comfortable or conforming to existing expectation, yet consciously engaging with the lively discourse of contemporary art, nationally and internationally.' Over the years, it has been home to some formidable teachers and has an extensive alumni of talented artists. It would have been a challenge for anyone, but more especially for this shy, rather placid and totally unprepared girl, to be cast headlong into a London hovering on the edge of that lucky dip of delicious irresponsibility known as the Swinging Sixties.

She would have arrived in London still thinking LSD stood for 'Pounds, Shillings and Pence,' not the mind-altering psychedelic drug that most young people thought 'Lucy in the Sky with Diamonds,' from the Beatles LP *Sergeant Pepper's Lonely Hearts Club Band*, referred to. This was the LSD that was spreading everywhere among the 'hip' generation in Britain.

Maggie returned to Waikanae in 1963 from her sojourn in London. What with boarding school and being six years younger and Maggie being a girl, I had hardly noticed she wasn't around. I was barely conscious that my father had taken one of his periodic overseas trips and then I came home for holidays and there was Maggie. We said hello and proceeded to ignore each other as usual. Maggie had kept her love of horses and still had a couple up in the back paddock. Soon she was back at gymkhanas and doing the show circuit.

I had spent my five years at Wanganui Collegiate doing the same things boys did at boarding schools everywhere. We were never really allowed beyond the school gates except with our parents (which was rare) or for sporting fixtures or to row on the river. At the end of my last year a diversion did at last appear. Some genius in a government marketing department somewhere decided it would be a good idea to have a 'Mr New Zealand' competition to find the most well rounded school boy in the country; they didn't think of girls of course. I was the Collegiate entry in the Wanganui preliminaries. All the entrants had to make speeches about who we would most like to sit next to at dinner. I said Jimmy 'Schnozzle' Durante, the American comedian and musician, because he had a bigger nose than me. Then I corrected myself and said Winston Churchill. As the only entrant to make a joke I was selected to go to the finals in Wellington.

We all collected in a Wellington theatre and had to present ourselves in dinner jackets and give our speech. I dropped the 'Schnozzle' but stayed with Winston; naturally so did everyone else except a smartarse Greek boy with flashing eyes who went on and on about Aristotle. 'Who was this Aristotle?' the rest of us asked each other. He won, of course. I had left my black shoes behind and appeared on stage in dinner jacket and Dunlop Volleys, which probably didn't help but I wouldn't have beaten Aristotle anyway.

My sister Maggie, for the few years she was in residence, lived upstairs, in the middle room overlooking the lawn and garden, where she occasionally did some painting, but without much enthusiasm. I should have wondered why, having returned from art school at the Slade, she didn't show more interest in art.

I spread my possessions extravagantly around the furniture and the floor of the larger room. Mother avoided the whole area, leaving it to Joan to try to rectify the mess.

Time passed and I was out of school and away to England and during this time, Maggie had a bad fall while showjumping. As far as I could piece the story together, the horse clipped the top of the jump, a plank flew up and somewhere in the tumult her helmet came off. She was in hospital for quite some time and when I next saw her she was semi-paralysed down her left side. She walked with a limp and had great difficulty holding anything in her left hand. She was still managing to ride but had switched to dressage and judging. The doctors told her if she had another fall, it could kill her.

In the mid 1960s while I was still in England, Maggie, with some help from Father, bought forty acres down the old dead-end road to the beach, with the cemetery on one side and the Waikanae dump, not very well hidden behind a row of macrocarpas, on the back boundary. It was only a few minutes' drive away from Te Rama. The idea was for her to run a riding school for which there would likely be demand from local families and the holiday-makers who were finding Waikanae.

She built a little one-bedroom house with a veranda facing the northern sun and looking out to a lake full of bulrushes and ducks, and started the riding school, 'Ferndale'. For company, when the kids were gone and the horses were out for the night she shared her home with a couple of Great Danes of her own and the odd cat. She named the Danes Ophelia and Hamlet. With her rural lifestyle Maggie soon looked like part of the scenery. She seemed to have given up on the idea of a husband or family. No amount of effort by Mother, Paris creations or expensive hairdos could make her look anything other than as if she had just finished cleaning the stables. But her life achieved a comfortable rhythm, punctuated by weekly visits up to Te Rama, where she would fall asleep over dinner after more than her fair share of Father's claret and lulled by Mother's endless tales of her triumphs great and, very rarely, small. She would wake up with a jerk, stumble to the kitchen with a plate or two, lurch out to her old car and rumble off down the drive to her dogs, which by this time were installed on her bed and not keen to move over. Fortunately, she had no great interest in housekeeping so the fact everything was coated in dog or cat hair, the dishes were piled in the sink with last week's omelette still encrusted in the frypan, and the cheddar cheese was looking like blue-vein, never much worried her.

Over the years my parents tried various cures for Maggie's disablement: acupuncture, physio, chiropractors, herbs and spices, and the occasional trip to London where surely someone in Harley Street could do something. Nothing availed and Maggie went on limping and enjoying her growing role as the village eccentric.

Maggie ran the riding school with a sort of partner, who did most of the teaching, since Maggie was selective about whom she wanted to teach and when she wanted to do it. She also did some dressage judging around the country at weekends, conveniently ignoring the economic reality that this was the best time for children to attend the riding classes. Naturally the financial results were hardly spectacular. The judging took her across the country and she used to head off towing her ancient horse float, dung coloured and rusting, and in which she slept when not offered a bed by a friendly local. Every now and then she would run off the road but thanks to the float's extremely slow speed, not much damage was ever done. Sometimes the dogs came too, the float being just comfortable for them. They provided good company, apart from their enormous, frequent farts. Maggie would wave her hand in front of her nose and swear at them, but they only looked offended and went on happily farting.

The one thing she never did was talk about her time in England attending the Slade.

During Maggie's time at the Ferndale, my parents' sixtieth wedding anniversary came around, in 1993 to be exact. They elected to have a party at Te Rama. Gail and I decided the whole family should come from Sydney, so the two of us plus our children, Mark, Sophie, Nicholas and Sam, trooped across the Tasman for the festivities. The children were furious. It turned out the party was on the same day as the announcement of the winning bid for the 2000 Olympics. Sydney was favoured but win, lose or draw there was going to be a huge party down at Circular Quay.

They stood around on one foot or played with the dogs while my parents enjoyed their place in the sun. This was followed by an excellent speech from my mother's friend Margaret Shields, Member of Parliament for Labour in Wellington and then I made a sadly uninspiring contribution punctuated by some feeble 'old people' jokes. The highlight was the next day. Apart from Sydney winning the right to host the Olympics, which only upset our children even more, my father had a call from the local telephone exchange in Waikanae. There were still no direct lines. The young girl at the exchange explained that a telegram had arrived for Sir Jack Harris. He asked her to read it out. 'Congratulations on a wonderful sixty years of marriage. Long may it continue,' was roughly the content. My father asked who it was from. The young girl replied that she couldn't exactly say as it hadn't been properly signed. It just said, 'Elizabeth R', she helpfully explained.

The Wanderer shows why men like "messing around in boats" as she streaks ahead of all the yachts in the Royal Port Nicholson Yacht Club's A class keeler race in the Wellington Harbour last Saturday. Note the casual stance of one of the members of Wanderer's crew as he stands on the gunwale of the sharply heeling cutter. At this stage of the race Wanderer was a good 100 yards in the lead.

My brother's yacht *Wanderer* was featured in *The Dominion*. The caption reads: 'The *Wanderer* shows why "men like messing around in boats" as she streaks ahead of all the yachts in the Royal Port Nicholson Yacht Club's A class keeler race in the Wellington Harbour last Saturday. Note the casual stance of one of the members of Wanderer's crew as he stands on the gunwale of the sharply heeling cutter. At this stage of the race *Wanderer* was a good 100 yards in the lead.'

11

CHRISTOPHER

Christopher had an important influence on me, of which I am sure he was unaware. He was ten years older, good looking, a fine athlete. The world was at his feet. I hardly ever saw him at Te Rama but after he was married he and Anna provided the sort of safe haven at their house in Wellington for a naughty teenager that wasn't available to me at Waikanae. We came from the same era, spoke the same language and, most importantly, he introduced me to another world: the world of sailing.

Christopher's yacht *Wanderer* was from an iconic line of locally built yachts. It was a Logan Classic 35-foot yacht, built back in 1905 by Logans, the premier yacht builders in Australasia from the 1890s until 1910 when they folded the business. Their yachts were works of art as much as they were yachts. They were triple skinned: two inner skins diagonal to each other and the outer skin running fore and aft, all made of beautiful kauri, made to last forever. Somewhere today *Wanderer* is probably some lucky yachtsman's prized possession. We used to race it around Wellington Harbour and cruise backwards and forwards across Cook Strait to holiday in the Marlborough Sounds.

Cook Strait can be calm, but at most times it's a challenging stretch of water with strong southerly winds, short steep seas, and a tide rip of up to six knots around Karori Lighthouse. Other times, conditions can be ferocious, with tides running for six to eight hours and seven-metre swells developing as the Tasman Sea on one side and the Pacific Ocean on the other are compressed through the 22-kilometre-wide strait. A few years before Christopher started sailing *Wanderer*, the Port Nicholson Yacht Club organised a race from Wellington down the east coast of the South Island to Lyttelton, the port for Christchurch. The weather turned nasty. Of twenty-two starters only one yacht finished. Two sank and ten lives were lost.

In a gale, to reduce sail area we would put four reefs in (most yachts have a maximum of three) and, with a pocket handkerchief of sail up, charge over the harbour, competing as much against ourselves as the other yachts we were racing. *Wanderer* had little free board, so freezing white water would come crashing down on us. All of us would be soaked to the skin, notwithstanding the sou'-westers we wore. No life jackets, and no safety rails. One day we overdid it. In gusts of fifty knots the wooden mast snapped near the top; stays, halyards and sails went everywhere. 'Boy,' shouted my brother, 'get up there and untangle it!' No argument.

It was always a relief to reach the other side of the Strait and tuck into the protected waters of the Marlborough Sounds or return to the shelter of Wellington Harbour. Crew usually included Professor Tim Beaglehole, whose father was a world authority on Captain Cook. Tim later became Chancellor of Victoria University. Also along would be another of my brother's friends, Doctor of Philosophy John Roberts, all six foot four and gangly, with a woolly beanie pulled down over his cauliflower ears. As we crossed the Strait the latter would entertain us, hanging on to the coach house, with a recital of the great Australian poem, 'The Man from Snowy River'. I listened intently while my brother gripped the tiller and steered us up over the white water on the lips of breaking waves rolling under the bow, then down into the trough on the other side, zigzagging across the Strait. Often, if we missed the tide, we were behind 'sched'. The sky would darken and stars would begin to break out, four of them anchoring the Southern Cross high in the sky, more beautiful than anything a battered earth could offer. The reflection of a thin moon would slide over the waves. John would change to 'Clancy of the Overflow': 'And he sees the vision splendid of the sunlit plains extended, and at night the wondrous glory of the everlasting stars.' Cook Strait was no 'sunlit plain' but a shifting mass of freezing salt water, but above us the stars hung still in their heaven tree. I was fifteen and 'Clancy of the Overflow' and 'The Man from Snowy River' were the greatest poems I had ever heard.

Conversation was pretty elevated for a bunch of sodden sailors. I clung on to a winch and listened.

Our hands and feet would be numb by the end of the day. Back at the Club, Christopher would administer a couple of rum and blackcurrants with a twist of lemon to warm us up. It would take quite a few to do the job.

Christopher only once took our father across the strait. On the way back to Wellington the wind was picking up speed. Father elected to stay below. To make it out of the protected waters of Queen Charlotte Sound into Cook Strait we had to navigate out of Tory Channel, where, as the myth relays, the mighty warrior Kupe in his canoe chased down and killed the giant octopus Te Wheke-a-Muturangi.

Yachts leaving the channel sail past the site of the last Cook Strait whaling station, the Perano family's decaying complex strung along the shore, and time the exit to avoid the eddies and rips that, in a fast-running tide, can throw a small yacht off course in seconds. It can get bumpy. We were just out of the channel into the strait when Christopher went to check on Father. He stuck his head up to report a medical emergency. Father was vomiting all over the cabin floor and the vomit contained purple bile, indicating he must have ruptured an organ or his stomach lining. We might need to turn back through the rip. Christopher disappeared below again then stuck his head back up. All was relatively well. The Old Man had been helping himself to the local plums back on the dock. There was plum residue everywhere. Christopher was furious.

Stroke of the 'rugger' boat in the 1966 May Bumps on the River Cam

12

CAMBRIDGE

It was only after I had been in England some time that I began to be curious about Great Grandfather Wolf Harris, the father of Pearl, Leslie and my grandfather Percy.

I had somehow been given a place at Trinity Hall, Cambridge, like my father and grandfather before me. This may have led to my acceptance at Trinity Hall, or perhaps my prowess at rugby or my headmaster being an old Cambridge man had played a part. I will never know. It was a life-changing experience for an eighteen-year-old from country New Zealand. I wasn't lonely because I had conquered those feelings during all the years at boarding school. What was difficult, apart from the work which I was ill-prepared for, was grasping the social climate I had landed in. Although my life at Te Rama had supplied me with endless sophisticated markers I had not spent enough time at home to absorb them. I was well aware though that there were things I should and shouldn't say or do, clothes I should or shouldn't wear, cutlery I shouldn't pick up and wine glasses I shouldn't drink from. How did tipping work? We didn't do that in New Zealand. Why did older men call me 'sir'? It didn't sound like respect, it sounded more like a threat. Someone called a 'Gyp' was assigned to look after me in my rooms in college. He wanted to clean my shoes. My attention had not been on these things in New Zealand. It had been on eels, or Great Danes, or Maori shearers, or how bad the crop would be and how the price of wool was terrible and of course on who won the Test match.

In my first few weeks at Cambridge I was invited by a new friend to partner his sister to a dinner dance at the Dorchester Hotel. I hired a dinner suit and thank goodness was talked into a real, not pre-tied bow tie. I had fortunately been warned this was an inexcusable solecism. I turned up in Park Lane, luckily a short stroll from Hyde Park underground station, and was immediately overawed by the lavishly dressed doorman, the richly panelled mahogany doors that swung open onto an outrageously lavish lobby, full of gold leaf, marble and elegant people. This was not six o'clock closing on Lambton Quay. I was introduced to my friend's sister who was pretty, self-possessed, and not likely to be enamoured by her country bumpkin companion. I was dragged onto the dance floor for something called the Eightsome Reel, a complicated Scottish jig which caused me to stumble all over her, mumbling apologies as I went. At dinner, I sat next to her aunt and was confronted with Beluga caviar as the entree. I confessed I had never heard of it. 'A little salty,' I ventured. Raising her eyebrows, she explained its origin and asked me if there was a preferred delicacy in New Zealand. I thought hard for something not commonplace. Whitebait was a possibility but then memories of the shearing shed came flooding back. 'Mountain oysters,' I ventured brightly. She looked nonplussed and asked me to explain. 'Lambs' testicles,' I elaborated, adding for colour that they were best obtained by biting them off with your teeth and then throwing them on a hot plate. This was not well received.

The English soon discovered my father was a baronet. This had meant nothing to me in New Zealand except occasional embarrassment. In England, it seemed important and I knew nothing about it. The parents of some of my Cambridge friends would occasionally ask me how the family had come to be in New Zealand and where the baronetcy had come from. It was embarrassing not to have the answers.

I settled into the university reasonably well. All the undergraduates ate together in the hall in the evening. I could sit anywhere and I found being a New Zealander made me virtually classless and therefore accepted, not like the Australians whom, I discovered later, many of the English thought were uncouth and descended from Irish whores and rabbit poachers. Occasionally I found myself among the Etonians who wanted to know how many acres we had and if I rode to hounds. One of my new Etonian companions turned out to be the Master of the Hunt. Presuming some athletic capacity in antipodeans he invited me to assist in the local Cambridge hunt. In the absence of foxes, he prevailed upon me, and a few other recalcitrants, to drag a rugby sock soaked in anisette and urine across the local paddocks to set a scent for the hounds, with the hunt to follow. We were subsequently invited to join the pink-coated huntsmen for smoked salmon and Pimms.

A postgraduate student who was studying politics once took me by surprise by accusing me of coming from a racist country. I had never considered such a thing; what the hell did he mean? Against the Maoris, he said. You've oppressed them, taking their land, confining them to just seven Maori electorates. I was astounded and pointed out that we all had Maori mates, we did what they did and vice versa and no one that I knew thought twice about it. I took it as a personal affront to my friendship with the Pomare family whose three boys I went to school with, whose sister went to Nga Tawa school with my sister, whose father Mick was a highly respected Maori member of parliament and whose mother Madge always made us welcome in her home. Looking back, it probably seems hard to believe that I had never even considered the subject of racism. Years later it seems an appropriate subject for debate but at that stage in my life I was in no mood for a lecture from a supercilious English public schoolboy. I wondered if he had looked in his own backyard.

I was most comfortable with the grammar school lads who seemed down to earth and easy to talk to. Tutorials, common dining and a whole variety of sports soon brought us together. I tried all sort of things, especially unfamiliar sports like soccer, which I had never played, water polo, squash and lacrosse, the latter being sanctioned belting each other over the head with sticks.

Generally, though, in those first few months in England, it was extremely discomforting to find myself in situations where I felt gauche and unsophisticated and without really knowing why. I thought perhaps one helpful response would be to learn my family's history. This became something of a mission and in fact I was unable to fill in the major details until I returned home years later.

'Hell no, we won't go.' Students protest in the USA in the 1960s. Protests were everywhere and in my experience mostly a lot more violent than this one. Photo credit: Lyndon B. Johnson Library/Frank Wolfe

13

THE US OF A

In the long 1965 summer vacation from university I found myself with only a few pounds to my name. Fortunately, a friend in East Sheen, a London suburb next to Twickenham, gave me a bed and I landed a job as a dustman in Twickenham, starting immediately.

I turned up bright and early on Monday and being new, young and foreign, I was put with a team collecting metal dustbins full of ash from behind the council blocks. In those days, everyone still had coal fires. The bins were amazingly heavy and I tried to carry two over my shoulder, one in each hand but my fingers involuntarily unwound and I dumped the lot on the footpath. My colleagues just laughed. It was an advantage being a New Zealander. They accepted me as another itinerant colonial. I soon became friendly with a tough stocky Cockney named Jimmy. 'Jimmy Riddle' as he liked to joke. It turned out Jimmy had been torpedoed twice during the war and found himself adrift in freezing water in the Atlantic. He had survived, married, had a couple of kids but took to the booze, much like my Uncle John. I thought he should emigrate to Australia, start again, and for a while we fantasised about 'life in the outback' over our mandatory Friday afternoon pint, or three. In the end, common sense prevailed. He was a Londoner through and through. His kids and most of his mates lived within a couple of miles of Big Ben. He was a rusted-on supporter of the Fulham Football Club, not caring that they hardly ever won a match. He thought rugby was for toffs but since I was a New Zealander he tolerated it.

When not hauling bins around I socialised with my Cambridge friends and their families. When asked what I was up to I described myself as a 'Waste Disposal Consultant' with Twickenham Council.

The following year, as it happened, I was playing rugby for the Harlequins' first team, based in the home of English Rugby Union, Twickenham. The Harlequins were the most established rugby side in the United Kingdom, famous for being the second rugby club ever to be formed and full of Oxbridge graduates. I wondered what the officials would think of having one of their players emptying their bins.

One of my more immediate reasons for needing cash that first long summer holiday from university was a plan some of my Cambridge friends had cooked up before the term ended. From Trinity Hall, Nigel Jones, a Mancunian, and Nick Heesom, a larger than life anglicised South African, plus David Bell from Gonville and Caius College, had discovered that a British Universities Club called BUNAC ran charter flights for students to and from New York for only seventy pounds return. Even better, the Greyhound Bus company had one of the all-time great travel deals, available only to non-US residents. For ninety-nine dollars you could travel for ninety-nine days anywhere in the United States or Canada. That did it. We were determined to go.

To get our visas we had to go to the US Embassy in Grosvenor Square in London. This imposing modern edifice with a huge eagle on top was morphing from a meeting point for the CND (Campaign for Nuclear Disarmament) supporters into the anti-Vietnam War supporters. We had to push our way through a crowd of hippies, students (particularly American students), Labour

Party and Communist Party members and anarchists, all milling about and waving banners. They were being watched by suspicious bobbies in helmets with truncheons by their sides. All students in England were well aware of the Vietnam conflict, but for us it was not an existential threat. Britain was not involved. The demonstrations were anti- the Vietnam War, anti- the US nuclear presence in England, anti-capitalist and just anti-.

BUNAC warned all of us not to work in the United States or we had a good chance of being called up and booted off to Vietnam.

A couple of New Zealand friends in London filled me in on what was happening at home. The New Zealand Government was in a dilemma. The British Government had called the Vietnam War a 'civil war' and refused to participate but New Zealand was a signatory to the Australia, New Zealand, United States Security Treaty (ANZUS).

The Australian and New Zealand Governments had to support the United States. Australia chose the path of conscription but Holyoake, the New Zealand prime minister at the time, a lot more cagey, was facing a hostile Labour opposition. New Zealand had conscription by ballot. All New Zealander men had to register on their twentieth birthdays and would be balloted by birthdate for compulsory military service: three months' full-time and three weeks' part-time for three years but Holyoake decided only full-time volunteer career military would be sent to Vietnam; no conscripts. He first sent the Royal NZ Artillery. He must have thought that would keep people quiet. It didn't. As in the United Kingdom, the United States and Australia, all hell broke loose. Students, communists, hippies, anarchists, old as well as young, took to the streets. The prime minister's suite in Parliament House was invaded. There were riots, baton charges, arrests, prison. Television arrived in New Zealand just in time to broadcast all this across the screen. It was never going to be 'kept quiet'. As the American commentator William Buckley phrased it, there was a 'contagion of protest'. In 1971, New Zealand finally withdrew. Nearly 4000 New Zealanders served, of whom 37 were killed; a good result, I suppose some would say.

We crammed onto the plane at Gatwick, our backpacks stuffed with just enough clothes to get by. At least it was summer. Since we had to work, as soon as we landed in New York we headed out of town to Canada. That was easy. Armed with our perpetual tickets, we hopped on a Greyhound bus and off we went to Toronto.

Toronto in 1965 was a very strict city. No drinking at all for anyone under twenty-one, not much night life that we could access, and a very starchy attitude to life in general. We soon had a job. We discovered a furniture store, on Bloor Street right in the middle of the city, that was insolvent. The owners thought it would be good, and obviously cheap, to hire some well-spoken students to move the furniture, crummy junk that had been especially purchased for the sale. We teamed up with some stroppy Glaswegian students who smelt a rip off and threw the furniture off the trucks. Soon there were only the four of us left. We unloaded furniture into the store, brushed our hair, and put on a jacket and tie to do the selling.

We lived in a partly furnished apartment and had had the foresight to forge our international driver's licences with a birthdate that said we were over twenty-one, and because we were the only ones who could buy booze we were invited to all the student parties. Every now and then the cops would arrive and everyone would hop out the windows or over the wall to escape. We just stood there and flashed our licences. They thumbed the multiple pages, looked twice at the page in Chinese, looked twice at our photographs, gave us a dirty look and left us to ourselves.

Pretty soon, despite having warned the old ladies who came in for a bargain that there was a better deal available down the street ('there's after-sale service,' we would say with a nod), we had sold all the furniture. We were ready to set off on our Greyhound bus to travel around the United States, Canada and Mexico, the latter a cheap add-on. We had three months before we needed to be back in New York.

Greyhound bus depots are always in the worst part of town so we saw the 'other' side of America. Not only that, they're ecumenical about who travels so we had some interesting travel companions. The Greyhounds carried old and young, black or white, Mexicans, Puerto Ricans and so on.

If we were stuck for somewhere to sleep we just hopped on a bus and curled up on a spare seat. The bus would head off into the night and as we rolled across the country we would gaze out the window at passing towns or mile after mile of black, unlit landscape, punctuated every now and then with a quick pit stop for hamburgers and Coke at some gas station. We were aware of the 1960 US Supreme Court Boynton v. Virginia case, in which the court had overturned a trespassing conviction against an African American for sitting in the whites section of a segregated bus terminal restaurant in Virginia but as we travelled south it didn't seem to be much enforced.

The bus followed the Trans-Canada Highway out of Toronto. We went through Regina, Calgary, over the Rockies to Banff, where we climbed up into the foothills of the mountains, then on to Vancouver, taking a side trip to Victoria, which made us feel nostalgic for England, and from there we caught a ferry to Seattle. A friend of a friend of Nick's had a house in Seattle, was away, and had invited Nick plus friends to camp out there so we did. It was luxury. We lounged around the pool until even Nick thought we might be overstaying our welcome.

We wanted to see Chicago so we hopped back on the trusty Greyhound and doubled back. In Chicago we met some local students who were in full anti-Vietnam mode, organising demonstrations, and we joined in. We had a certain amount of prestige thanks to the success of British pop stars at the time, such as the Rolling Stones, The Byrds, The Kinks, Gerry and the

Pacemakers; the most influential were The Beatles of course. They had toured in '64 and return toured in '65. Everyone remembered when John Lennon refused to play at Gator Bowl Stadium in Jacksonville, Florida before a segregated audience. The white promoters folded. It was unprecedented. Every now and then we were asked if we knew The Beatles. Of course we did; but my flat Kiwi vowels were no match for Nigel's soft Mancunian lilt. Besides, the talent wasn't all our way. Bob Dylan was holding up the American side.

Somewhere in the middle of all this, one late, late night, I caught a little John Coltrane, 'A Love Supreme'. What was that?

It was the early days of the protest movement, but Chicago Mayor Daley's police were already cracking heads and arresting protestors. Around the country, people were burning their draft cards, and this increasingly caught on as a simple and highly symbolic form of protest. We thought it was great stuff but it was all very well for us; we were never going to have to fight. The Vietnam call-up in the United States was by conscription so everyone had to go unless your dad had more than a lot of influence. Consequently, a lot of sons of doctors, professors, senior bureaucrats and even politicians were on their way to Saigon. These kids and their parents were articulate, thought they knew their rights and were prepared to fight back. Most of the talk over illegally bought beers was either about 'unjust' wars or the ways to dodge Vietnam, which included a variety of 'education' engagements and getting married, which suddenly became a whole lot more popular. No wonder the protests became violent. In the future the US Government preferred to 'recruit' volunteers, often unemployed, who otherwise couldn't get a job. In 1973 conscription was ditched.

We left Chicago and headed down the coastal highway to Los Angeles, where Nigel had a cousin who put us up and looked after us as we ventured into Downtown, where things were also getting violent between the LA Police and students, particularly black ones. This was more racially charged than being about Vietnam and the temperature was definitely rising.

Three of us were law students and somehow the local radio station found out about us. Nick unwisely accepted an invitation to debate a proposition along the lines of 'the law and justice have nothing in common' with a spiky local DJ. He was soundly beaten up trying to defend the law, which was not popular in LA at the time. No one under forty thought the law had anything to do with justice.

Again we hooked up with some students, this time from UCLA and 'Berzerkely', as Berkeley University was called. They were on the same journey as the students in Chicago. How to get out of the draft, how to get rid of fascists like Daley, and finding out from us if there were any jobs in Canada. There was an underlying seriousness about them, which was no surprise. They meant to change the world whereas we were just ambling through it. England had its mods and rockers, motorcycle gangs that dressed in leather jackets and brothel creepers, and turned up looking for a fight. In May they had congregated in Brighton and the brawling had gone on for two days, moving to Hastings along the way. The 'Second Battle of Hastings' it was called. Middle-class England went into panic; the newspapers labelled them 'louts' and 'vermin' and life went on pretty well undisturbed. Otherwise, protest in England consisted of long hair, flowered shirts and wide-bottomed trousers, and of course tons of pot, but you could still get a pint for a quid and the coppers called you 'sir' and never carried guns.

The student protests in America were often accompanied by a strong whiff of grass. It was ubiquitous, mostly appearing as roll-your-own joints. We tended to ignore it, especially me. I had never smoked. Well, I had once. In a futile effort to appeal to a boho hippie chick I had persuaded to go out with me in London, I bought a packet of Gauloise Disque Bleu, the fag, I presumed, of Camus, Sartre, Gide and co. I puffed away inexpertly all night to no useful effect upon my companion. In the morning, I woke up with a mouth like the bottom of a sandpit, a horrible headache and I vomited all over the floor. I never smoked again, pot or anything else.

We were on our way out of Los Angeles, on the bus again, when the Watts riots began. An African American had been stopped on suspicion of drunken driving. An argument ensued, became aggressive and fighting broke out. The next thing Watts was engulfed in six days of rioting and looting. The Californian National Guard was called out and in the end thirty-four people died and more than a thousand were injured.

We went down the Mexican peninsula to Mazatlán. Mexico was a lot more peaceful and we mooched in and out of cheap bars, occasionally visited a museum or peeped inside a Catholic Church. Eventually we persuaded the cheapest fishing boat in Mexico to take us fishing. Our boat was slower than anyone else's, about fifteen feet long and driven by an ancient outboard and more ancient owner. For a while we just followed around after the more professional fisherman but then, to our amazement, David hooked a sailfish and managed to land it. We celebrated by drinking cheap margaritas and trying to chat up the local birds.

We caught the bus for the long journey across the centre of Mexico through the border and into Texas. At our first stop, in Laredo, Nick wandered into the 'Negros Only' toilet and got heaved out. We just shrugged. America was turning out to be not just another country, it was another planet. On we went, back on the Greyhound, heading for New Orleans. Nick, our chattiest member, made an enduring friendship with a young man in the seat opposite. They chatted for hours as the bus rolled on towards New Orleans.

At the terminal, the young man invited all of us for dinner the next night at what turned out to be a very exclusive restaurant. Once all its 'guests' had arrived the door was closed. The restaurant specialised in delicious Creole food – gumbo soup and jambalaya – which was fantastic and our friend's shout (thank goodness).

Nick's friend had brought along his own friend, and one by one David and Nigel and I realised that these guys were gay. They were getting along famously with Nick but the three of us grew bored so we quietly exited one by one using a variety of pathetic excuses. The next morning Nick was furious. What did we mean by slinking off?

We made it up to him by taking him off to see the Preservation Hall Jazz Band, situated in the French Quarter and one of the few places not racially segregated. We stood in a dark smoky corner, entranced and trying to make one margarita last all night. Looking back we were privileged to be there at the birth of the Band, which is still touring the world.

Our next major destination was Washington and by luck Nigel's family friend in California had called up a friend of his who ran a mission in Washington. Free accommodation was available. We were in some trepidation about what we would find but it turned out to be a spick-and-span dormitory, with for some reason no other occupants – five star, as far as we were concerned. When Nigel's friend's friend found out our next stop was Philadelphia he offered to fix us up with accommodation with his friend, the warden of the mission in Philadelphia. As we headed to the Washington Greyhound station he gave us a note with our new host's name and the address, 5th and Vine St, not that much of a walk from the bus station, he assured us with a faint smirk.

We arrived in Philadelphia late afternoon. True to form, the bus station precinct looked pretty shabby. The station building was bare concrete and it looked like if anything broke, it was never fixed. There were beggars, drunks and derelicts lolling about but they tended to ignore us. We looked like a bunch of stupid students; we were even wearing our Mexican hats.

As we followed the directions things started to look worse. Derelict buildings, a few burned-out cars and rubbish piled up everywhere. The locals were looking at us now and they didn't look friendly. Even we thought this was not too encouraging. While conferring, it was decided I would go on alone unencumbered by backpack and Mexican hat and see what I could find. I was peering nervously around the corner on what finally seemed to be 5th and Vine when I was spotted by a tough-looking guy. He bounced over. 'You must be one of the Limey guys? I've been looking out for you. I'm the warden.' We went back together and collected the others. Inside the mission, which was a converted old brick warehouse, he locked our meagre possessions in the office and showed us up to four metal bunks in a dormitory on the third floor. Like Washington, there was no one else in residence. It was now dark and we proposed to wander around the neighbourhood until we found a cheap diner and get ourselves a hamburger. 'No way,' we were told. Too dangerous. So our host, whose name has receded far into the past, found us some sandwiches and by 7 pm we were up on our metal bunks. As the night progressed all sorts of odds and sods started to wander in and the bunks filled up. There was a bit of muttering, farting and laughter until about midnight when two huge African American guys lumbered in and lay down across from us. We peered over our blankets hoping not to be noticed. I was just nodding off when there was a massive crash. One of them had knocked over the vertical metal locker that stood beside each bed. The warden arrived, there was a bit of shouting, some pushing, and then things finally settled. In the morning, we were told to stay where we were until the dormitory cleared and only then allowed out.

    Chatting with our friend the warden, we soon got the message that this was pretty dangerous territory, full of petty criminals, dropouts, drug pushers and illegal hooch everywhere. He was full of the news that some local guy had just been convicted for manslaughter for selling something called Sterno, aka 'canned heat', from his cigar store to the local deros. Sterno was heating fuel containing fifty-four per cent wood alcohol. Thirty-four people had died from consuming it.

This adventure had a wry sequel. Dave Bell was in Gonville and Caius College and one of his friends was an American called John Lehman. Everyone in Caius knew John because not only was he American but he also came from Philadelphia, was a first cousin of Princess Grace of Monaco, the most beautiful woman in the world, *and* had been to her wedding to Prince Rainier. When Dave saw John back in Cambridge he had to tell him about our trip to 5th and Vine. John went white. He thought Dave was kidding. It turned out that 5th and Vine was pretty much the original Skid Row in Philadelphia. Nobody went there who didn't have to. John later became Secretary of the Navy back in the US but we decided not to look him up.

We took the Greyhound back to New York and caught the plane back to England with only a few of our ninety-nine days left. We were ready to go home. To us, the US of A was a country consumed by rage.

I had sort of forgotten about Waikanae, family and New Zealand, all except my determination to find out how Great-Grandfather Wolf had made it to New Zealand and why. Back in the UK it was time to start investigating.

Great-Grandfather Wolf Harris

14

WOLF

What, after years of often futile investigation, I eventually discovered about my great-grandfather turned into an epic story.

Wolf Hersh Schaglied was born in 1834 into a Jewish family in Poland. After leaving Poland, he changed his name to Harris, an anglicised form of Hersh. It was Wolf Harris who set the stage for future generations in 1858 when he started the family business in New Zealand.

Can there have been two more different communities in existence in the mid-nineteenth century than the new colony of New Zealand, situated almost at the exact opposite point on the globe to Poland, and the geographical entity that had once been and would in future again become Poland? Perhaps all they had in common was turmoil. But how did Wolf come to leave Poland at the age of fourteen?

Poland's misfortune is to lie between Russia in the east, and Prussia and Austria in the west and south. It is flat and unprotected by any favourable geographical features except the Baltic Sea coastland. Small in population, Poland has been constantly overrun and occupied by larger neighbours, mainly Austria, Prussia or Russia. Armies raged back and forth across Poland over the centuries as it defended itself as best it could with local alliances and that stubborn bravado that was tested so tragically in World War II, after the Nazi and Russian invasions.

In 1840s Poland there were two interlocked issues: the discrimination that was often a part of life for European Jews, particularly in Eastern Europe and Russia; and the more general turmoil caused by the rising tide of liberalism challenging the established monarchies.

From the time of the First Crusade, Jews had more often than not been subjected to a combination of mistrust, suspicion, fear and hatred as they herded together in little communities within larger nation states in Europe. Whether because of outside prejudice or their own desire to protect their religion, the Jews, or at least the most religious ones, had kept to themselves and lived within their own separate communities or ghettos. While well accepted in a number of European countries, in others, mainly in Eastern Europe or Russia, they were treated as unwelcome guests and subjected to repressive laws designed to discourage them and make their lives as difficult as possible. The majority lived in small rural settlements. Ownership of land was often difficult and subject to tariffs and taxes Christians were exempt from. Often Jews were not allowed to engage in mining or the smelting of metal, or any other major industrial enterprise, or to practise in any of the professions outside their faith. The only jobs that remained open to them were tailoring, peddling, small-time retailing in commodities, and money lending.

Many Christian denominations permitted Jews to deal in money lending. However, as commerce expanded and the Christian communities saw how much wealth it had created for the Jews, they began to relent of the prohibition. The prohibition was eventually relaxed by the Fifth Lateran Council of 1512 to 1518 but in places such as Switzerland this eventually made the principal function of the Jews unnecessary and the Swiss began to expel them. Later in Germany and Eastern Europe at the time of the post-Napoleonic revolutionary activity, the rural economies were declining so that more and more Jews were moving to the cities, where the severe legal restrictions on them made it harder for them to make ends meet.

Word spread of opportunities awaiting those who had the resources or daring to emigrate to America. This encouraged Jewish emigration to the New World, which had the overwhelming virtue of no ghettos and no discriminatory restrictions. The social discrimination that later arose, not only from the non-Jewish community in places like New York but astonishingly even from within their own communities, where issues of family status and cultural diversity could be as challenging for Jews as for the rest of the community, was a small price to pay for economic freedom.

Kraków, where Wolf was born in 1834, was a thriving trading town in the central part of what is now Poland, south-west of Warsaw. The 1840s were a time of ferment all over Europe but particularly in Poland and Kraków. Since the Napoleonic Wars (1803–1815), a rising contest between ideas of nationalism and liberalism had led to armed clashes and the constant redrawing of boundaries between states, complicated by a series of determined rearguard actions by the 'ancien régimes'. Poland and Kraków were in the centre of all this activity both geographically and philosophically.

The 'Greater Poland Uprising' took place in 1846 and ended in a fiasco. The uprising was driven by patriotism and revolution but all that resulted was the incorporation of the Republic of Kraków into the Austrian Partition. Class divisions were exploited by Austrian officials to encourage the serfs to rise up against the noble-dominated insurgents, which led to the serfs eventually slaughtering their overlords. Many Polish nobles fled from their homes and played a prominent part in liberal uprisings elsewhere in Europe, particularly following the 1848 'Spring of Nations' uprisings. These were a series of revolutions all over Europe, more attempts to remove feudalism and create independent states. Over fifty countries were affected although there was little coordinated action. Nationalism and freedom were the driving, sometimes clashing, forces. Apart from or perhaps because of the political turmoil, Europe in the 1840s was also enduring an economic recession, with failing crops and swelling ranks of unemployed. England would have seemed a haven among the turmoil.

Poland was a staunchly Catholic country. The combination of successive invasions and Catholicism made it an uncomfortable place to live for a Rabbi and his young family. Furthermore, in the 1840s Kraków, along with its political tribulations, was suffering one of its periodic upsurges of anti-Semitism (to manifest itself more tragically one hundred years later).

Wolf's father, Samuel Schlaglied, was a Rabbi, a prestigious position among the Jewish community in Kraków. He and Wolf's mother, Perla Chaia Frost, had three children: Feigel, Wolf (the middle child), and Gutel. But Samuel died in 1834 at about the time of the birth of Gutel. In 1838 Perla married for a second time to Feiwel Wachter and they had one son, Mojzesz. Feiwel died in 1849 and Perla remarried again, this time to Judel Grajower, and they had another child. As a teenager, it seems that Wolf could not stand his second stepfather and it may have been after a row with him that Wolf decided to leave Kraków.

Presumably the unrest in Poland was causing many young people to contemplate leaving the country. The Californian gold rush had subsided and new rumours were spreading of fabulous wealth to be had from gold in the South Pacific. This could have been a major attraction to Wolf. Not only that, Australia seemed to promise the freedom and opportunity once offered by America.

Wolf first travelled to England and there is some record of him in Todmorden, Yorkshire but in August 1854 he boarded the ship *James McHenry* in Liverpool, arriving in Melbourne in December after nineteen weeks of travel.

If indeed the lure of Australia was gold then he would have gone straight to either Ballarat or Bendigo, where gold was being mined in some quantity.

The Victorian goldfields attracted the usual mixture of adventurers, the destitute, romantics, thieves and ne'er-do-wells. Men were joined by wives, mistresses and children. Using what little resources they had, they made their way to the goldfields laden with not much more than a pack and the clothes they stood up in. Every form of transport was used: packhorses, wheelbarrows, prams or just traipsing through the mud or dust. A melting pot of nations was represented: Chinese, English, Scots, Irish and Europeans of all sorts. After arriving in Port Melbourne, it would take at least three days and, in winter, two freezing nights to reach the goldfields. Many slept rolled in a coarse blanket, their head on their pack, protecting it from theft.

Once they reached their destination, competition for a claim was intense, even on the surface. To sink a shaft took even more resources. They were surrounded by urgers offering goods or services for extortionate sums. Worse was the food: flyblown meat, tinned food, damper, or rotting vegetables. Three quarters of the diggers made little or nothing from their endeavours and a steady stream of the disappointed made their penniless way back to Melbourne.

No doubt Wolf was caught up in the frenzy of the time and joined the multinational hoard of 'diggers' on 'the track', which by 1853 had swelled Ballarat's population to over 20,000, but Wolf was resourceful and smart and he would not have taken long to work out that there was nothing there for him.

I don't know whether he was involved in the 1854 Eureka Stockade insurrection in December. This event, Australia's only civil rebellion, arose out of high government fees, rough justice and lack of representation. The rebels were quickly subdued, leaving twenty-two diggers and six soldiers dead. Probably Wolf would have sought to put some distance between himself and this querulous mob, and attuned his ear to other fabulous reports of gold around the world, and more especially the new gold finds in the remote Southern Alps of New Zealand. Wolf had realised that the money in the goldfields was far more easily obtained by trading with the miners than by being one of them. In Arrowtown near Queenstown, the centre of the prospecting, on New Zealand's South Island, most of the prospects were owned by Chinese or by local residents. But Arrowtown was tiny. He needed to be somewhere with a larger population if he was to set up in business.

By 1858 he reached Dunedin, some 300 kilometres further south. Dunedin was a sturdy port on the southern extremity of New Zealand, scoured by the southerly gales that swept up from the Antarctic. Its population was predominantly Scottish. To help blend in, Wolf changed his name to Harris. He probably spoke English with a Central European accent that would have made some of the Scots treat him with suspicion. It took him little time to find a Jewish partner for his business, a Mr Bing, and late in 1858 the business that was to remain in the Harris family for over one hundred years, Bing Harris & Co Ltd, was formed.

Wolf began the business by trading around the goldfields and the farming areas close to Dunedin. Seeking to expand, he returned to Australia and bought a shipment of goods, which was shipwrecked on the way back. No one seems quite sure which ship it was that was lost but it seems most likely to have been the *Port Glasgow*, which on 15 April 1858 was discovered a waterlogged wreck by Maoris on the shore of Fitzroy Bay, just outside Wellington Harbour. Wolf, undeterred, tried again.

Over the years, he proved himself an adept trader and gradually the business expanded north, to Christchurch, Wellington and Auckland, selling anything that first the aspiring miner and then the general citizen could want: boots, clothes of all descriptions, manchester, utensils, watches and so on. Sometime during this period the mysterious Mr Bing was somehow detached from the business, leaving Wolf Harris as the sole proprietor. My father says that Bing was unreliable, overstayed on a trip to Europe and failed to carry out his commissions. Wolf arranged a line of credit with the Union Bank of Australia and bought him out. With all this activity Wolf travelled the length and breadth of New Zealand, learning Maori on the way. It was no surprise that he began to spend more and more time in Auckland, the largest city, and also, that he should soon become acquainted with the Nathan family.

Lawrence Nathan's book on the history of the Nathan family in New Zealand

15

THE NATHANS

The Nathans were one of Auckland's leading families. They were strict Jews and, since they were in almost exactly the same line of business as Bing Harris, Wolf and old David Nathan must have had much to talk about. It was not long before Wolf came to meet Elizabeth, of whom it was said that she was tiny but quite beautiful with dark blue eyes, a mass of brown hair and a white complexion. After a brief courtship, they were married on 25 June 1872 in a synagogue in the district of St Pancras in London.

The Nathan family was a typical Jewish family from the East End of London. Elizabeth's grandfather, David Lion Nathan, was born in London in 1783 and her grandmother Sarah in 1787. Through hard work and ability they kept afloat, but without capital, profession or much education, life was not abundant with opportunities.

One of Sarah's nephews, Moses, found opportunity in an unwelcome direction. Born in 1802, Moses was an itinerant pedlar, mainly of small items of jewellery. In 1825, he was accused and convicted for stealing a trinket from a competitor's barrow in the market at Warwick, and transported for life to Botany Bay. Arriving in Australia in 1826, he determined to create a new life for himself and to right the wrong he felt had been committed. He eventually got a 'ticket of exemption', which allowed him to work as a clerk, and made enough money to open up a tobacconist's in Sydney. In 1832 he married his cousin Rosetta, who had travelled out from London to marry him in completion of a longstanding 'understanding' reached prior to his transportation.

News of the couple's success in Australia must have acted as a beacon to the rest of the family toiling away in London. In 1839 Elizabeth's future father, David, then twenty-three, having served his apprenticeship, joined Moses in Australia. It had been his intention to settle in Adelaide, but, hearing that business conditions were not good in South Australia, he decided to try the new colony of New Zealand.

In 1848 Moses was granted a free pardon, which meant he could return to London. But in the interim, he had managed to acquire considerable wealth in Sydney by farming, property and gold buying. By 1849, after twenty-three years in Australia, he owned 102,256 acres of sheep and cattle stations, as well as choice 'sections' in Bridge Street, Sydney and Collins Street, Melbourne. He bought land in Auckland to help his cousin David and in Wellington to set up his blind brother, Jacob Joseph.

By this time, the invasion of the Antipodes by the Nathan family was in full cry: two brothers and a sister in Van Diemen's Land (Tasmania), two sisters in Sydney, one sister in Melbourne, one brother in Adelaide and David in Auckland.

My great-great-grandfather David Nathan, who went on to found the family business of LD Nathan & Co Ltd (which is the direct parent of the giant New Zealand brewer, Lion Nathan), landed at Kororāreka on 21 February 1840, sailing from Sydney on the barque *Achilles*. It was only two weeks after the signing of the Treaty of Waitangi and a year before New Zealand's own charter came into effect, making the country a separate colony of Great Britain rather than a dependency of New South Wales.

The tiny settlement of Kororāreka in the Bay of Islands in the far north of the North Island is now the waterfront at Russell, but at that time it was the principal port and seat of government, a port of call for all visiting vessels from Australia or further afield and a provisioning point for the whaling fleet operating on the west coast of New Zealand's North Island. It was a rough and roistering little seaport. Every second building along the seafront was a saloon. The behaviour of the seamen ashore and the local inhabitants, including the Maori from neighbouring *pa*s (forts) who came to town to sell produce to the ships and drink in the saloons, was much disapproved of by the missionaries at Paihia, just across the harbour.

With sailors ashore spending money, visiting Maori with earnings from sale of produce and curios and with a thriving ship service business, Kororāreka was a likely place for David Nathan to set up business. He rented a waterfront shack on a section adjoining Pompallier House, unpacked the stock he had brought from London and supplemented in Sydney, and the Sydney Commercial House, as he rather grandly named his venture, was in business.

We know little of his activities in Kororāreka but an excerpt from a contemporary paper says something of his relationship with the local Maori. Two of these were discovered stealing from Nathan's store and brought before the magistrate. David Nathan refused to prosecute but the court ordered restitution of the goods. This was assessed as cost rather than sale price and the two men were heard to say as they left court, 'It is cheaper to steal from David Nathan than to buy from him.'

Commerce at Kororāreka was unsettled by Governor Hobson's decision that it was not a suitable place for the centre of government. He bought land at Okiato at the head of the Russell Peninsula as a temporary relocation for government offices and artisans who had arrived to get the new colony going.

Hobson called the new capital Russell and paid James Reddie Clendon, the American Consul, who owned the property, 15,000 pounds for the land and buildings, giving him fifteen per cent in cash and the rest in notes. In due course the governor of New South Wales, of which New Zealand was still a dependency, repudiated the notes, so Hobson granted Clendon 10,000 acres of land in the Tamaki isthmus in substitution.

The new capital was never built at Okiato. New settlements were beginning to be established at Port Nicholson (Wellington) and Nelson, and Hobson decided the new colonial capital should be situated somewhere more central.

He therefore sent exploratory parties south to find a protected harbour where it would be possible to buy land from the friendly Maori for a new settlement. The traders in Kororāreka were naturally fearful that their town could become a backwater. When reports came back that the survey party had looked at Whangarei Heads and Mahurangi Heads but were more impressed by the possibilities of the magnificent Waitemata River, an expedition of the more venturesome businessmen was organised to go south and see for themselves.

David Nathan was one of the party and they sailed to the Hauraki Gulf in the brig *Mary*. There was no port or settlement at Auckland and the party was put ashore at Waiomu, the *kainga* (village) of Chief Taraia Ngakuti te Tumuhia of the Ngati Tamatera tribe. From there they hired a canoe to take them thirty miles past Waiheke Island up the Waitemata.

The canoe landed them at Mokoia, the Ngati Paoa *pa* on the west bank of the Tamaki River, near today's Panmure, but the paddlers refused to go further up the Waitemata Harbour to where HMS *Herald* was anchored. The visitors were, however, able to scale a nearby hill (Mount Wellington) from which they could see the beautiful sheltered harbour in the distance. They were impressed. They could see the bracken-covered headland and the bush in the valleys between them and the volcanic peaks on the skyline.

But they could do nothing to influence the reports of the survey party or the final decision of the governor, so they returned to the Maori encampment and arranged a canoe to take them back to Big Bill Webster's Trading Post. From there they took the next ship back to the Bay of Islands.

In due course, the government surveyors reported to Governor Hobson that in their view a fine site for a city was available on the shores of the Waitemata, though they found it difficult to determine whether it should be built on the flat land of Hobsonville, at the adjoining bays (Point Britomart), or at the mouth of the Tamaki estuary, where the friendly Maori chief had his *pa*. Eventually Point Britomart was selected because the water was deep enough for shipping.

When the first settlers arrived, Auckland consisted of a number of fern-covered ridges sloping down to beaches in the three bays that were soon named Mechanics Bay, Official Bay and, on the western side of Port Britomart, Commercial Bay. The craftsmen who had been brought out under indenture to the government lived and worked in Mechanics Bay. Official Bay was home to government officials such as the colonial secretary and treasurer with the Governor's Residence on the hill behind and Princess Street as its main thoroughfare. Commercial Bay was, as its name suggests, intended to be the business centre of the new town.

Government House and the houses of government officials were pre-framed in timber in Sydney and only required assembly in Auckland. The settlers lived first in tents and then built *whare*s (huts) for themselves in local timber or raupo or reed in the Maori manner. The first houses were seldom lined or papered and were draughty. They were roofed with raupo or wooden shingles and were leaky in wet weather. Few houses had glass windows, some had oiled calico screens, and some only had wooden shutters. Furniture was almost non-existent and the water supply came from rainwater barrels or from wells. Sanitation was rudimentary.

Queen Street was only a clay road between Shortland Street and the court house and gaol on the corner of Victoria Street. From there a rough road led up to the Karangahape Road ridge. Down the side of Queen Street flowed the Horotiu Creek, which flooded in winter and became a noisome sewer in summer. This creek was later channelled and bridged and renamed the Ligar Canal.

David Nathan and Israel Joseph were observant Jews and from its inception the firm closed its doors on Saturdays and Jewish holidays. David's brothers and sisters soon found Jewish partners in Australia but when David reached Auckland there was only one Jew, Barnett Keesing, living there.

It was fortunate that David had retained his little store in Kororāreka because on a business trip there in October 1841 he learned that a young Jewish woman, Rosetta Aarons, had arrived with no friends or relatives ashore. She was the widow of Michael Aarons, a sea captain who had been lost at sea on the voyage out. David met Rosetta and they became fond of each other and soon decided to marry. Their marriage on 31 October 1841 was historic: it was the first Jewish marriage in New Zealand.

It must have been hard to organise a Jewish wedding so far from any Rabbi or synagogue, but all that is really required is a bride and bridegroom, a ring, a canopy to hold over the couple during the ceremony, and two Jewish witnesses, one of which can be the celebrant. All these were available. Israel Joseph acted as celebrant and the other vital Jewish witness was George Russell, the owner of the Russell Hotel at Kororāreka. Rosetta had with her the printed Hebrew marriage contract or *Ketubah*, which had been used for her first marriage, and this document, altered as necessary, was faithfully copied in pen and ink. This *Ketubah*, written in Hebrew is today a treasured possession of later generations of Nathans in Auckland. It is lodged for safekeeping in the Auckland Synagogue.

It would appear from newspaper accounts that the wedding celebration was quite an occasion in the small settlement and the wedding breakfast was attended by the officers and ship's company of a vessel in port, as well as by many local friends of the bridegroom.

David and Rosetta returned to Auckland and with Israel Joseph worked hard to establish their small store. David was twenty-five and Rosetta twenty-seven years old. A formal deed of partnership was entered into with Israel Joseph, but he soon decided that life in Auckland was not for him. In 1844 the partnership was dissolved. Israel Joseph departed, bound for California, married Rosetta Braham in Montreal, returned to Sydney and nine years later died there.

In 1842 David Nathan decided his store in Auckland was sufficiently established to justify relinquishing the one in Kororāreka. Travelling between the two was difficult and securing a suitable manager impossible, and with the development of the Auckland Port and the town which quickly grew up around it, trade in the north had withered away. My great-grandmother Elizabeth was born in 1848 in Auckland.

David sold his lease to William Lord, a saloonkeeper and in 1845 an important event in New Zealand history took place in these premises when one of Maori Chief Hone Heke's followers came into the saloon and asked if anyone had seen the chief. Someone in the room as a joke said, 'Oh, yes. I saw him out in the back store.' When the Maori went to look all they found was the carcass of a pig hanging on a hook. They reported the insult to Hone Heke who demanded *utu* or revenge and brought his tribesmen into the town to begin one of the most serious riots which ever occurred between Maori and Pakeha in New Zealand. The infamous insult resulted in a series of raids on Russell (shabby Kororāreka's new name) and the cutting down of the flagstaff on the hill above the settlement (which normally flew the Union Jack).

After Wolf Harris and Lizzie Nathan married in London in 1872, the family connection continued as a strong one. From the beginning of Wolf's time in London, Wolf acted as a buyer for both Bing Harris and LD Nathan, an arrangement that subsequent generations carried on until after World War II. David's grandson, David Laurence Nathan, was sent to be educated in England. At the age of nine he went to live with his Uncle Wolf and Aunt Lizzie at the house in Queen's Gate and later joined his cousin Percy, my grandfather, at Harrow.

Wolf and Lizzie had a daughter, Pearl, who married a prominent Parisian doctor, Raoul Bensaude. At their home in Paris, David met Dr Bensaude's niece, Simone Oulman, aged twenty, dark and vivacious. They married on her twenty-first birthday and returned to New Zealand. Auckland in 1910 must have been a considerable shock to someone brought up in Paris with little English and no knowledge of the colonies. Simone eventually returned to England to be with her daughter Sybil.

Newly wed, Wolf and Lizzie set up their family home near the head office in Dunedin. With Wolf often on the road, Dunedin's fierce winds must have been Elizabeth's dreary companions. Wolf's travels were now taking him to meet suppliers and these were largely in England, particularly the textile cities of the north. No doubt at some point Elizabeth accompanied him and, with a prospering business and some faithful retainers, she persuaded Wolf that his horizons would be immeasurably expanded by moving to London. We have no record of how profitable business was at this point but presumably there was little competition. In any event it must have been thriving in view of what happened next.

Early in the 1880s, the couple bought a huge house in Queens Gate which included a large ballroom and, under Elizabeth's influence, they were soon holding frequent formal balls for more than one hundred people and leading an active social life.

Their third child, my grandfather Percy, recalled the house as an 'invention of the Devil.' It had six floors and a basement and communication between floors was by ill-functioning speaking tubes. Comfort was sacrificed to entertainment. The basement was a terrific affair with a large kitchen, servant hall, pantry, to say nothing of rooms for butler and footman. Wolf became President of the Arts Academy and plastered the many walls with a great quantity of Victorian paintings that shortly afterwards became very unfashionable.

Sunday family dinner was part of the routine and in future years my father, who as he cheerfully admitted, was a 'very greedy little boy', enjoyed the rich food. By then the house was attended by two ancient retainers, Hannah the cook and Geisler the butler. Geisler, who was German, was interned during World War I and Wolf, born technically in Austria, was lucky to escape the same fate.

Wolf, when not occupied with the affairs of Bing Harris, busied himself with assisting the Jewish community in London, particularly in the East End. He was a fine gentleman, with strong features and a splendid beard, strong in purpose but with a real humanity.

Wolf took a great personal interest in Dunedin. He donated grand pictures to the Dunedin Art Gallery, and in 1903 gave 2000 pounds to set up a Chair of Physiology at Otago University. He gave his home and freehold property for the first Karitane hospital set up in 1907 by Sir Truby King, the founder of the Plunket Society. He also donated a rather beautiful fountain which is now in the Dunedin Botanic Garden, and was repaired only recently with some help from family members.

My father was fond of him and liked to reminisce about the many bridge games they played in the boudoir. The old man died in 1926, at ninety-three, a figure much loved by family and the Jewish community in the East End of London, whom he had served well. During the entire time of Bing Harris's existence until Wolf's death he remained the uncontested chairman.

The Christmas card painted in 1952 by Uncle Nicholas for Bing Harris & Co Ltd

16

BING HARRIS

One of the objects lost the night of the fire at Te Rama was the original seal of Bing Harris & Co Ltd, first used in 1858, and thereafter on all documents until its replacement late in the twentieth century by a seal using ink rather than wax.

The original seal had been a fine affair, carefully cast in bronze and with a delicately carved whalebone handle, kept reverently in an oak box with silk lining secured by a small brass key to deter unauthorised use, the latter a 'hanging' offence.

The seal would normally have been locked in the safe in the company secretary's office in Dunedin but upon its replacement by the more utilitarian ink model my parents bought the original as a reminder of the business that had survived for more than one hundred years – through the bonus years of the original gold rush and import licensing and the despair of the Depression, until its decline and eventual sale in the 1960s in the face of a changing business world that rendered the old family business obsolete.

As a child, I used to wonder about the seal's curious shape and why it weighed so much. It was not like any other object I had seen and my father's explanation did not enlighten me, since I had no understanding of the need to authenticate documents.

It wasn't till much later that I realised the need to authenticate ownership must have been one of the earliest requirements of city

Bing Harris, 1905

dwellers, for the use of seals can be traced back to Mesopotamia to the fourth century BC and to Egypt in the third century BC and was in widespread use among many civilisations.

Some of the figures for Bing Harris have survived from the early days of the company. In March 1903 (balance date), sales were £299,513, stock £113,209, gross profit £48,336 and net income £14,716. Trying to translate these figures to today is a very inexact science given matters such as inflation, tax and relative values of currencies but a very rough guide to today's values can be obtained by multiplying by between 50 and 100, so for instance sales might have equated to between 15 and 30 million pounds sterling. Business was a leisurely affair, country customers were provided with drinks at the warehouse (soft I am sure), and the same occurred in country towns when the traveller arrived with his dray. The boss went off for his five-course lunch at his club, ending with brandy and cigars.

In spite of the six weeks' delay in correspondence, Wolf controlled things with an iron grip from London, exercising excellent judgement on the buying side, though it appears the standard of his partners in New Zealand was not always satisfactory, the last two appearing to have been an alcoholic and then a thief.

Wolf saw the business as strictly importing and frowned at suggestions for local manufacture. He also vetoed an idea to pull down the Dunedin warehouse, built in 1861, and replace it with a building with retail shops in the front. The old building is still occupied and is the last of the grey stone buildings that so grandly represented the days of prosperity in early Dunedin.

While the business kept to its purpose of importing produced good profits for many years, competition from local manufacturing and an aggregation of small retailers was steadily developing.

Tired of problems with local managers, in the early 1900s Wolf despatched his oldest child, Leslie, to the colony to see if he could do any better. Leslie, in his twenties, was not stupid, but he was easygoing and not predisposed to argue with Papa. He soon found his constructive suggestions treated with scorn by the old man. It was only a matter of time before Leslie became discouraged and spent less and less time in New Zealand until he returned permanently to England after World War I. In due course, the owners of the business all resided in England, in a dusty Victorian office on the ground floor and basement of 8 Philip Lane, London from which issued a stream of good advice to the management in New Zealand, who studiously ignored it. As Wolf aged he handed over the buying to subordinates with a less sure feel for the far-off markets and, having little knowledge of textiles, they were often sold inferior goods.

The management of the business then devolved to three men, a Mr Lees, chairman and Wellington manager, Mr Benson, Dunedin manager, and Mr Trimnell, in Christchurch. Mr Lees was an accountant whom my father, who disapproved of accountants, recalled as saying 'no' to all proposals, ignoring all opportunities and strangling the business.

Mr Benson came to New Zealand in 1902 as manager of the Manchester department and later Dunedin manager. He was apparently a trained warehouse man and devoted to the interests of the business. He trained the staff thoroughly in business procedures and it was his enthusiasm which carried the firm through the long period of neglect, not to mention the Depression, until 1935. He was predictably very conservative and probably resented the arrival of an upstart Pom with no business experience. My father remembers many violent arguments at board meetings.

The fortunes of the firm had deteriorated in the early years of the twentieth century, but it was saved from collapse by the advent of World War I. New Zealand was mainly dependent on Britain for imports and supplies were difficult to source. Having a London office was a great advantage and Bing's took good advantage of their ability to dictate prices to customers. In their eagerness to profit from this fortunate position, the buyers placed orders for delivery at the first opportunity, however far out that might be. By 1920 supply had caught up with demand and in 1921 disaster struck when all of the importers were found to have been adopting the same practices. British manufacturers finally started to get to orders that had been placed four or five years earlier at wartime prices, which had since dropped. British manufacturers ruthlessly enforced their contracts, and Wolf, in London, had to go cap in hand to suppliers and offer up to thirty per cent of the price by way of cancellation fee. In the year 1921, the firm lost half its capital and all the reserves built up during the war. It survived only because Wolf pledged his personal fortune as security to the Bank.

In 1923 Wolf died at the age of ninety-three. Until the last few years he had controlled every facet of the business but he had lost touch with the market in far off New Zealand, and with the staff who worked for him on the other side of the world. In a scenario played out time and time again in family businesses, he refused to trust his sons to take over from him, with the result that they lost interest in the activities of the family firm.

In the years after his death the firm managed to carry on, making modest profits, but it was in no condition for facing the Great Depression, which lasted five years from 1929. Nothing to this date that has occurred since in the West in economic terms has equalled the misery unleashed by the poor economic decisions made by governments. New Zealand, as a country benefiting from free trade and unrestricted access to international markets for primary produce, fared particularly badly. Orthodox thinking at the time was to pay the unemployed a dole, just enough to keep them alive, and supplement this with soup kitchens organised by charities. Meat and dairy products were often destroyed in the face of a hungry population and wool was sold for sixpence a pound. There was little in the way of state services and the phrase 'social security' had not yet been coined. There was also little public sector employment to cushion the declining purchasing power of laid-off private sector workers. The Liberal prime minister, George Forbes, was a bull-necked rugby player and farmer. Forbes' virtue was doggedness and his vice was stupidity. As future prime minister Keith Holyoake said, 'The only way George graduated from school was that the school had burned down.'

Forbes cut wages, cut spending and cut public works. The worse things became, the more he cut. Unemployment relief was also cut and eventually around forty per cent of the workforce was unemployed. Much of the population were living in not much more than hovels and under these conditions the normally law-abiding citizens of New Zealand rebelled. In 1932 there was rioting in Wellington and Auckland and serious damage was done.

And this was how, when my father arrived in New Zealand in 1931, aged twenty-four, he was confronted by an emergency and, at first, an unsympathetic bank. While Jack was acclimatising himself, the company was being 'run' by an associate of Mr Lees, an accountant with the unlikely name of Mr Junk. Bad debts piled up as did obsolete stock. Half the company's capital was gone. The bank, which held a first mortgage, was contemplating closing down the business. After listening to my father's case, they agreed to give him a chance to engineer a revival and appointed a representative, a prominent Wellington accountant, Jack Griffin, to oversee him. Jack Griffin was highly capable and together they gradually brought down the litany of bad debts and sold off, for a pittance, the collection of out-of-date and badly selected stock that had been cluttering the warehouse.

He found little help from the grim Mr Lees and less from Mr Junk, who was principally otherwise occupied in the business of saving souls. Benson was more helpful in Dunedin, not so ably assisted by an old gentleman named Mr Portman, who had a large walrus moustache. Mr Portman sat in a high chair in the office writing out the accounts with a quill pen. He used to wear a flat cap, and rode home on a bicycle, nodding to the passing citizens. The collection of Victorian relics, many sporting magnificent side whiskers, who made up much of the remainder of the staff, were unable to assist beyond selling at half price to every crummy hawker who appeared.

About this time George Milne, my grandmother Frieda's nephew, arrived, and he and my father were able to restore some order. But the situation was not helped by appeals to the family in England. As my father noted:

> *I wrote repeatedly to my father and uncle suggesting that one of them should come out to NZ. They were Joint Governing Directors, and as they also owned all the shares they could have done as they liked. Neither of them would budge. My father used to write out to tell me to wind the business up, it was an old man of the sea. In this case, there would have been precious little for shareholders, but this did not seem to worry him. My uncle took a slightly different line. He would write each year and say triumphantly that he had told us we would make a loss and now we had made one. He would then add sagely that we must be careful and not spend too much money.*

It was clear to my father and his uncle that no one intended to do anything until the bank stepped in. My father finally took things into his own hands and went to the Union Bank. He explained the situation, saying he wished to do something before the business went bankrupt. He was taken upstairs to see the general manager, a Mr Fotheringham. After several interviews, it became apparent that Fotheringham understood his position, and he was invited to run the company with the Bank's support. It was Fotheringham who suggested the appointment of Mr Griffin, a friend and colleague who had just completed a major assignment for the Bank, to assist as a consultant and board member.

Jack Griffin undertook a review of the business and finally recommended to the Bank that my father be given the opportunity to run the business with his assistance. Shortly afterwards, he joined the board and became joint governing director in 1944 until 1968 when he retired. He was my father's most trusted adviser during that long period of recovery and development.

Tight budgets were enforced on all buying, stocks reduced and attempts were made to collect the book debts, many of which were bad. The executive directors oversaw every aspect of the firm's activities. Once credit and stock control improved some cash began to be generated and it was probably only this that allowed the company to survive.

At the end of 1935 a general election was held and the Coates/Forbes Government was heavily defeated by Labour. My father remembers them as richly deserving their defeat. It was his view that they were nothing but a bunch of 'very stupid farmers' who had done nothing to alleviate the suffering of the population during the Depression.

According to my father, the incumbent, Michael Savage, 'had a soapy voice and a mournful manner capable of reducing his audience to tears.' His successor, Peter Fraser, a dour Scotsman, had the same qualities and my father remembered the former speaker, a Mr Algie, remarking that he would put any undertakers out of business if he

The entrance to the head office of Bing Harris & Co Ltd in Wellington

commenced in that profession. These characteristics must have suited the mood of the times for Labour continued to be elected.

The Savage Labour Government nationalised the Reserve Bank, opened teachers' colleges and made primary and secondary education free. The dairy price was guaranteed and unionism made compulsory. In 1938 parliament passed the Social Security Act, which promised security 'from cradle to grave', including a free health system and old age pensions for those over sixty. It was the first Labour government in New Zealand and many of its supporters, steeped in socialist ideology, believed it would herald the nationalisation of all the means of production, distribution and exchange. As it turned out the government was quite pragmatic and tried to balance its budgets and limit their overseas borrowing. Following good Keynesian policy, they embarked on an extensive policy of public works, and in particular a massive program of public housing. They even tried to acquire the fledgling Fletcher Organisation, then the only company in New Zealand capable of mass-building houses. They also began large-scale planting of pine plantations, which was to supply the paper industry in years to come. Primary production export sales continued to languish and the country soon began to run short of foreign reserves. To protect what remained and encourage local manufacture, a tight system of import licensing was introduced. Entitlements were based on past sales so Bing's started from a low base but the limited availability of foreign products meant these products were in high demand. Special licences were obtainable and Bing's did well by putting a director and my father's cousin, George Milne, in charge of getting them. George had an avuncular air about him but behind his jolly demeanour he was very shrewd. He hired the most attractive female models available, put them in their smartest dresses, and took them to see the Department of Industries and Commerce. This so enlivened the day of the department bureaucrats that the licences were immediately granted.

In the prevailing climate, it was a logical move for the company to begin some local manufacturing, as well. Wolf Harris had always resisted this and in fact had sold the clothing and footwear factories that the firm had acquired years before in Dunedin.

The first venture was ladies outerwear. A representative of a German manufacturer, Mr Rosen, had arrived in New Zealand with his wife. As German Jews they were, luckily for them, stranded there by the rise of the Nazi Party. Bing's set up a manufacturing company named Bond Street Models, and put Rosen in charge. Although having no manufacturing experience, Rosen had an eye for women's clothes and was good with staff. He hired a capable designer and, when war broke out and imported product became impossible to obtain, the business prospered.

After the war, Mr Rosen, whose wife had never acquired a taste for New Zealand, returned to Germany. Bing's bought a new business, Ethel Kay Mantles Ltd, which made ladies' coats and skirts. It was in the same building as Bond Street Models and was owned by an enormous fat Cockney Jew. He used to say you make your money out of 'cabbage'. He meant garbage and was referring to the over recovery that is made on fabrics. The business did quite well until the heated car reduced the need for ladies' coats.

During the war years Bing's was lucky to have a London office, as the key to prosperity was the obtaining of desirable goods for export to New Zealand. There were virtually no other sources of manufactured goods, apart from a few textiles from India, so everything that could be sourced could be sold.

Bing's survived quite well throughout the war, despite most of its staff being called up. By war's end the overdraft had been repaid and a credit balance established. This enabled expansion. Jobs were found for almost all the old staff as they were released from service, and my father found many of them much improved by the discipline and sense of purpose they had acquired from the wartime experiences. George Milne returned from services in the Pacific Islands and became a director. Sam McLernon came from a firm of accountants as company secretary and later manager and a director of the Christchurch branch.

Governments of either persuasion, instead of removing wartime controls, tightened them. Petrol rationing remained in place far longer than it was needed. A doctrinaire socialist, Dr Sutch, became head of the Trade and Industry Department and the most influential advocate for post-war economic policy. He envisaged a self-sufficient New Zealand, capable of manufacturing all its needs inside a wall of tariffs and creating jobs for all. The result was a series of totally uneconomic small manufacturers, a tight labour market, and a powerful union movement.

Bing Harris began setting up a series of tiny manufacturing companies. For instance, Chilco, which made children's wear and women's frocks, was set up in Wanganui. It was not very efficient, but employed at one time a staff of a hundred and fifty. Labour was cheap, partly Polynesian or Maori, but it was not long before competition began to bite and the restrictive demands of the unions made it almost impossible to respond. Bing's set up more small units: Guardsmen in New Plymouth, to make sports coats; a factory in Christchurch to make boys' shirts and girls' blouses and, later, knitwear and men's boots; another in Levin, making interlock underwear; in Palmerston North children's wear and bobby socks. Finally, Bing's acquired the Rainster factory, making rainwear, in Auckland. Bing's obtained import licences for fabrics. Initially most of the fabrics came from the textile factories in the north of England but my father and George Milne explored for better quality at cheaper prices: George in Japan and North America, and my father in India and Hong Kong.

In pursuit of his goal of full employment in the island fortress of New Zealand, Dr Sutch went to extraordinary lengths. For instance, Bing's was forced to import towels in large rolls, cut them and package them, even though the finished product could be imported much cheaper. The same process applied to ribbon fabric. In the case of ribbons the factory could only make a small range of products and had to try to import made-up ribbons for a myriad of uses none of which would have sufficient demand to justify local manufacture. Small runs of product and constant changes to the goods produced combined to undermine profitability that was never more than marginal.

Bing's found the operations of these tiny factories a logistical nightmare. They were dotted all over the country in towns that often had a population of only a few thousand. Sourcing competent managers was almost impossible, controlling their expenditure difficult and suppressing their ambitions to buy the latest (imported) machinery a constant battle. On top of this the accounting and reporting mechanisms in those pre-computer days were antiquated so that for instance, it was only after a primitive computer was installed that they discovered that all sales by the large tobacco division were made at a loss. Looking back, it is hard to appreciate how any of these businesses could have made a profit, even behind a huge tariff wall.

Sir Percy Harris, Bt, PC, DL, LCC

17

SIR PERCY

My grandfather Percy Harris, Wolf and Lizzie's youngest, was born on 6 March, the same date as me, only in 1876. He was educated at Harrow, where he was a near contemporary of Sir Winston Churchill. Years later when they shared the House of Commons together, Winston would remind him that 'Old Harrovians stick together', a suggestion that Percy would not always feel able to honour.

Wolf had not taken long to apprise himself of the Byzantine social stratification that determined English society at the end of the nineteenth century. He determined that his son should have the best opportunity to overcome his background by attending that most establishment of English schools, Harrow, and then going on to read history and economics at Trinity Hall, Cambridge. Once this had been accomplished, Wolf sent Percy to New Zealand, where his newly appointed manager had just died in the fire which destroyed the Royal Oak Hotel in Wellington. This mini-tragedy was reported in the *Wellington Evening Post* on 10 December 1898. The deceased, Mr George Blandford, was described as having a 'genial manner which made him most popular, winning for him the sincere regard of all those with whom he came in contact' and a man of 'undoubted business ability'. Given what followed he would have been sadly missed not only by his family but also by Bing Harris & Co Ltd.

Thus it was that, just before the turn of the century, Percy set out for New Zealand. The journey took six weeks, and he travelled via Marseilles, Suez, Colombo, across the Indian Ocean to Australia, and then via Tasmania to Dunedin.

He had already formed an affection for Frieda, the second daughter of Dr Bloxam, but their engagement had not been permitted for some reason he never divulged. Quite likely it was because his father was Jewish. However, Frieda's sister Sarah was married to the first master at Winchester College and had become friendly with Percy. When Sarah sensed the appearance of a rival, she wrote to Percy urging him to return. Percy headed back to England on a small steamer ('small and old-fashioned, and not one to be tolerated by passengers these days') via a delightful stopover in Hawaii, where he noted, 'The Yank had not yet taken possession, there were no skyscrapers and monster hotels.' He remembered vividly going out in the native catamaran (probably an outrigger canoe) and, nearing the shore, being dropped overboard, to be swept ashore by the surf.

After Hawaii, the next stop was Canada, presumably Vancouver, by rail across the Rockies, and on to London by boat. Back in England he wasted no time reclaiming Frieda, and on no less a date than 1 April 1901 they were married and spent their honeymoon retracing his steps to New Zealand. Percy first took Frieda to Paris. Frieda had professed a desire to ride in a motor car. These were virtually prohibited in England. No mechanically propelled vehicle could go on the road unless preceded by a man with a red flag. Percy searched Paris and, as a great treat for his bride, took her for a half-hour drive in the Bois.

On arrival in New Zealand they continued their honeymoon by embarking on one of the first hikes across the mountains to Milford Sound. This is quite a challenge even now. They followed a rough track and slept in the primitive bushman's huts, using ferns for bedding, and carrying their food. He remembers the scenery as unrivalled anywhere in the world, but they were attacked by sandflies and had to wear thick nets over their heads, which they could never remove without being instantly attacked by swarms of these tiny insects with vicious bites. Percy found it a particular inconvenience, persisting in trying to light his pipe through the netting. They bathed under the numerous waterfalls, climbed above the snowline and finally walked down into Milford Sound. One of the 'finest fjords in the world, comparing well with anything in Norway.' During the hike they visited Sutherland Falls, one of the highest in the world, and met Donald Sutherland, a gold prospector, who had discovered the falls in 1880 and was now living in one of the bushman's huts. Percy and Frieda developed a love of the country and used to spend weekends exploring on horseback accompanied by their faithful cocker spaniel.

Percy was to spend three years taking what must have been, given his lifelong indifference to the affairs of commerce, a cursory interest in the activities of Bing Harris. However, his time was not wasted for at that time New Zealand had some of the most advanced social policies in the British Empire: universal suffrage, old age pensions and cooperative farming. This and the egalitarian lifestyle of the population made a strong impression on the young Percy, echoed many years later in his reforms in his electorate of Bethnal Green. Frieda must also have found the experience interesting once she had become used to the lack of sophistication, for she was interested in women's rights and New Zealand was well ahead of much of the rest of the world, including Britain. As far as I know she only visited New Zealand on one other occasion, in the 1950s, when she gave me the pocketknife that I soon lost.

In 1903 Percy took a trip from Wellington to Auckland, and recorded the details. He caught a train from Wellington to Wanganui. Since the train line runs through Waikanae immediately past the front gate, he must have passed within a few hundred metres of Te Rama's predecessor, Waimahoe, at about the time the old house burned to the ground.

Percy took a steamer up the Wanganui River, which, as he notes, is not easy to navigate, as it narrows into a series of rapids and fast currents. By another of the little coincidences that seem to be dotted through life, it was these upper reaches of the Wanganui River on which I used to row in the Collegiate School VIII in the early 1960s.

I can just imagine how remote it would have been to Percy. Wanganui even in my time at the end of the 1950s was a sleepy little town and in fact the school would have been one of the largest employers, probably followed by Bing Harris & Co, which had one of its tiny factories there. The river would have provided much of the activity in the early days, steamers coming and going and fishing boats bringing in their catch, but there was little of that by the time I went to school.

After leaving the river, Percy and his fellow passengers boarded a coach, 'quite primitive', Percy wrote, having five, rather than four horses, with three leaders in front. They drove straight across the bush, guided only by cart tracks. Pushed beside him, as a travelling companion, was a carcass of mutton, but Percy was becoming used to the travelling habits of New Zealanders and minded not at all. They stayed at wayside inns, where there was always plenty of food, but 'not particularly well cooked'. He noted New Zealanders' propensity to drink tea constantly. As Percy recorded, 'He has it when he gets up in the morning, he takes it at eleven o'clock, has it with his midday meal and again at four o'clock. He has it with his supper and, before he goes to bed, he has a final cup.'

Back in England in 1905 Percy wasted no time joining the political fray. The Liberal Party under William Gladstone was the home of free trade and dedicated to introducing radical social welfare reforms to Britain. It was Percy's natural home. Under the new leader HH Asquith, Percy was chosen to stand as a Liberal in the solidly Conservative seat of Ashford and came within 400 votes of winning. Thwarted in his ambition to become a Member of Parliament, Percy turned to the opportunities presented in local government.

In 1889 the Conservative government, despairing about London, had hit on the idea of turning it into a county, even though it was entirely urban. And so was born the LCC. The London County Council was a unique institution. Prior to its incorporation London was run, more or less by default, by the City of London. The one square mile the City represented also represented the wealth of London. It was supported by the power of its merchants and financiers and the wealth of the city guilds. Business was its remit. However, conditions outside the square mile were appalling. In 1854 a series of parishes were grouped together as vestries but had limited powers so nothing was done for the poorest people outside the City's boundaries. After incorporation, in an attempt to rectify this, the LCC was charged principally with overseeing education, city planning and council housing.

It rapidly attracted 'a splendid lot of young men', who contested the election representing either the Progressives, allied to the Liberal Party, or the Moderates, allied to the Conservatives. The Progressives won hands down and held power for eighteen years until 1906, when, just as the Liberals had their finest result in a general election, the Conservatives managed to capture the LCC and kept hold of it till it was won by Labour in 1934.

In 1907 the local progressives, or Liberals, in Bethnal Green, the Cockney suburb not far from the City of London, wanted a candidate to run with the Rev. Stewart Headlam for the London County Council. Percy volunteered. With two others, Percy had to face some hundreds of Liberals at the Old Town Hall, and after a volley of questions, he was selected as their candidate.

The soundness of their choice, as the *Times* recalled it, was proved by his 'triumphant' return. In spite of many three-cornered fights, Percy remained in the LCC from 1907, through two world wars, but after World War II, it became evident that the LCC was too small to cope with the greater demands being placed on local government by the new welfare state. After prolonged debate, in 1963 a new Greater London Council and thirty-two new London

The cartoon published by the London Times celebrating Percy holding the balance of power on the London County Council

boroughs were finally set up. The LCC ran concurrently with the GLC for a year but in 1965 it was finally abolished. The Greater London Council was itself abolished by Margaret Thatcher in 1986 after one too many clashes between Thatcher and the socialist Mayor, 'Red' Ken Livingstone.

To return to national politics, at the beginning of the twentieth century the two major parties in British politics were the Liberals and the Conservatives. Following Gladstone, the Liberal leader was HH Asquith and he led Britain in the early years of World War I but he was replaced as prime minister, but not party leader, by a more vigorous David Lloyd George in coalition with the Conservatives in 1916.

While these internal Liberal Party struggles took place Percy pursued his political career. There was nothing to prevent him being a Member of Parliament at the same time as he was a member of the LCC. Percy, retaining his position on the LCC, entered Parliament at Westminster in 1916. He stood for Harborough as a Liberal and, in spite of strong opposition, was elected. He won a reputation in the House of Commons for industry and independence, not entirely to the liking of the Coalition machine. Asserting his independence, he backed Asquith in the 1918 election rather than Lloyd George. Lloyd George and Bonar Law, the Conservative leader, took their revenge contriving to endorse a Tory candidate against him in Harborough. This was at the 'Coupon Election'. (The Coupon Election was the immediate post-war election in which the leaders of the Coalition, Lloyd George and Bonar Law, sent coupons or letters to the electorate asking for their support as a patriotic duty.) It must have been unnerving for constituents to see the leader of Percy's own party endorsing another candidate. The result was that Percy was defeated by a handful of votes.

But Harborough's loss was Bethnal Green's gain for in 1922 Percy won Bethnal Green back for Liberalism, defeating both the Tory member and the redoubtable ex-mayor, Councillor Vaughn.

Fellow Liberals for their entire careers, Percy and Lloyd George had first found themselves in parliament together in 1915, when Lloyd George was Minister for Munitions and Asquith Prime Minister in what looked like an impregnable Coalition. This peaceful appearance did not last long. Pressure from a war that was not going well and questions about Asquith's restrained style of leadership soon led to Lloyd George taking over the reins as prime minister, supported by the Conservatives. Apart from Churchill, who we will return to, the other great character Percy shadowed all through his political career was Lloyd George. Lloyd George was a true liberal. In 1909 as Chancellor of the Exchequer under Asquith he had introduced the 'people's budget', which proposed higher taxes. It was rejected by the House of Lords and resulted in a struggle for power between the two houses of parliament, which eventually led to restrictions under the Parliament Act of 1911 on the power of the House of Lords.

Percy described Asquith as a man with a fine mind and balanced judgement, but shy and reserved. By contrast:

> [Lloyd George] had all the arts of a demagogue, and knew how to fire the popular imagination. Asquith and Lloyd George had worked well together. Asquith was nothing if not tolerant, and would overlook his colleague's foibles, whereas LG believed in his own star, was ambitious, and would not hesitate to do anything to get his own way. There was too the sinister figure of Beaverbrook, who was ready to act as Lady Macbeth to LG's desire for power. I do think Asquith was treated badly, but when the political game is being played, loyalties seem to count for little. The curious thing is that the Tories had more in common with Asquith than LG, and one would have thought they would not have lent themselves to Asquith's destruction. Bonar Law, as their leader, had much to do with the decision.

Percy saw the move by the Conservatives to support Lloyd George as a deliberate attempt to split the Liberal Party, and in this it succeeded admirably. The Liberals never recovered and from the 1920s politics in Britain became increasingly a contest between Conservatives and Labour. Many Liberals, who in any event were scarcely represented in the Coalition government, developed a lifelong dislike for Lloyd George, tinged with a hint of snobbery at the expense of the effervescent little Welshman. Percy was much saddened over what the future might have held for Liberalism had the split not occurred. Nevertheless, Lloyd George proved a capable wartime leader, and, with superb skills as an orator, he was inspiring.

Lloyd George met with great success at the Paris Peace Conference, but at home the country was facing an economic shock and the return of almost four million soldiers to civilian life. In Ireland violence led to the establishment in 1920 of the Irish Free State. The Conservatives were unhappy and the Coalition began to fall apart. A scandal over campaign finance worsened the situation and led in 1922 to Lloyd George's resignation.

He never served in government again. He led the Liberal Party from 1926 to 1931 but, with the split not healed, they continued to lose at the polls. He is remembered as the man who led Britain to victory in World War I and who ousted Asquith in 1916.

Bethnal Green was an interesting electorate for Percy to choose after his 1918 loss in Harborough. Bethnal Green is about three miles from Charing Cross and anyone born there is a Cockney. It has a long history but by the end of the nineteenth century it was one of the poorest slums in London. By the time Percy became involved, things there had improved a little and it was home to a whole mix of races, particularly Jews. During World War II Bethnal Green was a constant unintentional target for German bombs, being so close to the Square Mile. On one night in 1943, 173 people died in an underground train station, their deaths attributed to a German bomb. It was not until 1946 that the English authorities admitted that the deaths had been caused by a stampede brought on by panic.

Bethnal Green was in Percy's time very poor and in dire need of major reconstruction, so in many ways Percy, who had a strong commitment to social justice, was its ideal representative. Bethnal Green became his second home and his life. Percy was inspired by his love for the humanity and diversity of its people and their stoic acceptance of poverty and the trials of war. In celebrations to mark twenty-five years on the LCC he remarked, to a tremendous ovation, 'After all. It is a sort of silver wedding. Bethnal Green and I have been married twenty-five years, and I think we have been a happy couple all through. We have never quarrelled, we have always remained good friends; and I believe out of our marriage has come some happiness.' His wife Frieda's comments are not reported, however the assembly was right royally entertained. Dancing music was provided by Johnny Silver's 'Rhythmic Aces', Councillor Thoms, it was reported, making a very able master of ceremony. Between the dances variety tunes were presented under the direction of Mr TJ Ellis, and a display of ballet 'evoked considerable enthusiasm.'

On 24 January 1932, Percy was created a baronet. To most people today, especially those who live in the Southern Hemisphere, the baronetcy is a strange affair, especially as it remains in place after the initial recipient's death and is inherited by the eldest son. This arrangement can continue forever in theory so it is worth exploring a little of the background.

In 1611 King James I of England and VI of Scotland was having trouble with his Irish subjects in the North of Ireland or Ulster. The Earldom of Ulster had been created in the North of Ireland in 1205 by the English King John Plantagenet. By the late sixteenth century Protestant Scottish and English settlers had begun to arrive in Ireland in increasing numbers, with the economic strength to allow them, bit by bit, to dominate the original Catholic population. Inevitably resentment increased among the Catholic serfs and violence soon broke out. Instead of leaving them to work it out for themselves and saving four hundred years of sectarian murder, rape and pillage James sent an army to regain control. But James, like all the Stewarts, was chronically short of money and developed the bright idea of selling honours to help finance his army. He created the baronetcy to rank between barons and knights and made it more enticing by allowing the title to be inherited by the eldest male heir. The price for the honour was set at £1095 which was supposedly the amount that would maintain thirty soldiers in Ulster for three years. The first baronet was the Baron of Redgrave, bestowed on 22 May 1611, and in the initial years, 200 baronets were created. Redgrave's baronetcy is still in existence. Of seventeen others from 1611, eight still survive.

Charles I, extended the system to cover the whole of Scotland, with the particular intent of assisting the colonisation of Nova Scotia. This time the purchaser paid £2000 (the amount said to support six colonists) plus £1000 to the Earl of Sterling, to whom Nova Scotia was granted in 1621. In return the purchaser received 16,000 acres of land, the title and a grand badge displaying the arms of Nova Scotia with a Latin motto, *Fax mentis honestae Gloria*

('Glory is the torch that leads on the honourable mind'), to be hung around the neck from an orange ribbon. To keep the Ulster baronets quiet, he also granted them the right to display the Red Hand of Ulster, known as the 'bloody hand', upon a silver escutcheon, on their shields. The symbol was adopted for the neck badge authorised in 1929 by George V for baronets.

The 'bloody hand' was to make an unexpected intrusion into our lives in New Zealand nearly one hundred years later. In the fire that demolished Te Rama a tiny pair of red coral and gold earrings shaped in the form of two delicate 'bloody hands' had disappeared, or so we all thought. Subsequently we learned they had not been in the house and years later my mother gave them to my wife Gail, who by coincidence was a Stewart by birth. So now the 'bloody hands', at least these ones, are back in the hands of the Stewarts.

The coral earrings in the form of the bloody hand and signifying the baronetcy

By 1707 there were 984 English baronets and 344 Scottish baronets. Once Scotland and Ireland became part of Great Britain the titles merged and from 1801 only baronets of the United Kingdom were created.

By the start of the twentieth century, it became apparent that there were some fake baronets around. Since the title had no constitutional function attached to it no one had paid attention to the successors to the title until 1910 when Edward VII legislated to prevent 'the assumption of the title of baronet by persons who have no right thereto' and a registrar was appointed to control abuses.

The *Times*, speaking upon Percy's death in Kensington in 1952, gave a warm endorsement of his long career in both Parliament and the LCC.

> *Besides looking like a benevolent Dickens character, he really behaved like one. Among the slums and overcrowded tenements, he secured for the poor families of the East End the Collingwood Housing Estate – the first to be built after the 1914–18 War – the Bethnal Green Men's Institute, the first LCC nursery school, the Bethnal Green day nursery and many other amenities. He had a vision for a new London 'with fine streets, great new bridges – a town of sunshine and air instead of fog and squalor, a smokeless city, a gay town with boats on the river and gaiety in the parks,' an image creating some difficulty in modern parlance. After the air raids so sadly hit the East End streets he loved he was among the first to see the opportunities for the town planner. The people of Bethnal Green loved him, for he campaigned against high rents and overcrowding and he paid them this tribute in 1936: 'There is no more peaceful part of the world than Bethnal Green. I have known it during strikes and in the Great War, and can testify that there is no more law abiding, tolerant people than in the East End. Irish and English, Jew and Gentile, shopkeepers and street traders, though there are many causes of friction, manage to live in harmony and goodwill.'*

In photographs, he looks the conservative gentleman but he clearly had a sense of fun and enjoyed the good humour of his constituents. To wit, to quote the *Times* again:

> Sir Percy [he had by then become a baronet] held a big party at the Empress Hall, Great Tower Street. The guests were Bethnal Green Liberals old and young, and the special visitors included Lady Sinclair. I am told that the liveliest spectacle of the evening was Sir Percy dancing 'Knees-up Mother Brown' and somewhere near midnight, his effort in the middle of a circle of people doing a frolic that could only be called the 'Bethnal Green Special'.

Finally, like Churchill, Percy lost his seat in the Labour Party tidal wave of 1945. Predictably Percy grew bored with life out of politics. Frieda immersed herself in her own affairs and her painting, which, he confided, seemed to occupy her twelve hours a day. It was scarcely surprising that he succumbed to an invitation to stand for the Liberals as a candidate in the 1946 London County Council elections against the might of the Labour machine. Percy was turning seventy and it was his twenty-first election, but he was known and loved in Bethnal Green and when the votes were counted he and his fellow candidate, Captain Edward Martell, were returned. For much of the time the Liberals were in the minority, but in the 1949 elections Percy found himself holding the balance of power when both Labour and Tory had sixty-four seats. Finally, he was defeated in the 1950 election, which saw the end of his political career. He died in 1952 in Kensington aged seventy-six.

My father always claimed that Percy would have been made a Member of the House of Lords if it had not been for Frieda. When I raised the question of Percy becoming a baronet my father said the government had all immediate members of the family checked. He notes that of course he and my mother were perfectly acceptable but Frieda's activities were something of a problem and that later, when the Lords was on offer, her bizarre activities were unacceptable.

Percy may have been a successful politician, but the niggardly salaries of the day would not have provided him with his comfortable lifestyle. On his return from New Zealand in 1903 Wolf provided Percy with a small office and stipend while he pursued his political ambitions. It is clear that to the end of his days the Old Man quietly subsidised him, no doubt enjoying the pleasure of seeing Percy so well-loved by his constituents. As Wolf grew older he began to take his religion more seriously as the allure of the material world began to dim, and he spent both more time and money among the many Jews of Bethnal Green. I remember seeing records of letters and awards given to him by the Synagogue but sadly these were destroyed in the fire.

Although Percy's life was largely devoted to politics, his family were also of great importance to him. Percy and Frieda stayed in France during the summer of 1929 in Saint-Jean-de-Luz. Joan Harris, the daughter of Percy's older brother Leslie, who was staying in Paris, decided to join them. Bored with the casino and beach, Percy and Frieda headed for the mountains in Spain and, to their surprise, Joan, as Percy wrote, 'most unsuitably dressed in high-heeled shoes and clothes of the latest Paris fashions', followed them. They took her for a long walk, exhausted her, and she elected to remain behind as they headed out for another hike the next day. They had noticed in the hotel a 'fine, well set-up young man, having the appearance of a naval officer.' When they returned from their hike Joan was nowhere to be found and they were told that she had gone to lunch with a young gentleman. It transpired that the young man was a White Russian, Constantin Slioussarenko, who had served in Deniken's Army. (Deniken was the Commander of the White Volunteer Army that arose in 1917 after the Russian Revolution. It briefly resisted the Bolsheviks before in 1920 being destroyed. The few that survived fled to the West.) Slioussarenko had escaped and joined the French Foreign

Legion, in which he was now serving in North Africa. Percy and Frieda found him 'a most attractive man rather of the strong, silent type, but with excellent manners.' Percy and Frieda returned to London and Percy's brother Leslie was heard to complain that he couldn't get any sense out of his daughter, who had found a sudden attraction for mountain air. Joan and her captain became engaged, and they corresponded for a year while he served in North Africa. Joan finally married her captain in Paris. Constantin was then posted to Indochina (Vietnam) and she accompanied him. In 1940, Indochina was overrun by the Japanese and Constantin had to get out fast, leaving his family behind. He disappeared and nothing was heard of him until his reappearance in the French Foreign Legion after the war was over. For four years Joan and her children managed to sit out the Japanese occupation. After the war, they returned to France via Fez, in the mountains of Morocco. Constantin reappeared. The youngest son Alex many years later emigrated to New Zealand where he wisely decided to follow Wolf's example, and changed his name to Harris. There is a story here but no one will talk about what happened. Being under Japanese occupation could not have been pleasant so maybe it is one of those stories, of which all too many took place during the war, where the truth will never be known. Alex still lives with his family in Auckland.

Percy had unique insight into many of the great political figures of Britain in the twentieth century. As already noted, he was particularly close to Lloyd George and Winston Churchill. In 1946, when Percy wrote his book, memories of each of these characters would have been fresh in his mind. Little original perhaps remains to be said particularly about Churchill. But Percy's personal reflections manage to throw a perspective from a point close in time and place. Some of his reflections seem quite quaint from the beginning of the twenty-first century. Percy wrote in his memoirs:

In 1890, at the age of fourteen, I went from Hardie's (School) to the famous school on Harrow Hill.

1890 to 1894 were years of excellent vintage at Harrow. Weldon, afterwards Bishop of Calcutta and Dean of Durham, was Headmaster, and amongst the boys were Winston Churchill and Amery. I have a vivid memory of Winston, who was a year or two older than I, but was perpetually stuck in the lower form of the school. Many years afterwards at a dinner at the House of Commons, presided over by Stanley Baldwin, Winston made a characteristic speech about his Harrow days. Baldwin had said that he had left no special mark, and insisted that he had not distinguished himself at Harrow. 'What Baldwin did not tell you,' said Winston, 'was that he was in the upper sixth and was second or third in the school. I did distinguish myself: I was longer bottom of the lower fourth than any boy in the history of the school.'

Amery, by contrast, won distinction from his earliest days. He was head of the school, and a distinguished one at that. He has very little changed through the process of time. Unlike most of us, his hair has not gone grey, and he is the same stocky little figure that graced the platform on speech days and said his words in the same way as he did as Secretary of State for India, standing at the Box in the House of Commons.

Churchill in bulk and bearing has very much more altered in appearance, but he has still the same personality I became familiar with as a small boy. He was very fond of attaching himself to some junior master, and he could often be seen walking along the High Street with one, speaking in that familiar raucous voice, no doubt about the exploits of his father. Except [when] a boy was exceptionally tall, boys, until they reached the lower fifth, had to wear Eton's, and as far as I can recollect, Winston wore them and had the appearance of an overgrown schoolboy bulging out of his Eton jacket. Often when I have sat opposite him as Prime Minister and seen him indulge in those characteristic displays of temper and petulance, I have felt he had changed little and was still the overgrown schoolboy of his

Harrow days. In many of his moods he has a very boyish face, and I have always felt he has never completely grown up. That is one of his charms. There always remains in him something of the schoolboy. He loves to go abroad wearing all kinds of uniforms. His spirit of adventure has something of the schoolboy touch, which is most lovable and charming. He has never spared himself or bothered about appearances. One day he is wearing the uniform of a Colonel of the Hussars and the next a siren suit with equal confidence and pleasure. He would be a great man to go tiger shooting with but not equally safe on a dull journey – I am sure he would lead one into mischief. All his life has been one great adventure. He has never spared himself or avoided any risk. Most men who at the height of their careers had suffered twice from bad attacks of pneumonia would go slow, but not Winston. Hardly had he recovered from a severe illness, than off he would go again on some long journey with cigar in his mouth and a double whisky to fortify him. But, to go back to his school days, certainly he did not distinguish himself at Harrow.

Percy was in and out of Parliament from the time of Churchill's first appearance until they were both defeated in 1945 when England turned away from its wartime leader and embarked on a new course to rebuild the shattered country. He recalled little vignettes. In 1924, as Chancellor of the Exchequer, vituperative debates with Philip Snowden, a caustic socialist in the Labour ranks. In 1936, Baldwin, whom Percy accused of 'moral cowardice' for not facing up to the Germans, refusing to have Churchill in the Government, telling Percy, 'Winston is a blister: and I have come to the conclusion it is better to have a blister outside than inside.' Percy sagely agreed that probably Winston would not be a good subordinate. Percy recalled that in 1938 he championed Winston, telling his own party, 'When I compare the pygmies now sitting on the Treasury Bench with the great figures of past Liberal Governments, Mr Asquith, Sir Edward Grey, Lord Haldane and Lloyd George. These names are remembered, but who will know the names of the present

Government twenty years hence? I have omitted the name of your own member: he was a great First Lord of the Admiralty in a Liberal Government. He is quite the greatest Parliamentarian we have got, but I sometimes think that, patriotic as our ministers are, they would rather lose the war than have him as a colleague. These Lilliputians don't like Gulliver; he makes them feel small.' Fighting words for Percy. He went on to write, 'I am not going to assert that anyone could have averted the war, but I am sure Chamberlain did not understand Mussolini, or Franco, or Hitler, or Stalin. I think if Lloyd George or Winston had been Prime Minister, our relations with all those persons would have been different. Chamberlain was pained and surprised when all these foreigners did not conform to the standards he was accustomed to.'

Finally, in May 1940, Parliament had had enough of the Chamberlain Government, which resigned to make way for the Churchill National Government. The Liberals, after the support they had provided, were disappointed not to have a ministerial appointment. Percy, Chief Whip of the Liberals since 1935, was entitled to hold the position as representative of the third arm of the government. But he declined, seeing it as an appointment that would have reduced him to silence. Churchill accepted the decision and it was shortly after that he recommended Percy for the Privy Council.

Percy remembered 1940 as the 'blackest year of the War.' As it emerged there was even talk of evacuation of Parliament to the provinces. Percy strongly disapproved. He was 'satisfied nothing would have a worse reaction on the people of London in particular, and the British Commonwealth as a whole, than if we were to leave the capital. In due course I received satisfactory assurances: Churchill had made up his mind that on no account should we change the seat of Government. Churchill will always have his critics, but I am satisfied his iron nerve, coupled with his brilliant oratory, did much to rally the nation and pull through the critical months of that year.'

Over Christmas 1940 the London office of Bing Harris was hit by a bomb and completely obliterated. As Percy recalled, 'you could not even trace the lines of the street where it was situated.' In April 1941 he wrote the following in his diary:

> *I went to Bethnal Green. Turin Street and the narrow lanes and alleys I have canvassed and walked through during the last thirty years in an awful mess and most of the wretched houses, long overdue for clearance, reduced to rubble and dust. Rescue work still going on but little hope of the buried being dug out, but some marvellous escapes. Visited the rest centres and found people quite content to be alive, though they had lost their all. A general cheerfulness and absence of complaint.*

Some glimmer of light was needed and it came from the most unexpected quarter. Percy particularly remembered Sunday, 22 June 1941. It was the day the:

> *astonishing news of the invasion of Russia by Germany broke. Everyone was completely taken by surprise. Then, that afternoon we heard Churchill's declaration. I think, considering the circumstances, that speech was the finest he made during the war. It was not only the content, but the clear and decisive statement of support. The people listening at the hotel (in Southampton where he had gone to visit youngest son Nicholas) were mostly middle class, frightened of communism and Russia, but Churchill's lead heartened all of us and gave the nation a real new ally and broke our isolation. I believe the historian will say that Winston Churchill's clear and definite promise of active help had much to do with the stoutness of the Russian resistance. And there was something magnificent in his gesture.*
>
> *He hated Communism and everything it stood for, but he swallowed his prejudices, conscious that however hateful its doctrines might be to him, they were a lesser evil than the Nazi threat to civilisation. But if Great Britain alone had offered help I doubt if it*

could have been effective. President Roosevelt could claim equal credit. Our resources were not great enough and were too badly needed by ourselves to have been adequate.

By December 1941 the United States had entered the war and Britain began to feel less isolated. Percy was quick to involve himself in the formation of a British American Association, which went on to form alliances between its parliamentary members and Congress. The importance of the alliance was obvious, and Percy was all too aware of the importance of Churchill's relationship with Roosevelt. Percy remembered Winston returning to Britain after meeting with Roosevelt in Washington:

I came into the dining room (at the House of Commons) a bit late and found Alexander, the First Lord of the Admiralty, at my table. I complained and told him to go to his proper seat at the Minister's table. Winston, hearing the conversation, invited me to go over and sit with him. I at first refused as the Minister's table is regarded as sacrosanct, but he insisted and as a result I had an amusing conversation. I asked him how he had got on with Roosevelt and he replied, 'Almost too well. In fact,' he said, 'we were always in and out of each other's rooms. He caught me,' he explained 'one morning with nothing on but my bath towel.'

As the war dragged on and the allies continued to be hard-pressed, criticism inevitably developed, often from the backbenchers of all three parties. Churchill was highly sensitive to this and although Percy tried to smooth over it, Winston was obviously not placated. Churchill was attacked from both sides – from the far left by Aneurin Bevan, inevitably provoking a splenetic response, and from the far right by Wardlaw-Milne, who spoiled a well-reasoned criticism of the war strategy by proposing that a suitable aristocrat in the shape of the Duke of Gloucester be made Commander-in-Chief. Following the Japanese attack on Pearl Harbour, Percy made a speech emphasising that the Pacific and therefore the Empire now had to defend its own region and that it was a mistake to relax because the Americans would now shoulder the main burden. He went on:

> *More and more we shall be thrown on our own resources. We must, therefore, close ranks and show our solidarity behind the Government. More than ever this is a struggle between civilisation and barbarism, and I have no doubt that civilisation will win.*

Percy wrote little about the latter years of the war because, as he wrote from the vantage point of 1946, 'they are so near at hand that they are familiar to all of us,' which is a pity for us some seventy years later.

He did express further admiration for Churchill for keeping cool in the face of increasing left-wing pressure to announce the forming of the second front. When D-Day did arrive, Percy admitted to having no prior knowledge.

Finally, on 7 May 1945 the Armistice was signed. Churchill stood in Parliament and repeated the statement just read to the nation. Percy recalled that:

> *Not one of us present could but feel deep emotion. No one was more moved than Churchill himself. Quite informally he crossed the floor of the House and shook hands with some of us senior Members. Then we filed out of the House in procession across Parliament Square, through cheering crowds, headed by Mr Speaker, preceded by the Sergeant at Arms bearing the Mace, to the Church of St Margaret, Westminster, where the Speaker's Chaplain moved us to thanksgiving.*

Percy recalled the crowd being more subdued than they were after the end of World War I. He walked down to Bethnal Green, surveying the death and destruction that had been wrought among his beloved constituents:

> *It was a happy crowd that rejoiced that day. They enjoyed themselves but there were none of those excesses that marred Armistice Day in 1918. The people had suffered so much and been through so many ordeals that they took peace quietly.*

In the face of the dissolution of the National Coalition, Churchill quickly called for an election. Percy felt it was a mistake and one of Winston's own doing – although once the results were through Winston tried to blame the Labour Party. In the event, Winston was out, and so was Percy.

Percy found himself in compulsory retirement and for a time contented himself with gardening in his house at Chiswick, growing apples, strawberries and raspberries, most of which went to the local birds. He spent the remainder of his time writing his memoirs, *Forty Years In and Out of Parliament*, which I've been quoting from.

Percy ended his book with barely a nod to his family, something he either thought was out of place in his book about politics, or decided not to go into. All he said was in a few paragraphs right at the end of his 197 pages. The same was true of my father Jack's own book.

Te Rama after the fire

18

THE BLOXAMS

When Wolf Harris came to London in about 1870 almost the first person he met was a John Porter. John Porter was a prosperous partner in a London wholesale firm. Given that they were both in almost the same business it was not a surprise that they became lifelong friends. They must have spent endless hours talking about trade, the risks and rewards of the business of buying and selling goods, the 'Art of the Deal'.

One of John Porter's daughters, Jessica, married a John Astley Bloxam. John Bloxam was born at Highgate on 26 May 1843, the son of Charles Bloxam and Elizabeth Tucker. John became a celebrated surgeon. Because he was a member of the Royal College of Surgeons we know much more about him than about the Porters. My grandmother Frieda was John and Jessica's daughter.

The Bloxam family came from the Cotswolds, where they had lived almost back to the time of the Norman Conquest. Early records speculate that the original name was de Bloxham, shortened to Bloxham and finally Bloxam.

The first official record of the family is of the marriage on 13 September 1550 of Ralph Bloxam to Magaret Southerne. Traditionally the Bloxams worked in the legal profession and were associated with the wool trade. They had large, long-living families.

John Bloxam's father had moved to Marlow and set up as a solicitor there. As a boy John went to school in Maidenhead; later he went to Highgate School, a tradition of the Bloxams. He went to school in a coach and then to Maidenhead by train. In the back of the coach was a man armed with a blunderbuss to protect them from highwaymen as they passed through Maidenhead Thicket.

The young John paid for his medical studies at St Bartholomew's Hospital by playing billiards for money around the pubs. Such was his enthusiasm for his medical studies, he was thrown out of his home for dissecting a body on the dining-room table.

After serving as surgeon to the Royal Horse Guards or 'the Blues' for about two years, he became, for many years, senior surgeon of Charing Cross Hospital. He practised at Grosvenor Street and had a smart clientele, but he never cultivated the bedside manner and would give short shrift to other doctors who consulted him. It must have been during this period he began to study syphilis, an unmentionable subject in Victorian England. He published three papers on the disease. He was also the first person in England to use skin grafts, necessary to repair the noses and lips of those who had been the victim of syphilitic ulceration. During one of his more notorious operations, a patient arrived and was told in a stentorian voice to take his pants down. In a lightning move a piece of skin was removed from the patient's bottom and transferred to the affected place. The operation was a success, and the patient mollified when told that if the procedure had been explained in advance he would never have given permission. He also pioneered the practice that became known as plastic surgery, once transplanting a part of a finger to form the basis of a new nose.

John Bloxam retired early and bought a house in Bourne End, a picturesque village on the banks of the river Thames, not far from Henley. My father remembered the house with affection.

It was an Elizabethan house and had once been an inn. There was a cockfighting room and a billiard room (which Bloxam added) decorated with a huge pike he had caught. The house had a beautiful garden where he exercised his surgical skills in grafting plants. He had distinguished friends in the country, where he would go hunting and fishing.

He was a convinced atheist and would shout people down with 'God damn rot bloody nonsense.' Jessica on the other hand was very religious. Surgeons were not well paid in Victorian England so in reality it was Jessica Porter's dowry that largely allowed the family to live in such comfortable circumstances.

Plarr's Lives of the Fellows contains a list of over 9000 obituaries of members of the Royal College of Surgeons. It was first published by the College's Librarian, Victor Plarr, who served from 1897 until his death. John Bloxam died at Bourne End in 1926. His obituary describes Bloxam as 'a man of striking appearance, tall, slender, and of upright carriage, and preserved in old age many of the characteristics his early training in a crack regiment; above all things he valued punctuality.' The obituary continues, 'At 2 o'clock every day of duty he drove up to the door of the hospital in the smartest private hansom in London, and woe betide his house surgeon and dressers if they were not waiting ready to receive him.' This obsession about punctuality and almost everything else we know about him could not have been more different than Frieda. What on earth did he make of her?

Percy was brought up with the Bloxam's four sons and four daughters and spent many happy hours riding with them over the heath at Highgate. He had known Frieda for some years before they became engaged.

Portrait of Lady Harris (Frieda)

19

FRIEDA

Frieda, born in 1877, was a year younger than Percy. In accordance with Victorian tradition she was sent to a classical school near the family home in Bourne End where it appears her education, under the guidance of the Lehman family, may have been more unorthodox than usual for young Victorian ladies of good birth. Her teacher was an American and fellow Bourne End resident, Alice Marie Davis. She was the mother of the novelist Rosamond Lehmann, Cambridge graduate and infamous for writing a novel about gay and lesbian relationships which was a major 'succès de scandale'. Rosamond's life included two marriages and two high-profile affairs but was largely defined by the death of her beloved daughter Sally at twenty-six. Rosamond took to making psychic contact with her daughter, something that continued for years. Alice's other daughter was the successful actress Beatrix Alice Lehmann. More importantly for Frieda, Alice was married to Rudy Lehmann. Rudy Lehmann was an ex-President of the Cambridge Union, a barrister and, from 1906 a Liberal Member of Parliament and thus he and Percy spent considerable time together. He also was an editor for *Punch* magazine to which he contributed for over thirty years, including writing a series of parodies of the

Sherlock Holmes novels. More importantly from Frieda's viewpoint he was dedicated to the sport of rowing, notwithstanding finishing last in every heat he entered at the Henley Royal Regatta. He intermittently coached both Oxford and Cambridge Universities, the Berlin Rowing Club and later Harvard University. He was also captain of one of the world's first rowing clubs, the Leander Club, based at Henley and founded in 1818. Frieda must have met him through Alice and thus been introduced to rowing. It was Rudy Lehmann who sent the first women's eight to Henley, in which Frieda and her sister performed attired in long skirts to prevent anyone seeing their legs. My father doesn't know whom they rowed against but he remembers Frieda later wearing a scarf from Leander Rowing Club, much to his embarrassment. One can sense this may have been frowned upon since the Leander Club did not admit women until 1998.

In looking at Frieda's later life it seems mysterious that someone whose parents were on the one hand a tough, no-nonsense military surgeon and on the other someone with a strong commitment to her religion, could have become so tangled in the occult and Aleister Crowley, but when you delve into the Lehmann family maybe there is a clue. A family in which one daughter is a feminist writer, decades before her time, and the other a highly successful actress, is one thing, but then there is her rowing coach Rudy. Rudy Lehmann's photographs show a handsome young man with a fine moustache who obviously had a charismatic personality. On top of this his obituary in of all things the *Arthur Conan Doyle Encyclopedia* of 1930 refers, after his death in 1929, to RC Lehmann, MD, Kt, LLD: sportsman, writer, poet, politician, jurist, and spiritualist. The addition of the description 'spiritualist' is striking since we know of his close connection with Conan Doyle and Conan Doyle was first a Freemason and then, after resigning, a spiritualist obsessed with psychic events and the existence of life after death. Conan Doyle was the author of *The History of Spiritualism*. Lehmann's wife Alice was of course also

Frieda's teacher so the influence of the Lehmann family must have been considerable, particularly taking into account that there is no evidence of Frieda in any other period showing any interest in sport. How was it she suddenly became so involved with rowing?

After Percy and Frieda were married Percy pursued his political career while Frieda maintained a vibrant social life in Edwardian London, based around their house in Sloane Square. My father as a small boy suffered badly from tonsillitis and adenoids and had difficulty breathing. Frieda had become infatuated with the works of Mary Baker Eddy, the founder in the United States of Christian Science, and instead of having his tonsils removed he was prayed over by a Christian Science practitioner. When this failed to provide a remedy, the tonsils and adenoids were eventually removed when he was sixteen. He claims, with considerable truth, never to have had a day's sickness since, and he harboured an antagonism to what he described as 'medical quackery' for the remainder of his life.

There is not much available about the relationship between Frieda and her two boys. The main source is my father's book.

My father does record that when she was young, Frieda developed a strong desire to be an artist and went off to art school. It could well have been the Slade, set up in London in 1871 and attended much later by my sister Maggie. Frieda married Percy in 1901 and Jack was born in 1906 and his brother Thomas Nicholas in 1908 but it appears that her main interests were really her art and her struggles on behalf of the suffragettes. Nannies were the way to bring up children. Her pictures, in my father Jack's opinion, were interesting but not good enough to achieve fame. When Frieda and my father were in Paris, he suggested to her that she paint the scenes in the apartment they were renting. She did this using, for some reason, the name of Jesus Chutney and achieving, as he says, some notoriety, although it is not clear whether this arose from the name or the paintings.

With a background like Frieda's she was always likely to be attracted by the women's suffrage movement, or, more correctly, the Women's Social and Political Union (WSPU) founded in Manchester in 1903 by Emmeline 'Emily' Pankhurst. Frieda would have been a great catch for the movement; as the wife of a prominent Liberal MP she had access where it really mattered. Frieda and Emily even looked alike. A painting of Emily done by Georgina Brockenbury in 1927 shows a handsome woman staring confidently back at the world with the prominent nose and strong profile that could almost have been Frieda's. She is grasping something in her right hand and though we can only see the handle, it looks suspiciously like a fan. The picture is not clear enough to ascertain whether it is the same fan still in my sister's house at Waikanae.

Since the Great Reform Act of 1832 democracy had slowly advanced so that by the turn of the century two thirds of British males could vote. However, women could not, notwithstanding that in the colonies New Zealand had granted full voting rights to women in 1893 and in Australia voting rights were granted in 1902 but restricted to non-Indigenous women.

For forty years, a group of mostly upper and middle-class English women had been protesting in vain. In 1889 Emily Pankhurst had founded the Women's Franchise League, which by 1908 had succeeded in gaining the vote for women in local elections. But universal suffrage was a tougher target and the WSPU was to be the means to reaching it. In the spirit of their motto 'Deeds, not words', they began to make their physical presence felt. Led by Emily Pankhurst they held public meetings, interrupted elections and accosted more and more politicians in their day-to-day business. They pointed out that a woman could be a nurse, a doctor, a teacher, or a mayor. How could it be right that they could not vote?

None of the political parties would support the suffragettes, not even the Liberals, then led by Asquith. Although the trade unions, which by now had over two million members, supported socialism and had some leverage due to their support of the Liberal government, now under Lloyd George, the real objective was welfare provisions for the poor, not votes for what many viewed as a privileged group of educated women.

The louder the women protested the more the forces of law and order reacted, but the more women the movement attracted. They chained themselves to fences outside government offices, marched in the street with placards (risking arrest for obstruction), and threw bricks through opponent's windows. Soon many had been arrested and their leaders had received gaol sentences. The women then adopted a strategy to be copied with great effect some years later by Ghandi in his struggle to free India without violence. They went on hunger strike. Before long some of the women became seriously ill, so determined were they in their cause. The authorities became alarmed and fought back. They force-fed the women. This involved men wrenching open their jaws, if necessary breaking a few teeth, and forcing a tube down their throats. The women gagged and struggled but to no avail. The tube was quite abrasive and left the women with painful damage to their throats, not to mention the pain of the humiliation. Between 1908 and 1914 Emily Pankhurst went to gaol on a number of occasions, accompanied by many of her leading supporters. Strangely though, however involved Frieda became, she somehow always escaped arrest. Lloyd George's government could hardly afford to have the wife of a prominent member gaoled, especially since Percy's experience in New Zealand had left him more than sympathetic to the cause, and Percy might not easily be muzzled.

In June 1911, after the death of Edward VII, the suffragettes decided on a wonderful strategy. They planned a large pre-coronation procession to upstage the coronation of George V. The procession stretched over four miles around inner London. The women wore white with purple and green sashes, the movement's colours. At the procession's head was a figure on horseback dressed as Joan of Arc, whom the movement had adopted as their own saint. Still the political leaders would not bend and, more infuriating still, Lloyd George, whose sympathy they might have expected, changed his stance not a jot. Protest increased. Houses were burned down, including Lloyd George's, and finally Emily Wilding Davison threw herself under the King's horse at Ascot and was killed.

The struggle was brought to an end by a much greater threat. In 1914 war broke out with Germany and the women put their cause on hold to help the war effort, along the way proving beyond doubt that they could match it with anyone in their contribution to society. Shortly before Emily died in 1928 British women at last gained full voting rights.

How close had Frieda and Emily really been? At this distance it is hard to tell but there must have been something special for Emily to give Frieda the fan that my sister found in the embers of the fire at Waikanae.

Frieda collected a number of artists as friends, and my father Jack, with his lifelong interest in art, remembers that he had the opportunity to buy some paintings by names that later became famous but he could not afford even the inexpensive prices of the time, a situation rectified later when he had the financial capacity to indulge himself a bit more. Among her contacts was Aleister Crowley, in his time notorious as one of the world's leading occultists and therefore a dangerous associate for anyone in polite society. According to my father, Frieda in her search for novelty joined a witch's coven which Crowley had created. My father was caustic in his memoirs about the whole business, and jotted down various incidents which make it sound ridiculous, to wit:

> *Members of the Coven were undoubtedly given hallucinatory drugs. On one occasion, it was agreed that Frieda had been turned into a frog and on another she and other members of the Coven danced on the cliffs at Dover to keep the Nazis away.*

My father Jack refused to have anything to do with Crowley, and would not meet him. Whatever he may have thought, it clearly became Frieda's major preoccupation, and though she may have been eccentric she was not a fool, so these incidents, while amusing, obscure what was really at stake for her in this perilous friendship.

My father related how it came about that, recovering from Crowley, Frieda became entangled in Ceylon with the famous classical Indian dancer Ram Gopal. He recalled that Frieda had painted the backdrop to Ram Gopal's Dance Company's postwar London tour. She became infatuated with Gopal and helped him with his finances, finally following him to Ceylon, to where he had gone for the making of a Hollywood film.

In typical Frieda style, she never bothered to record either when the diary was written, say what the name of the film was, or anything about it. The focus was on Gopal. My father said it was *Elephant Man*. Fortunately, the power of the internet solved the mystery. In fact, the movie was *Elephant Walk* and it was made in 1954 by William Dieterle for Paramount Pictures. It was supposed to star both Sir Laurence Olivier and his wife, Vivien Leigh. Olivier pulled out and was replaced by Australian Peter Finch. Leigh had to leave the set, struck down by bipolar disorder and going to California for 'electro-convulsion therapy'. A few long shots of her remain in the film. Her role was taken by a young Elizabeth Taylor. The film received 'mixed' reviews.

The exotic attractions of the East were always likely to seduce someone as whimsical as Frieda, especially after the death of her husband and the demise of Aleister Crowley, so when the filming finished she had little reason to return to England. She made her way north through India until finally arriving on the shores of Lake Srinigar, beneath the peaks of the Himalayas, in Kashmir. In those days, this remote lake must have been overwhelmingly beautiful. Believing she had found nirvana, she promptly bought the houseboat *Starlight* and installed a young Kashmiri named

Shaban. In his notes written mainly for the benefit of family, my father continues the tale of his visit to the houseboat and beyond:

> *Shaban would sleep on the floor outside her door in case he was needed and despite the fact he had a family in Srinigar. He learned to cook the awful milk puddings she liked in addition to the fruit and vegetables, which were grown on the floating island on the lake.*
>
> *Shaban was very careful that I should be protected against anything he considered unsuitable for a Sahib. Frieda was not permitted to introduce me to her Guru. Shaban was a very pious Muslim and I suspect he hated Hindus. On one occasion, I visited a Hindu village in which there was a huge spring and a pool in the middle of a temple. Apparently, this was a sacred area and I should have taken my shoes off. I was asked by a priest in perfect English to remove them and he invited me for tea. Shaban appeared from nowhere and with a horrified expression removed me.*
>
> *Frieda was getting more and more eccentric and we were much embarrassed by her behaviour on a short visit to England. On one occasion, we lost her and I found her hanging onto a marine outside the American Embassy. She returned to India and died shortly afterwards. My wife and I visited Kashmir and the houseboat, which was large and dank. The houseboat next to ours sank in the middle of the night and we had some very charming English visitors. We were much amused by dozens of Kashmiris trying to raise the boat by manpower.*
>
> *Frieda had become some sort of Saint and her portrait was in the sitting room surrounded by flowers. She was buried in the Church of England cemetery but there was no headstone so we arranged for a headstone to be placed over the grave containing the first couplet from Cymbeline: 'Fear no more the heat of the sun, nor the furious winter's rages. Thou thy worldly work hath done. Home art gone and ta'en thy wages.' It was a very moving little ceremony joined in by some of the locals. That night Frieda appeared to come and sit on my bed. Her appearance was very vivid and she said that she had come to thank me for remembering her.*

FRIEDA

She was very psychic. When I first left for Australia she came to see me off on the Orient Liner. As I was about to go on board she pointed out a party ahead and said 'that girl is your future wife.' That girl is the mother of my children.

Kashmir is very beautiful with lakes, high mountains and chestnut forests the wood from which is used to make furniture. It is floated down the rivers. Unfortunately the climate is very variable. When I arrived with Frieda and your mother there was snow on the mountains although it was nearly midsummer. Two or three days later it was very hot and your mother caught pneumonia which she could have died from but fortunately we had brought some antibiotics, and Shaban lighted a huge fire to dry her out. Shaban himself later died of pneumonia.

In these days it was an alternative place for tourists but it was, and probably still is, full of drugs. We were visited by an official, a very pleasant man, but he was on the lookout for drugs. Because of the ridiculous fighting over a bit of mountain there are no more tourists and the place has to be maintained by the Indian Government.

Frieda's last home on Lake Srinagar in Kashmir

20

CROWLEY

Aleister Crowley had a mesmerising effect on Frieda and dominated her life from the time when she took up his assignment to paint the tarot cards in 1937 until his death in 1947. Sir Percy was left to struggle with his parliamentary duties and the war on his own.

Aleister Crowley was born in 1875 to a wealthy family in Warwickshire. His parents were members of the sect known as 'Plymouth Brethren', believers in the literal truth of the Bible but Alistair, or Aleister, as he renamed himself, rebelled from the rigidity of his upbringing from the start.

He distinguished himself as a child by nearly killing himself with homemade fireworks and torturing a cat in several horrible ways to see if it really did have nine lives. He is, at fourteen, reported to have lost his virginity with a maid who worked for his family. At seventeen he contracted gonorrhoea.

He was something of an intellectual prodigy, and he went to Cambridge where, in the ample free time available between studies, he continued to indulge in sexual activities with either sex as frequently as possible. He left Cambridge after the normal period of three years required for a degree but in fact never matriculated.

In 1898, aged twenty-three, Crowley joined the Hermetic Order of the Golden Dawn, led by Samuel Mathers. This organisation was based on a synthesis of a number of philosophical strains all loosely revolving around magic, alchemy and ritual symbolism. Adopting the name Frater Perdurabo ('I will endure') Crowley moved swiftly through the organisation to the rank of Adeptus Minor, but, shocked by his overt homosexuality (though bisexuality is probably a more accurate label), the London order refused to confer the position.

Crowley installed himself in a ceremony in Paris, causing further outrage to his English colleagues. Things went from bad to worse. Mathers was expelled for acknowledging that the English body had been formed on the basis of forged German documents. Crowley attempted to highjack the Order's property, appearing at one of their meetings dressed in full Highland regalia and a black hood. The Highland regalia arose from his decision to call himself Lord Boleskine, the self-appointed Laird of a fine Scottish estate he had somehow bought in 1899. The estate was associated both before and after Crowley's purchase with black magic rituals. The executed head of Lord Lovat can apparently be heard rolling around on the floor. The house ended up being bought by Jimmy Page of Led Zeppelin.

The dispute between occultists finally led to astral attacks, which resulted in Crowley's raincoat spontaneously catching fire, and causing bouts of uncontrollable temper. These altercations were resolved by the police, and Crowley was expelled, mainly through the efforts of one longstanding member, the Irish poet William Butler Yeats.

Crowley wisely decided to travel, and in 1901 found himself in Kandy in the mountains of Ceylon, which may help further explain Frieda's pilgrimage to this region. Much argument took place over the power of the god Shiva, the Destroyer, with Mathers and Arnold Bennett, who at that time was a guru to Crowley and instructed him in the art of yoga, where he reached the status of

Dhyana, in which the ego is annihilated. Bennett later went off to become a Buddhist monk and Crowley took his .303 rifle and, regaining his ego, went big-game hunting. It was also while in Kandy that Crowley refers to taking, for the first time, '225 drops of Laudanum in five hours.' He then went on to say that 'I think that we may dismiss the alleged danger of acquiring the hashish habit as fantastic. Nobody will acquire the habit but the destined drug slave; and he may just as well have the hashish habit as any other; he is sure to fall under the power of some enchantress.' It was his view that the drug 'is to be combated by a highly, may I say magically, trained will.' In his novel *Diary of a Drug Fiend*, he expressed the same view about combating heroin. Symonds observes tartly that Crowley did not have such a will.

In Scotland in 1903 Crowley met Rose Kelly through the agency of her brother Gerald Kelly, later to become President of the Royal Academy. Rose Kelly was as impetuous as Crowley. On a visit to Scotland Crowley was introduced by Gerald, and discovering Rose's life had been a disaster to date, and that in fact she was about to be claimed by two suitors, both of whom she had promised to marry, he did the gentlemanly thing and asked her to marry him. She immediately agreed. They thought they would have to wait three weeks but when he enquired Crowley discovered that in Scotland the sherriff could authorise an immediate marriage. Undaunted they sought him out the next morning, roused the mystified sherriff from his bed and were told that any lawyer would do. A local lawyer was found in the town. The marriage took place before lunch. Gerald, when he found out, was furious.

In 1904 Crowley and Rose set out for Cairo and in March he and Rose spent the night in the King's Chamber of the Great Pyramid. He needed her to help him access the god of wisdom, Thoth. Rose showed little interest in the visit but then claimed, while in a trance, and while she and Crowley were surrounded by the soft glow of astral light, to have received a message, 'They're waiting for you.' Later she mentioned the presence of both Thoth and Horus. Crowley was sceptical but Rose was able to recite a number of details about Horus which she could not possibly have known. In April she went further, beginning to recite messages dictated to her by the Gods. Over three days, April 8, 9 and 10, Crowley took down secret messages, via Rose, and sent by Aiwass, who Crowley later referred to as his own 'Holy Guardian Angel'. He used these as the foundation of *The Book of Law*, which was, in turn, based on the three central concepts he had received from Horus, namely 'Do What Thou Wilt Shall Be The Whole Of The Law,' 'Love is The Law, Love Under Will,' and 'Every Man and Every Woman is a Star.' The text prophesies the end of the old religions. The philosophical precept appears to be, as often, self-knowledge, the primacy of the will, and exploration of the 'higher self'. The more cynical of observers were inclined to interpret it as 'do whatever you feel like'.

With Crowley in Egypt, Samuel Mathers must have thought he had got rid of Crowley, but he was confronted back in England by Crowley brandishing a letter announcing that the Equinox of the Gods had come and granting him supreme magical authority. This naturally led to further astral duels, which Crowley won. An idea of this encounter can be gleaned from Crowley's report that Mathers had sent a vampire disguised as a beautiful woman to tempt him, but Crowley had summarily turned her into 'a hag of sixty, bent and decrepit.' Mathers then sent a current of evil, which struck Crowley's bloodhounds dead and made his servants ill. Crowley retaliated by summoning Beelzebub and forty-nine of his attendant fiends. The battle was clearly fierce, with Crowley the victor.

Crowley, in search of more recognition, offered a prize for the best essay about himself. The only entry came from a Captain Fuller, a devotee whose opinion was that 'It has taken 100,000,000 years to produce Aleister Crowley. The world has indeed laboured, and has at last brought forth a man.' Fuller eventually became a major general, wrote excellent books on military history, and transferred his admiration to Adolf Hitler. Symonds records that Fuller was one of two Englishmen invited to Hitler's fiftieth birthday party, the other being Arthur Ronald Nall-Cain, the second Baron Brocket of Brocket Hall, Eton and Oxford, Member of Parliament and later member of the House of Lords.

In search of a change of pace, Crowley went climbing in the Himalayas. The expedition led to the death of several fellow climbers plus a high-level brawl when Crowley's temper, presumably urged on by the malevolent Mathers, led him to pull a pistol on one of his companions. In fact, Crowley was a remarkably skilled climber, considering his asthma and that his lifestyle would hardly have assisted his physical preparations for anything as arduous as mountain climbing. In 1902, he was second in command of a party formed to climb K2 or Chhogori, the second highest mountain in the world. A caravan of 230 men, 18 sheep, 15 goats, and more than 20 chickens, plus a large and heavy pile of books for Crowley, made its way up the mountain. Crowley on his own reached 18,733 feet and two of the Austrians in the party finally reached 22,000 feet. Finally, in the face of deteriorating weather, illness, and continuing disputes between Crowley and the party leader, a Swiss named Oscar Eckenstein, the attempt had to be abandoned. The mountain was not to be climbed until 1954.

In 1905, Crowley, undeterred by his K2 experience, decided to lead an assault on Kangchenjunga, 100 feet lower than K2 and arguably the most difficult to climb. Many of his K2 companions refused to go, including Eckenstein and Knowles, who was the climber Crowley had pulled a gun on. The climb set off in the midst of a furious dispute with the Alpine Club in the UK, which Crowley with his usual tact had initiated. Predictably, Crowley's unsubstantiated optimism about the ease of his venture turned out to be grossly misplaced. His arrogant leadership and total disregard for his porters, many of whom had no shoes, led to a split, at 21,000 feet, with Crowley left on his own with Charles Reymond, a Swiss army officer and experienced climber. The others, led by

Dr Jacot-Guillarmod, who had been on the K2 expedition, and was Crowley's number two, tried to find their way down. There were six on a rope; three Europeans and three ill-shod porters. On a vertical part of the mountain they were submerged in one of the constant avalanches that sweep the mountain and Jacot-Guillarmod, at the top of the rope and anchored by his ice axe and crampons, felt the other members of the party slip and disappear under the snow. He found his Italian companion unconscious and revived him but of the others nothing remained but the end of a rope descending into a crevasse. Crowley and Reymond had remained above and heard the screams for help. Crowley later claimed that Reymond had gone down to investigate but had not returned and Crowley records, 'I went to sleep and rose next morning at dawn and went down to see.'

Crowley returned separately to Darjeeling where he immediately set about justifying his own lack of action and criticising the other members of the party. Four were dead: Pache, the Swiss army officer, and three 'coolies'. The ensuing row involved the Alpine Club and again Crowley's lack of feeling, and the reports of his failure to lend assistance, when it became known, led to universal condemnation. As Symonds says, 'If it was Crowley's intention to make himself odious in the eyes of all mountaineers, he succeeded completely.'

An incident, which occurred just before the expedition was formed, illustrates why Jacot-Guillarmod, a humourless Swiss medic, and Crowley were unlikely to get along. Jacot-Guillarmod came to visit Crowley in Scotland where, as noted, Crowley was masquerading as a genuine Scottish Laird under the name of 'the Laird of Boleskine and Abertarff'. Jacot-Guillarmod was a keen shooter and determined to hunt grouse, notwithstanding Crowley's protestations that there were none on the property and in any case it was out of season. To placate him Crowley, after discussion with his gillie, mentioned the existence of a very rare mountain sheep, which much excited Jacot-Guillarmod. A few days later the gillie rushed in to report a possible sighting and, wasting no time, Crowley dragged Jacot-Guillarmod on his knees through pouring rain across the fields, where looming through the mist a strange animal appeared, whereupon Jacot-Guillarmod blew its head off with his shotgun. Crowley whisked Jacot-Guillarmod away, congratulating him on his dispatch of the rare mountain haggis while the gillie cleaned up the remains of Farmer McNab's prize ram. In Crowley's words, 'the next scene lies in Neufchatel. The doctor had the head mounted (presumably repaired) with a gold plate suitably inscribed. Naturally, he told the story everywhere.'

Unlikely as it seems, Crowley's marriage survived for six years and, together with their child, Rose accompanied him on further journeys to various exotic places, culminating in his taking up residence in the United States. The stress of life on the road with Crowley finally took its toll in 1909, when Crowley divorced his wife, who by this time was suffering from alcoholic dementia. This better allowed him to indulge his passion for magic, drugs and women.

In 1916 Crowley promoted himself to the rank of Magus, reportedly at a ceremony of his own devising which involved baptising a toad as Jesus of Nazareth and then crucifying it. Crowley wisely sat out World War I in the United States, where he passed the time by writing in support of the Kaiser. After the war, he fathered a daughter (Poupee) with Lea Hirsig. They moved to Sicily and the Abbey of Thelema in the little coastal town of Cefalù. Ensconced in this 'unsanitary hovel' his addiction to cocaine and heroin raged out of control. Poupee died and then one of his students, Raoul Loveday, also died, apparently from an affliction which arose from drinking the contaminated water. Loveday's wife, Betty May, went back to England and sold the story to the *Sunday Express*. The papers were filled with allegations of black magic rituals and other scandalous acts, including at one stage child sacrifice. These events occurred in 1932, at the time of the rise of Mussolini, and, since apparently Crowley's activities did not accord with the Duce's views of how he wished Italy to be seen by the foreign press, Crowley was quickly expelled. He returned to England and there devoted his attentions to *The Book of Thoth* and its accompanying tarot cards. Hence began, in an increasing haze of drugs, his association with Frieda.

A story which novelist and poet Martin Booth tells in his book on Crowley concerns the defection of Hitler's Deputy and Secretary, Rudolf Hess. Hess had persuaded himself that if he went to England he could get the British Government to see reason and negotiate a settlement of the war. Being very superstitious, he often consulted astrologers. The British knew this and infiltrated an astrologer into Hess' circle. The astrologer pronounced it timely, on 10 May 1941, for Hess to attempt this unlikely feat. He was convinced that he would meet with the Duke of Hamilton, who would assist him to meet with Churchill. He flew across the North Sea and landed in Scotland, where he was promptly arrested. He was imprisoned at Trent Park, a country estate north of London. Ian Fleming, the creator of James Bond, who was working for the Director of British Naval Intelligence, conceived the idea of having Crowley interview Hess to try to find out how influenced the Nazis and, in particular, Hitler were by the occult. Crowley readily agreed but the idea was eventually vetoed. However, it is claimed by Fleming's biographer that Fleming used Crowley as the model for Le Chiffre, the villain in his first James Bond story, *Casino Royale*. As Booth points out, 'Le Chiffre is a sadist, addicted to inhaling Benzedrine (rather than ether) and with a craving for women: he was also overweight, ugly and, like Crowley, addressed other men as 'dear boy'.

Crowley was a sixties' child born before his time, and his spectre was to be revived in the sixties and seventies as an inspiration for many of the more outrageous bands, most notably Led Zeppelin and Black Sabbath. The equally outrageous, but lesser known, Graham Bond, who met his personal abyss under an underground train, claimed to be Crowley's illegitimate son.

Probably his most specific influence came from the eventual publication of a Rabelaisian summary of his creed called *Liber OZ*, which was written in 1941 but not published until thirty years later. Frieda was alarmed when she read the typescript; 'Do What Thou Wilt' was all very well but 'Man has the right to kill those who would thwart these rights' was a bit much for the wife of an MP to stomach. Its eventual publication influenced many young people, including the bands referred to above and even the emerging 1960s phenomenon, The Beatles. Crowley's influence is confirmed by his appearance, peering owlishly from the back row along with the likes of Mae West, Carl Jung and Edgar Allan Poe, from the cover of the Beatles' LP *Sergeant Pepper's Lonely Hearts Club Band*.

In 1947 Crowley (who was also known as the Wickedest Man in the World, the Great Beast, Baphomet) died. His earlier experiments with drugs of all sorts – opium, hashish, alcohol, cocaine, laudanum – while contributing to his bizarre visions, had also destroyed his health. It was not the same with heroin, which was prescribed for him by a Harley Street doctor to combat his asthma, which worsened after his mountaineering expeditions. He was unable to rid himself of this addiction, though he tried often. He died alone, aged seventy-two, in a small bedroom in Hastings. His last words, somewhat out of character, are reported as being, 'I am perplexed.'

The funeral ceremony at Brighton was celebrated by the reading of Crowley's 'Hymn to Pan':

And I rave and I rape and I rip and I rend,
Everlasting; world without end.

Crowley penned his own obituary. 'I am The Beast, I am the world of the Aeon. I spend my soul in blazing torrents that roar into night, streams that with molten tongues hiss as they lick.'

'Rage, rage against the dying of the light,' seems puny in comparison.

The Hierophant tarot card painted by Frieda for Crowley's Thoth tarot deck

CROWLEY'S TAROT
(AS EXPLAINED BY 'LIGHTOFISIS')

According to ancient tradition *The Book of Thoth* was the legendary repository of the Egyptian mysteries; as such it is forever connected with occult knowledge, mystery schools and the esoteric secrets and magical systems that these schools taught. It has long been associated with the tarot, which is said by many to be the embodiment of its teachings.

Crowley was undoubtedly one of the finest occult minds of our time and soon realised that despite the historical interest in the tarot that occultists harboured, there was a distinct lack of authentic texts that explored the cards, let alone develop them. He resolved to rectify that omission by creating one definitive text that would make the tarot accessible to everyone who had the desire to learn. Guided by the intelligence that had directed him throughout his life, Crowley penned a legend, an extensive treatise on the tarot, which he named *The Book of Thoth*, after the tradition of wisdom itself. The book incorporates the wisdom and philosophy of Egypt. It unites cabbalistic tradition, tarot, philosophy, science, magic, to create a complete tool to explore the microcosm and macrocosm. It represents the entire sum of not only Crowley's knowledge but also the knowledge of the masters themselves.

Crowley commissioned the surrealist artist Lady Frieda Harris to undertake the artwork. The Thoth deck itself was a labour of love, an undertaking that took over five years of painstaking work with many of the seventy-eight cards being redesigned up to eight times before Crowley was satisfied. To create the vision, she first had to understand it herself. The result is a deck in which every single card contains a wealth of esoteric symbolism. Essentially each symbol stands on its own as a complete idea and each card reveals a key to a specific area of knowledge, a symbolic picture of the universe. It is the fractal model of the universe that many mathematicians and physicists use to study cosmology, and Crowley uses the tarot to validate the understanding of the universe. *The Book of Thoth* is the road map to the new aeon, the knowledge lost by humankind that needs to be rediscovered. The numbering of the pack is based on the idea that each number is a concept in its own right. The tarot is a pictorial representation of the tree of life, the Kabbalah. The sequencing of the Thoth Tarot is unique and based on his *Book of the Law*, a unique sequencing correcting mistakes and changing the attributions of the Star and Emperor. He also incorporated three Magus cards, bringing the total number of cards to eighty-one.

The Book reflects Crowley's legacy of Thelema. In essence, the message is to discover and follow your own way and create a lifestyle that is in harmony with the energy of the universe. The Thoth deck is the tool which allows you to do just that. The book represents an instruction manual that will guide the initiate on their journey to self-knowledge and enlightenment.

Crowley believed that we are all individuals just like the symbols and therefore we each have a unique path to walk; in the words of his Thelemic doctrine, 'every man and every woman is a star'.

The above is an abridged version of the description of the evolution of the Thoth Tarot, which is set out in considerably more detail on a website principally dedicated to the Goddess Isis: www.lightofisis.com

I have already referred to the loss of the paintings or antiques that dotted the house, not to mention the family history. Also lost was the extensive library packed with books, valuable hardbacks and first or second editions, and later paperbacks, from an eclectic mix of writers, poets and artists. There was plenty of choice, but if Father had wanted to pick one book to explain to me it probably would have been the strangest book on the shelves, an original signed copy of Crowley's *The Book of Thoth*. This book, bound in Moroccan leather, was one of only 200 in the limited original edition and was signed by Crowley, written by Crowley, and published in 1944. The Te Rama copy had been owned by Frieda. It was the key to Crowley's writings on tarot. I had looked at it a few times but never been able to get beyond a few incomprehensible pages. Perhaps my father just thought it was the ravings of a lunatic under the influence of seriously mind-bending 'medication'. Whatever the case the genesis of Crowley's tarot cards was the 'truths' he believed *The Book of Thoth* contained. The original 'Book of Thoth' dates back to at least the Ptolemaic period around 330 BC and is not so much one book but a collection of Egyptian texts, heavily influenced by ancient Greece. The Egyptian historian Manetto claims Thoth, the Egyptian god of writing and knowledge, 'wrote' 36,525 books. Clement of Alexandria mentions forty-two.

There were many different Thoth Tarot cards, early sets often based on the Kabbalah, suggesting their origin back to more than 5000 BC. Crowley's tarot incorporates the wisdom, philosophy, science and magic of Egypt, melding East and West traditions to create a complete method for studying the tarot. Crowley's is the 'classic' text.

Crowley had the idea of writing the book about the tarot and at the same time creating his own tarot set using Frieda to do the illustrations for the cards. He was meticulous in insisting they were correct to the smallest detail and Frieda had to make many copies to correct minor mistakes. These tarot cards became standard for fortune-telling. The original illustrations are in the Warburg Institute in Greenwich, London. We have a pack in the house and the strange illustrations still raise many questions that for a non-initiate are impossible to answer.

I had originally come across the cards fossicking about in Te Rama years before the fire. At first, I thought they were some sort of normal playing cards but when I asked my father he dismissed them as just some of his mother's eccentricities. I looked more closely and could see that some of the cards were decorated with the paintings by Frieda that hung in the corridor of Te Rama. I looked at the paintings and back at the cards, but it was clear that although the cards were fascinating they could mean nothing without understanding the tarot on which they were based. At that stage, I was not interested enough to investigate. It was not until many years later, after my father had died that I explored a bit further. I tried showing the family the cards. They were intrigued by what they depicted but they could find no meaning without explanation. What did the cards depicting the Hanged Man, the Knight of Swords, and Ace of Disks stand for? What about the 'Aeon'? Why does the 'Art' card depict an androgynous figure standing over an Orphic egg? If you shuffle and cut the pack and the 'Devil' comes up, depicted as a goat with a smirking face, what does it signify? What about the fascinating depiction of the Hierophant?

The Hierophant, much like the Pope, forms a bridge between heaven and earth. The Hierophant card showed a high priest, in flowing robes. Between his thighs is a priestess holding a sword. He 'carries' a child. Is it Horus? He is surrounded by bulls, elephants, gargoyles, and the like and contained within the outline of a pentagram. Two fingers of his left hand are extended, perhaps in benediction.

Crowley has provided meanings to the tarot in his book but in many cases the answers are as mystifying as the cards. To take just one example, the Knight of Swords is described as representing the 'fiery part of air'. Further, the image is of 'the extended flame of mind', a 'light shaft of the Ideal absorbing the entire life in concentrated aspiration, passing from earthly Taurus to exalted Gemini' et cetera.

There were seventy-eight cards plus three Magus cards and they included twenty-two trumps, of which the Hierophant was the fifth trump. Each card contained a message and each card related in some way to each of the others. What was the formula that connected them?

When I showed them to Gail she shook her head. Coming from a family from the north of England, many of them members of the Uniting Church or the Congregational Church, religions based on lack of flamboyance and an austere outlook on life, she probably didn't feel much like exploring tarot. However, there was a strange connection between her family, brought up in strict Methodist households, and Crowley's bizarre activities.

Her father and grandfather were members of the local Manchester chapter of the Freemasons. The Masons, originally derived from the fraternities of stonemasons, were then, and still remain, a very significant organisation in both Britain and in many parts of Europe, the old colonies and the United States.

Crowley and, later, Frieda were members of an organisation called the Ordo Templi Orientis (OTO) which was formed in the late nineteenth century by two German members of the Masons. It was originally closely modelled on the Masonic traditions but, unlike the Masons, it allowed women. Six of the nine 'degrees' were Masonic and it aped their elaborate secret ceremonies. Crowley joined OTO, as it was called in 1903, and it was soon under his influence. He seized control of it just before the start of World War I. More and more, its activities became entwined with his own *Book of the Law* and with Crowley's own obsessions including *The Book of Thoth* and the tarot. The connection with the Masons became more tenuous and eventually ceased.

Frieda's membership of OTO in 1938, which formalised her relationship with Crowley, occurred after she entered her commitment to painting the tarot cards for him. She had become his 'disciple'.

What was it that made Crowley so spellbinding for Frieda?

It seems that Frieda and Crowley came to know each other when Crowley was searching for an artist who, apart from having artistic ability, could interpret his complex instructions for his tarot cards. It was Crowley's persistence which induced Frieda's great work. The cards appear to trace back not only to Thoth and ancient Egypt, but to more recent influences on Crowley via the Rosicrucians in the seventeenth century and particularly Alphonse Constant. Constant was an Abbé of the Roman Church who changed his name to the Jewish Eliphas Levi. Crowley claimed to be reincarnated. He insisted that his past incarnations included Eliphas Levi, Count Cagliostro (an eighteenth-century occultist), Alexander VI (the Borgia Pope), and Edward Kelly (an Elizabethan Court magician). Levi's principal work was to reconstitute and redesign the tarot, which itself was based on the Holy Kabbalah. The 'Holy' or Jewish 'Kabbalah' is referred to as the 'Tree of Life'. The secrets of the Kabbalah were purportedly given to Moses on Mount Sinai at the same time that Moses received the five books of the Old Testament, which included within them the 'Ten Commandments', the formative documents of the Jewish religion. The followers of the Kabbalah to this day believe it contains the 'true' secrets of the universe.

Frieda was already sixty when she first became seriously involved, but she took her assignment very seriously, responding to

Crowley's criticism and producing endless drafts of each painting. In trying to unravel the mathematical and philosophical nature of tarot, she was persuaded to study such opaque subject as 'projective synthetic geometry', based originally on Goethe, and something called 'Anthroposophy.' She took up the name 'Tzabo' or 'Hosts', which adds up to ninety-three, the number of the Thelemic current which she appeared to believe would assist her. At Crowley's suggestion, she studied the I Ching, the ancient Chinese divination text, much of it based on sets of random numbers. The I Ching is closely linked to both Confucianism and Daoism, so Frieda was getting herself into a very deep philosophical ocean. All the time she provided Crowley with a stipend of varying amounts, presumably coming from her Porter side since Percy would not have wanted his modest parliamentary salary used for such a purpose.

Frieda claimed that 'The Tarot could be described as God's picture book, or could be likened to a celestial chess game.' Crowley had this to say: 'The Tarot is a pictorial representation of the Forces of Nature as conceived by the Ancients according to a conventional symbolism. At first sight, one would suppose this arrangement to be arbitrary but it is not. It is necessitated by the structure of the universe, and in particular, of the Solar System, as symbolised by the Holy Kabbalah.'

The tarot set took over five years and was not in fact published until after both Crowley and Frieda had died. There were many meetings at Crowley's home in Jermyn Street, but most of the work was done at the Hyde Park home of mutual friend and London socialite, Greta Valentine. Frieda was with Crowley at his death. She wrote, 'I saw him on the day he died. But he did not recognise me. I shall miss him terribly. An irreplaceable loss. Love is the Law, love under will.' After her death, she bequeathed the paintings to Gerald Yorke and he in turn gave those he had not sold to the Warburg Institute in London, where they still remain.

Frieda was clearly infatuated with Crowley, in awe of his intellectual capacity, his compelling and dominating personality, and very much aware of his rampant bisexuality which bewitched women but which seems not to have involved her in any physical intimacy. However, it is also clear that she was prepared to defend herself if pressed. Her letter to Crowley on 10 May 1939, reads as follows:

> *Your secretary forgot to send the letter you wrote to me & she has rung me to read it. I am, also, sorry that I have to write plainly to you because I enjoy our friendship & your instruction very much, but it is entirely spoilt by your attempts to use me as your bank and financial adviser. I have frequently told you that I have nothing, but a weekly allowance & that out of it I have given you all I can spare.*
>
> *If you are expecting the Tarot to be a means of getting money, or my position as useful for pushing it – I am sorry I am not the right vehicle for such an enterprise as I intend to remain anonymous when the cards are shown as I dislike any notoriety.*
>
> *Your books are wonderful but you must not expect the reading or money-making world to buy them as they don't want to think.*

The rest is somehow lost.

Complicating the relationship between Frieda and Crowley, and certainly one reason for Frieda keeping a low profile, was of course the presence of Sir Percy, Frieda's husband and a respectable Member of the House of Commons. Percy and Crowley would have had almost nothing in common and presumably Percy was concerned about the relationship becoming common knowledge and damaging his career. Just how tricky the relationship was is highlighted in some extracts from Crowley's diaries, which were reproduced in the distinguished British writer John Symonds' book about Crowley, *The King of the Shadow Realm*: '6 January 1942. Almost driven insane by Frieda: raving nearly half hour on the telephone.'

He did not say what she was raving about but when she had finished raving she invited him to lunch at The Savoy, which he pronounced a great success. Symonds notes Crowley saying Frieda, who was paying the bills, continued to provoke him. 'She upsets me. All day "under the weather",' he wrote. On 10 January 1942: 'Frieda's invitation to dinner merely infuriates me. I wish I had somebody to kick and the energy to kick them.' Two days later he renewed his abuse of Frieda: 'Frieda Harris insane, bullying and threatening. The tantrums of a spoiled schoolgirl.' A shot of heroin administered by the doctor revived him. He concluded that Frieda 'actually brought on a serious prolonged attack [of asthma], destroying my inner resistance.' Crowley continues in his diary, Frieda, 'Egomaniac ingratitude and insolence – I am so ashamed of her that I dare not trust myself to act' and later, 'FH's churlish hysteria…it is only her insane reactions about money that do harm.'

'11 March. 4.30pm. FH here. It took about half an hour to ease her of fantastic rage and misery, fagged by Percy and Morton House. I brought her round nicely and the last two hours were delightful.'

All of the above took place during the height of World War II, yet only the most oblique references are made about the war. Percy is scarcely mentioned and it is safe to assume that Percy and Frieda saw little of each other since Percy was almost wholly engaged at Parliament in the prosecution of the war. He was, for five years from the formation of the Churchill Government in May 1940, acting leader of the Liberal Party in the House of Commons and Liberal Chief Whip. Later in 1940 Churchill made him a Member of the Privy Council which entitled him to the prefix 'Right Honourable.' 'I therefore became a regular Pooh Bah,' as he says in his book. However, it is interesting to read his reference to Frieda in his memoirs, and compare them to the letters above. That Percy had an aversion to Crowley is hardly a surprise, but his book suggests a fairly serene situation or was Percy just being naive?

My wife is an artist and a good one. She takes her art seriously, in fact works at her paintings seven days a week and generally twelve hours out of twenty-four. She has had an immense output of pictures and has painted attractive landscapes and some portraits under the signature Frieda Harris. When, however, critics discover she is my wife she is immediately written down as an amateur and accordingly disparaged, of which there is evidence in an incident that occurred in a show she had at a Chelsea Gallery. She was exhibiting a number of serious pictures but she included a few that she had painted for a lark and signed them J. Chuckney. [Actually, many of them were signed Jesus Chutney which my family all found much more amusing.] One critic, after being very condescending about Frieda Harris's pictures said he much preferred the ones by her young friend Chuckney.

Of recent years she has been interested in mainly abstract paintings. Besides, she has produced some sixty designs for the Tarot Cards, which were shown at the Royal Water Colour Societies' Gallery, and they have been published in a book on the history of these cards.

This perhaps appears irrelevant to my postscript, but the fact that my wife was busy with her painting made it difficult for me to enjoy idleness.

My wife has never been a political woman. I have seen too many public men followed about by their spouses, who act as their shadows, sing their praises and push their claims to advancement. To me it has always been a relief that I can find recreation in talking to her on subjects outside political life. But she has been splendid at election time, when she generally worked herself to the bone.

She believes in my political star and she could not bear to see it dimmed. Anyway, I was urged by her to get back into the political arena.

In Symonds' book, in his even-handed way, he paints a portrait of Crowley as a maniacal genius; a self-publicist consumed by the need for recognition whatever the cost and whose occasionally inspired writings were the product of a completely unrestrained experimentation with every combination of available drug. Until 1921 when the Dangerous Drugs Act was passed in the United Kingdom, these drugs could be acquired whenever needed. The biography makes some interesting asides about Frieda. One of the most interesting, in view of Percy's comments above, relates to one of Crowley's endless dinner parties with his 'friends.' It confirms much of what Symonds has to say, related above.

> *Frieda, Lady Harris, wife of Sir Percy Harris, Baronet and Liberal Party whip, was another of his friends, one from whom he received in his last dreadful years much kindness and a regular stipend of two pounds a week, a small but not insignificant sum in those days. In the summer of 1937 her name appears in The Beast's journal. '13TH August 1937. Great lunch with Frieda. Great dinner with Tom Driberg.' [Tom Driberg was a Labour Member of Parliament.] And on 11 November of the same year 'Frieda Harris, Morton House, The Mall, Chiswick.' On 3 May 1938 he was able to record with triumph, 'Frieda at 4. She is now quite definitely a pupil.' A week later, 'Her visions are quite remarkably good. She agrees to affiliate to the OTO (Crowley).' She gave him ten guineas, was given in return the magical name of Tzaba, 'hosts', which adds up to 93, the number of the Thelema current which she was edging towards. But very soon a querulous note about her appears in his journal. 'Frieda kicking about cost of supper. Terribly depressed: weather vile. Driberg inaccessible.' He asked her for 200 pounds, she demurred and gave as an excuse she would have to ask Percy's permission first. However, she gave him two pounds and promised eight.*

There then appears four extracts straight from Crowley's journal, reproduced without comment; namely:

> *3 December 1938. Peg again to dinner. Hours and hours of cunnilingus. She is really rather a juicy sow.*

> *4 December. Lunch with Sir Percy Harris.*
> *22 December. Why do women resent being praised for their fucking? What else is there to praise?*
> *26 March 1939. Peggy foully drunk again. Luckily, I wasn't there.*
> *30 March. What shall I do about Peggy? 24 Fu. Give Peggy a really severe flogging.*

Apart from both having been to Cambridge, it is hard to imagine what Crowley and Percy would have found to talk about over lunch. A few paragraphs after the above diary entries, Symonds observes:

> *I asked Frieda how she had managed to stick with Percy, her husband, for so long; he was a thoroughly decent man but rather dull. She replied briefly in an undertone that she had had a lover. And when her lover died, she filled the gap with Aleister Crowley. She was not his mistress but the 'Artist Executant' of his last major work,* The Book of Thoth. *She painted the many stilted pictures the book contains. She was also his treasurer, courier, companion. They were an extraordinary middle-aged couple: he, with his occult learning and forebodings of awful things to come (as predicted in the* Book of the Law*); she with her nose that reminded me of a parrot's beak, protruding blue eyes, and unconventional views. She had played a supportive role to her husband in his activities in the Liberal Party; and with the Party's decline, she had slipped into boredom, from which the Beast 666 had aroused her.*

Symonds' comments about Percy being rather 'dull' are confirmed by the story that Percy was nicknamed 'The Housemaid' by his fellow parliamentarians, due to his ability to 'empty the Chamber' every time he rose to speak. Clearly Frieda filled her life by entertaining the glitterati of the day at her top floor studio in Marylebone while Percy toiled diligently in the House.

All in all, we have one of the weirdest threesomes it would be possible to imagine. It gives pause for thought to consider how her two young boys would have grown up in that atmosphere. Boarding school and nurse might have been a blessing. Perhaps it helps to explain what happened next.

The book and its central commandment provided a loose justification for Crowley's life of mayhem and murder, not to mention its influence on the hip generations of the sixties.

Frieda's painting of the Hierophant held pride of place among her other Tarot card paintings on the corridor wall in Te Rama. Although it was incinerated of course it can still be seen in the tarot pack. The Hierophant is one of twenty-two trumps from a pack of seventy-eight tarot cards. It is numbered fifth and is described by Aleister Crowley thus:

> *Offer thyself virgin to the Knowledge and Conversation of thine Holy Guardian Angel. All else is a snare. Be thou athlete with the eight limbs of Yoga: for without these thou are not disciplined for any fight.*

What we have no way of knowing is how far Frieda, in pursuit of greater knowledge, decided to participate in Crowley's pursuit of the occult, and in particular his experiments with mind-altering substances. But reading her letters and considering the circumstances she must have been under some pressure to do so. One thing seems clear, although Crowley treated most women with contempt and as sexual playthings, confirmed in his own diaries, his relationship with Frieda was platonic and he ended up having great affection for her; presumably this was one reason he made her one of two executors of his will, a task that she was ill-equipped for and which placed her at the centre of a maelstrom of squabbling claimants.

An epitaph for Frieda was placed inside an edition of *The Book of Thoth*. It read, 'May the passionate "Love under Will" which she has stored in the Treasury of Truth and Beauty flow forth from the splendour and strength of her work to enlighten the world; may this Tarot serve as a chart for the Gold Seamen of the new Aeon to guide them across the Great Sea of Understanding to the City of the Pyramids.'

Maggie on horseback

22

MAGGIE AND MATTHEW

Suddenly not only was Te Rama gone from Waikanae but so were our parents: my father and mother, aged ninety and eighty-six respectively, opted, in a fit of whimsy, for life in an apartment at the top of a high-rise tower in Sydney, a city in which he had never lived and which she had left in 1933, some sixty-three years earlier.

With her parents in Australia, Maggie found herself treated by the Waikanae locals as a person in her own right instead of Sir Jack and Lady Harris's daughter. She blossomed, became rather more vague, a little more eccentric and happily switched her social life to the potters, writers and eclectic collection of oddballs who shared their interests with Maggie together with a strong and continuing odour of horse. Maggie was content as she clomped about her property and watched her new garden grow, and the ducks and the dogs get fatter. The general state of disrepair did not improve much. Ducks shit almost nonstop and the Great Danes produced copious turds like a pile of large brown cucumbers, but Maggie was so at home in her bucolic existence that she began to draw again.

One item Maggie did look after: Emmeline Pankhurst's fan. The illustration on the fan depicts a village in China with all the village people and their animals. All the faces are mother-of-pearl, and the fan itself is of ivory and silk. In the 1990s Maggie had the fan set in a frame. The framer who was also an antique dealer thought the fan was eighteenth century Chinese. Maggie displayed it on her wall.

And so more time passed in Waikanae so that it was quite out of the blue, and over thirty years after she had returned from London, when, one evening, I received a phone call from Maggie. This was rare. She wasn't in the habit of wasting her small income on fripperies like international communications. Breathlessly, and with an air of mystery, she revealed she had received a letter.

'From whom?' I inquired.

'From my son,' was the reply. And so, the story emerged.

Maggie had found herself, aged eighteen, alone in a London which was exuberantly celebrating the transient freedoms of the sixties. There was such a lot to do. There was the Campaign for Nuclear Disarmament (CND) for starters. For CND, the focus became the protest marches from Aldermaston, the Atomic Weapons establishment eighty kilometres outside London, to Grosvenor Square. In 1959 as many as 60,000 people marched. By 1963, when Maggie was in London, it was 150,000 people. The CND was a significant organisation. It was headed by the philosopher and Nobel Peace Prize winner Lord Bertrand Russell, and among its prominent members were many artists, writers and academics: JB Priestley, Benjamin Britten, Michael Foot MP, and Dame Edith Evans, Frieda's great friend, to name a few. Its insignia, a little like the Mercedes logo, became instantly recognisable around the world. Predating the anti-Vietnam protests, the outraged army of the 'bien pensants' invaded Trafalgar Square, outside the US Embassy, and wrestled with bemused lines of bobbies, and knocked their helmets off. The smell of marijuana was in the air, Aussie plonk was dirt cheap and the young had found a powerful cause.

MAGGIE AND MATTHEW

The Beatles or Rolling Stones belted out of the radios of hundreds of minis or tiny sports cars as they hurtled round London from one trendy pub to another. Dress was duffel coats and miles of beads. And sex was fun and free and the right of anyone who felt the urge, provided they weren't old. It was bliss to be alive if you were hip and beautiful. But for Maggie, with her boarding school upbringing in rural New Zealand, it must have been quite bewildering. Exciting, but if you were going to be honest, a little scary; and lonely when she woke up in her tiny flat and the rain pelted down outside and all the fabulous new friends, who often talked about things she had no understanding or experience of, were already off at some coffee house in Chelsea making a whole lot of new friends. So, Maggie would have pulled on her poloneck and denim skirt, five feet of wooden beads she wore round her neck, the suede boots and the duffel coat with the bone buttons and the peace badge, and taken the tube to the Slade to learn all about feminist symbolism in post-impressionist art.

When the obligatory student trip to Spain, which was even cheaper than London, came up she wouldn't have wanted to miss out. And what with sun and booze and this and that and too much excitement you could easily end up preggers and she did. Of course, she couldn't tell anyone in the family, and the father, whoever the hell he was, certainly didn't want to know. By the time she finally told her kindly uncle and aunt, respectably residing in their Oast House in Kent, it was a little too late to do anything even had she been so minded. And then there was the problem of the parents. Uncle Nick said she had to tell them but Maggie would do anything to avoid the moment. By the time she broke the news there was just time for my father to rush to London and make arrangements with Dr Bernados, who of course, after the baby's birth made damn sure they got the mother out of the way as soon as possible. She was shipped back home and the less said the better.

It appears that mother and son had each decided to try to find each other at about the same time and his letter had reached her as her inquiries were leading her to him. It turned out in the end, to be a small modern fairytale. His name was Matthew Taylor. He was born on 3 January 1963. He had been adopted in 1967 by a couple living in Cornwall on the south coast of England. His father, Ken (now deceased), was a playwright and television scriptwriter and he and his wife Jill had a suitably complex family – a daughter from his first marriage, Pam, and then a daughter from their own marriage, Vikki. They were unable to have further children, which led to the adoption of Matthew and, eighteen months later, to the adoption of a second boy, Simon. Matthew's upbringing seems to have been a very happy one. He gained a scholarship to Oxford and after graduating with a degree in Politics, Philosophy and Economics and having been President of the Oxford Students Union, he became research assistant to David Penhaligon, Liberal Member for Truro, who was tragically killed in a car accident. Matthew took over as candidate and, in 1987, was elected by a record majority. He was then aged twenty-four and became, for ten years, the youngest Member of Parliament in the House of Commons. He has from time to time been party spokesman for almost everything: Energy, Trade and Industry, Education, Environment and Shadow Chancellor. In 1994, he was awarded the 'Green Ribbon Award' for Britain's most effective environmental Member of Parliament. And so, as she needlessly explained, he was a direct heir to his great grandfather's forty years in and out of Parliament for the Liberal Party.

Matthew arranged to come to New Zealand to meet his newly found natural mother. My brother and I and our wives were agog; this was an event on no account to be missed. Maggie decided to have a party in her house to welcome Matthew and introduce him to everyone she had ever met. We managed to keep our parents in Sydney for we knew Maggie's party would become their party if they arrived.

The night of the party, the house was crowded with what seemed, given the minute size of the house, a vast crowd. The general chaos was added to by the Great Danes, ducks, and a goose or two, one of which disappeared squawking into the night when accidentally trodden on. There were dozens of people mostly dressed like residents of an ashram. In the middle of all this Matthew, more soberly attired but tastefully, as befitted a rural member of parliament, made it his business to talk to all and sundry, and charmed the pants off everyone. Part of his tradecraft, as he explained later.

Calls came from everywhere for a speech and Maggie, who had waited forty years for an audience, strode beaming to the centre of the floor. She told at length of her excitement at finding Matthew (rapturous and prolonged applause); of what a wonderful and successful son he was (cries of 'here, here' and more rapturous applause); of how thrilled she was to have all her friends and family present – from Australia, Auckland, Wellington, locals et cetera (applause); how excited she was to have found Matthew and he her (more applause); and finally, as people were drifting back to the bar she stopped them by saying how thrilled she was to see everyone (muffled sound of people trying to clap with glass in one hand and bottle in the other). It was a vintage performance; one very rarely sees happiness in such an uninhibited form.

Matthew Taylor in Sydney

There is not much more to tell. Matthew took a trip around New Zealand and then came to stay in Australia, where he finally caught up with his grandparents. Our mother introduced herself by offering to show him her living will, which tested even his powers of diplomacy. But the meeting went very well and they were most satisfied that he had clearly inherited almost all of their attributes although, as my brother sourly remarked to me, 'It would have been a bit different if he had been a fucking bus driver.' They went on to insist that they had been perfectly willing to bring him up as their own in Waikanae but, had this occurred, it would not have involved more than following Mother's normal procedure of handing him over to a nurse as quickly as possible. Maggie would never have had a look in. In fact, it is much more likely they were mortified by the unexpected arrival of a grandson. Certainly, it was never mentioned on any occasion my brother or I can remember. I found out about the baby by accident from my uncle in England. In the social environment of rural New Zealand in the 1960s a bastard child would not have been good for their social position and, had it got out, the locals would have enjoyed my parents' discomfit immensely.

From the moment of Matthew's departure, Maggie was planning her trip to England. The following year she met Matthew in London, had dinner in the Members' dining room in the House of Commons, and met his parents, who welcomed her without apparently any of the restraint they could have been forgiven for feeling. She exudes happiness in a way that amazes each of us who remember her early introspection.

Maggie continued to live in her house in Waikanae among the rubble and she seemed now quite contented although chronically short of money, which she had never really had to worry about before. She had her local friends, the two Great Danes, the cat, and she bought a red Honda Zot. Now, for someone with two Great Danes and an aversion to ever washing her car a red Honda Zot was possibly not the ideal choice. She also developed a liking for touch parking, meaning she stopped when she touched something. The red paint and the panel work soon needed attention.

I experienced one of her favourite pastimes. She would find a remote section of road and let the Danes out for a run alongside the car. When they were tiring, she would pull over and shoehorn them into the back seat. One day I went with her, sitting in the front seat. After the run was over the two Danes leaned their heads on my shoulder. Great Danes like to dribble and, pretty soon, a pool of mucus had slid down the inside of my shirt, which I tried to remove with one hand while putting the other over my ear to dissuade the affectionate licking. To add to the fun, Great Danes as I may have mentioned like to fart, and what with the dribble, the licking and the farting, I was soon wondering if I might be allowed to hop out and run alongside the car.

Maggie continues with her rural life and has taken up drawing and painting again. Matthew continues to rise up the Liberal Party hierarchy. He stood down recently from the Commons and has now been elevated to the House of Lords. He sent us a photograph of himself dressed in a ridiculous ermine gown with an enigmatic smirk on his face. Perhaps old Percy watches with quiet satisfaction as at last one of the family picks up his mantle. Maggie is naturally bursting with pride.

> *POSTSCRIPT: EMAIL AUGUST 2017:*
> *I am crying! When I was in hospital they told me that in no circumstances could I drive any more. For good! Tried to sell my car! No one wanted it. Went to all agents. No interest at all!! It eventually went to the agents and they came and looked. It, by this stage, had spent three or four weeks in the garage. They walked around and said 'bumps, scratches, smelt of dogs, and even worse had 250,000 on the dial.' The best price they would give me was $300 for scrap. I had to take it. It really hurt. Luckily there are lots of buses and friends but, but, but! Maggie.*

Sir Jack aged 100 and granddaughter Sophie

23

THE AFTERMATH

In Sydney, my parents set about finding an apartment and Gail located a new two-bedroom, third-floor apartment in Mosman which had some discrete facilities to cater for older people. It seemed ideal. My father liked it but Mother threw a huge tantrum. She shouted at him she would leave him immediately if he went ahead. No reason was given. Not sufficient 'presence' perhaps?

A week or so later Gail received a call from an old friend who happened to be a real estate agent. The friend assumed, she said, that we knew my parents were about to buy a penthouse apartment in Kirribilli. In fact, we knew nothing about it. She didn't want to poke her nose in, but she was surprised that my parents had just accepted the asking price. She knew about the fire and was trying to save them some money.

We very obliquely raised the issue but my parents ignored us. They thought 'haggling' undignified and they paid the price.

It wasn't long before they found the apartment was unsuitable. They moved to something with more help available; they moved again. Each time, they managed to lose money in the Sydney real estate market, not that easy to do. Eventually they moved into two self-contained units in a retirement village in Mosman.

That didn't work either. They couldn't afford it. They thought they were living in a hotel and kept calling to get little jobs done, food brought, tea made. The retirement village charged for everything, including time, in fifteen-minute intervals and on top of that they hadn't made any friends and were dependent on our family. Even my father realised this was not going to end well. Our home phone started to ring constantly. We tried to persuade them that perhaps they should go back to Waikanae.

One inducement was that Pat's brother John was living there in the village. John had been a Lancaster pilot and in World War II, had flown twenty-seven missions over Germany, mainly over Hamburg and Dresden. Of every one hundred airmen in Bomber Command, fifty-five were killed, three injured, thirteen taken prisoner, two shot down but evaded capture, and twenty-seven survived a 'tour of operations'. A Bomber Command crew had a worse chance of survival than an infantry officer in World War I.

John came home to Sydney after the war, married the daughter of Sir Norman Cowper, the senior partner of Sydney's largest law firm, and took to the booze. The marriage disintegrated as John's alcoholism worsened. He headed over to Te Rama but the family couldn't control him and eventually he found himself in a hospital for alcoholics in Dunedin, back where the whole Harris saga started. In hospital, he met and married another reforming alcoholic, Dinah, and they went to live in Waikanae where they had a son, Jack. Neither of them went back to drinking and all was well until she got cancer. There was a remission and John, knowing Dinah had an ambition to visit Sydney, and sit eating prawns overlooking the harbour, brought her over. After a few days, she became increasingly unwell. The cancer flared up and she was taken to a Sydney hospital where, three weeks later and aged just thirty-nine, she died. John stayed with us through the whole saga and Gail looked after him as the crisis deepened. He never even glanced at the grog cabinet. The war must have taught him well how to confront death. When it was over he sat at our kitchen bench drinking tea. 'You shouldn't be in it if you can't take a joke,' was all he would say. Now he was back with his son in Waikanae, trying to get on with his life.

My parents finally set off back to Waikanae on Easter Thursday. Gail and I took them to the airport and tried to look mortified as they disappeared through customs. Mother had a nurse to help. She needed incontinent pads and they might need to be changed. My mother was distracted by a confrontation with the Easter Bunny which bemused both of them.

The whole departure was clouded in disaster. Not long before, preparing them for the move, none of us could find her jewellery. It had vanished. A large emerald and some diamond earrings. Since we had no idea how long it was since she had last had any of her jewellery no one we asked could help and nothing could be done. As usual, no insurance.

Their sojourn in Sydney was never going to work. They knew no one except us, the city was too big, too fast and too expensive. Not quite no one: one companion Pat did spend time with was Nancy Kerr, the wife of one-time governor general Sir John Kerr. They had known each other for years. On one occasion Gail and I were invited to join the four of them for lunch. After Pat gave a running commentary on the woeful state of politics, Sir John leaned over to me and whispered, 'Do you think she really believes all that rubbish?'

With little to keep them amused, they had leaned on us and especially my wife. Gail constantly and, at least at first, without complaint had responded to their increasing demands for assistance notwithstanding having four young children and a husband to get out of the house every day, but they had mistaken politeness for acquiescence. She started to say 'no' and when she said 'no' she meant it. The low point was probably sitting around our dining room table one evening entertaining them yet again. Jack contemplated our four children, and in an expansive mood, leaned over to her to pronounce that I had 'sired well,' a phrase that seemed in two words to encapsulate misogyny, gross insensitivity, Nazi genetics and confusion with the bloodstock industry.

The brutal truth was we had nothing in common. Ties of blood were no ties at all. We were just another house full of over-exuberant kids, with parents trying to get them to school on time, do our jobs and pay the bills. They vaguely thought I did something in what my father called 'the City,' mistaking Sydney for London, I suppose. Conversations went around and around on the same subject until we were reduced to making up more and more absurd excuses for being somewhere else.

Christopher, Maggie and I must have been quite a disappointment. Our parents would have expected at least a judge in the family, perhaps a professor or a surgeon, even a high commissioner. What had they ended up with? Not much to boast about.

To pass the time they rewrote their wills and we reluctantly passed them to our friend and family solicitor. Pat constantly harassed him with ever-diminishing codicils, which cost more in his time than the codicils were worth. A few months later, when we caught up with him, he put his hand over Gail's and pronounced, 'You have the mother-in-law from hell.'

Gail and I had noticed increasing stacks of stamps and envelopes being mailed plus forms everywhere which seemed to relate to some kind of lottery. We investigated as best we could and found Pat was entering these lotteries and it wasn't just one or two, it was dozens. One day we were there and she announced she had won 5,000 dollars. My father was cock-a-hoop. I picked up the winning ticket. What it said was words to the effect of 'Lady Harris. CONGRATULATIONS!!!! You have won the $5000 special prize. All you need to do is send a processing cheque for $100 and you can collect your winnings.' I tried to convince them it was a scam. They got angry and so did I. I pointed out that when I looked closely the scam operated out of Canada and was in US dollars. All her cheques were in Australian dollars so none of her entries were for the right amount but they had been cashed anyway. We tried to stop it but nothing would make either of them listen, even when the police confirmed my suspicions. My father accused me of being rude and ungrateful. On and on it went.

It was after they returned to New Zealand that we managed to get access to her bank account. She had over a period written nearly 1000 cheques. Most were small, ten to thirty dollars but some were over one hundred dollars. It appeared my father had decided to join in. Neither of them ever won anything.

A few months after moving back to New Zealand, my father on a visit to Sydney requested my presence for lunch at the Union Club in the city. I hated lunching in clubs, mostly because I had to wear a tie and the food reminded me of boarding school. I turned up somewhat apprehensive. Sure enough, some time after the Windsor soup, he began taking me to task about neglecting them; not discharging my responsibilities as a son. I sat for a while and then stood up. 'You're too late, Dad,' I announced. 'If you wanted to play "Happy Families" you should have started fifty years ago.' I stalked out.

About a month later our son Mark called in to see us. He had received a letter from my father.

> *Dear Mark,*
> *I think you must have observed some eccentric behaviour by your father. I fear that he is deeply mentally disturbed. When I was in NZ[?] he came to the apartment and violently attacked your grandmother and she was deeply upset.*
>
> *I took Paul to the Club and told him we had not been invited to the house for a long time. I was greeted by a violent diatribe in which he alleged that he had been neglected as a child. According to his version he had been left in charge of a nurse, sent to boarding school and finally to Cambridge to get rid of him. He then rushed out and it seems he has forbidden Gail to contact us which must be very distressing for her.*

> *We know this illness which is not unusual among middle-age men, not disconnected to female menopause, it can be alleviated but will you ever get your father to take medical advice? We all have a fair idea what caused it.*

He then goes on about all the children being invited to 'Mother's' (Pat's) birthday party and goes on to say that he doesn't know Mark's address and then adds darkly, 'I have taken certain precautions.' Finally, he finishes by saying, 'I hope that you will be able to arrange to come to have a private talk to me.'

Mark immediately sent a copy to me and my brother Christopher. Our reactions were of amazement mingled with a good laugh. My brother thought it was particularly hilarious; but actually, it was not so funny.

Finally, after long discussion with all of us Mark wrote back.

Dear Grandfather,
I have spent a few days thinking about the best way to reply to your letter. Although my initial reaction was one of complete shock, I now feel saddened that you feel this way about your son.

Having spoken with my sister and my two brothers about your suggestion I cannot believe that you think he is in any way mentally disturbed.

Our father is held in the highest respect by not only by his own family but also by his friends, peers and business acquaintances alike. Indeed, he is known for his humility…It certainly distresses me to think that you cannot see what is behind this upset. I know that whenever he and I have a disagreement we talk it through and manage to get on with being part of the happy family we all enjoy so much.

> *Given that it seems you do not wish to open your arms to his concerns, I will come and meet with you in his place. I do hope this situation can be resolved as it is very upsetting to find myself a mediator between a father and a son.*
> *With kind regards,*
> *Mark Harris.*

Nothing ever eventuated from this.

Maggie's portrait of Sir Jack for his 100th birthday

24

THE END

Reflecting all these years later on Pat and Jack it has dawned on me that I hardly knew them. I had a nurse from the day I was born, went to boarding school for eleven years straight from the age of seven and left for overseas within six months of leaving school, never to return to New Zealand to live.

I never discussed my future with them but I know I must have been subtly influenced. My mother expressed contempt for advertising agents and stockbrokers and barely tolerated lawyers. Most people she considered 'shopkeepers.' Mining engineers, in view of her father's profession, were acceptable. Discussing money they considered vulgar so I never learned anything from them about the grubby business of commerce although that was what Bing Harris & Co Ltd did. When I was at university in England with only a few pounds I heard the bank would lend money. I went to see the bank manager and was astonished to learn that not only would I need to supply security but also pay interest. I sold my typewriter for twenty-five quid instead. A diminishing list of options for future employment seemed to confront me.

When my parents died in New Zealand, she at 93 and he at 103, my only reaction was nothing much at all. I remember wondering if something was wrong with me. Was I an emotional cripple? Why didn't I feel sad? I had seen other friends and family devastated by family illnesses and death so how could I feel so nonchalant? If anything threatening to my wife or my four children occurred I was overwhelmed with apprehension; to my eleven grandchildren, wracked with concern.

Going to New Zealand for the funerals it dawned on me that my brother and sister seemed to have much the same lack of reaction. In fact, my brother hated our parents and never said a good word about either of them. It's an interesting reflection on nature versus nurture. Giving birth is not on its own enough. Below are a few words from me at my father's funeral.

VALE JACK HARRIS 26/8/09.

'Welcome to all of you who have come to say farewell to our father. Thank you from Maggie, Christopher and me, and from his many grandchildren and great grandchildren, for being here. I know how much he would have appreciated a 'good turn out' as he would term it.

'You all knew Jack to various degrees but, as I am sure you will also know from your own experiences, knowing someone as a friend or acquaintance is quite different from knowing them as a family member, let alone as a father. So, what was he like as a father?

'On the night Jack died, as it happens Gail and I were at a lecture by the historian Antony Beevor, and in the course of his lecture he reminded us how unfair it is to look at historical figures through contemporary eyes. So it is important to remember the times in which Jack lived. When he was born so long ago in 1906 Britain ruled the world and to be an Englishman was indeed a rare privilege, but all that was about to change violently with the outbreak of World War I. He once told me he remembered being at boarding school in Kent in 1916 and he could hear the guns firing in France. The wounded came to the little town dressed in some sort of blue overalls. He particularly remembered those who had been blinded by mustard gas. After boarding school, there was the University of Cambridge, then the Great Depression, including the General Strike, at which he was accepted as a "Special Constable". This was followed by some time in Germany where he witnessed the rise of Hitler. During this time he had married Pat, taken over Bing Harris, and moved to live in New Zealand. The years after the war were mostly occupied with Bing Harris until the firm's sale and a long and busy retirement.

'To see him through his formative years he had a highly respectable Victorian father, busy in Parliament, and a highly disreputable mother, busy with the occult. From his accounts, they were quite remote from him and his brother Nicholas. Neither of them would have been at all concerned with the modern concept of bonding with their children or involving themselves in the minutiae of child-rearing. Victorians didn't do that. They hired formidable nannies and often deviant schoolmasters to instil proper values, "character" as they called it, while they got on with things grown-ups did. Jack quite naturally seems to have taken much the same view on leaving child-rearing mainly to others. Safe to say, being present at his child's birth would have seemed to him a bizarre intrusion into women's business and as for nappies, I can only say that the only poo he ever tangled with was Winnie the Pooh. So for him and Pat there was no debate; probably just as well. I think their view was that parenthood required giving birth as expeditiously as possible, immediately appointing a nanny, and arranging a couple of satisfactory boarding schools, in my case to commence at the age of seven. As soon as school was over it was off to university on the other side of the world. That was it. The job of parenting conscientiously discharged.

'Needless to say, this doesn't lead to a close-knit family life. My last birthday at home in Waikanae was in 1950 just before I left for boarding school in the Waikato. We didn't really do family things like holidays; after all, we had Te Rama, and for me, until it burned down, who could have conceived of wanting anything more than to roam unsupervised around Te Rama?

'Looking back, as I grew older, even though I was living in Australia, there were things I began to admire. One could hardly call Jack tactful nor was false modesty a problem but his Victorian certainty about what was right and wrong, and the belief that principle comes before personal gain or popularity, led him to stand up for some tough causes.

'Publicly opposing a vindictive bastard like Muldoon was definitely not a career-enhancing move; marching with hippies in anti-apartheid rallies would I expect have been marginal among his fellow Wellington Club members, and leading the campaign to save Manapouri probably had him branded a greenie ratbag by many of his peers. Today they seem hardly radical causes at all but when he embraced them they certainly were. But on all these issues I'm proud of my father.

'So we have in him a real conundrum. By appearance he might have been a Victorian Englishman, but underneath he was quite radical in his social attitudes. His life really revolved around Pattie, his various dogs, Bing Harris, politics, travel, his paintings, his books, the theatre and good food and wine, the more the better. I'm sure he loved us children too, although showing it wasn't his strong suit. Like his father, he was a Liberal to his bootstraps, but underneath he was also a modern man, loved New Zealand and was proud to call himself a New Zealander, notwithstanding being one of the few men in New Zealand utterly indifferent to sport. Sometimes he could be insensitive, sometimes practical, and sometimes quite eccentric. Sometimes he was kind and generous, and, like all of us, sometimes not. One thing's for certain, his unique personal aura, to use a word his mother Frieda would have approved of, left an indelible impression on all those who knew him, whether family, friends or especially his children. The twenty-first century for better or worse will likely not produce any more characters like him, and personally, finding myself to my surprise

THE END

and alarm rather old-fashioned, I think it's for the worse. With his passing it really does feel to me as if he was the very last of a unique generation.'

When the speeches were over I glanced across at my brother, sitting with his arms folded and his head on one side and the ghost of a smile. He was now Sir Christopher Harris Bt, the third baronet. I wondered what would eventually happen to the title. Christopher had one son, but he is estranged from the family and living somewhere in Germany. He will one day presumably be Sir Andrew, and, since the title follows the male heirs (legitimate naturally) next in the chain if I should live so long is me. What a hoot.

Frieda's cycle of life painting

Appendix: A souffle for Ganesha by Frieda Harris

I am told that before I embark on this book of travel in Ceylon and India, I must explain myself, and how I came to be acquainted with the leading Indian dancer, Ram Gopal, who initiated me a little into Indian religion and philosophy.

Before I met him, I had dabbled a bit in vague magic. I had designed a pack of tarot cards and illustrated 'The Chemical marriage of Christian Rosencrantz with academic symbols'. But this was done only in calm intervals between raging elections and the interruptions incident on my husband's parliamentary career that forced me to busy myself as kind of 'obliger' or curate to him and was not congenial to my temperament as a painter.

I began to be educated to the ways of the stage as well as of those of the House of Commons. Both these paths in human affairs seemed to me to be a mimicry of real life as I found in them no religion and very little gaiety and I wanted both then.

One momentous evening I went to see Ram Gopal dance. I knew nothing about Indian technique, nothing about the hidden ritual he was dancing, nothing about him, but I did know I was looking at beauty controlled by will and, for me, that was the aim of perfected art. A week later I was invited to meet Ram at lunch.

Arriving I found fourteen other guests assembled, all distinguished and successful people and, as I did not sit near Ram, I had little chance to speak to him beyond the mere formal introduction. After lunch, I retreated into a corner, as I am shy of bearding lions. Suddenly I found Ram standing next to me.

'When were you in India?' he inquired. 'Never,' I replied, somewhat startled. He looked at me broodily. 'Oh yes, you were and we have a lot of work to do together.' Before I could inquire what kind of job he fancied I could do he was grabbed by our host and removed.

Later he sent me tickets for his ballet. After the show I went behind the stage to thank him. There he was resplendent in his golden winged Shiva costume and thronged by lovely ladies all saying, 'Darling, you were marvellous.' I shambled into the background but he saw me. 'Frieda,' he said, 'come here.'

How did he know my name was Frieda; this was one of his queer occult flashes that I do not understand. He grasped me by the hand and said 'Wait' and I waited. Then, when the adoring crowd had melted away he said, 'We have so much work to do together.'

'What work?' I said.

'Have you ever painted scenery?' and this inquiry was odd since he knew nothing about me and I had no reputation as a set designer.

'Well, a bit, rather badly,' I stuttered.

'Please do some for me,' was his response.

I went home and thought about it, looked at some Indian miniatures and worked out a lotus theme he had suggested. I then showed him a few rough sketches for sets. Ram was enchanted. 'How did you know? This is not a Western setting, it is genuine East.' Presently we were working together, quarrelling together, and setting to work again. Finally he outlined a large ballet incorporating the life of Shah Jahan with a background of the Taj Mahal. It was to be done with traditional Indian dances, each scene to be dominated by a different planet or sign of the zodiac. I found out that Ram believes he has a mission to endeavour to fuse Western and Eastern thought by a mutual emotion engendered by evocative dancing.

Luckily I was able to grasp this and interpret for him. When I thought the designs were finished I went triumphantly to his dressing room in the theatre where he was dancing. He was praying to his image of Shiva and Ganesha before going on the stage. All round him were cardboard professional models of my scenery. I looked at them in horror, every well thought-out curve which had a relative meaning was wrong. In spite of remonstrances I destroyed them all. Now I had to start and make those models myself. It took me years before we were all satisfied and I was tired out. My husband had died, I was alone and without responsibilities.

Ram had gone to supervise the choreographer in a big American production in Ceylon. I made up my mind to return alone via India to study the system of relaxation which I had sensed in the swamis I had met in England and recognised in that strange creature, Ram Gopal.

I wrote this frivolous yet partly serious account of my impressions as an old amateur in the arts of religion and dancing and gave it the title 'A souffle for Ganesha' to suggest the frothiness of my short acquaintance with the little Indian god of wisdom.

1

So I bolted by jet-plane to Ceylon for fun, and I went to India in search of a God.

Had Ram Gopal forgotten I was coming? Where would I stay? I disembarked stone deaf, to be greeted by two beautiful women in saris, smiling a welcome. They had been deputed by Ram to look after me. Before I could grasp what was happening to me, one of my travelling companions, a typical Englishwoman of the best type, who had taken me under her wing en route, whisked me off in her car driven by her son in dazzling white European clothes. He seemed to take it for granted that he should go out of his way to deposit me at the Galle Face Hotel and wait to find out if Ram had organised a room for me.

Overtired from my journey, I went to my room alone where an old room-servant with a turban, flowing white robes and the expression of an aging apostle, inquired, 'Did Lady want anything?'

'Sleep and a bath and could I have lunch and dinner in bed?'

'Yes, Lady can have whatever she requires.' Unbelievable, after the struggle for existence in London. 'Lady' had everything she wanted and slept the day and night around. Then a message from Ram Gopal – he was arriving for breakfast.

I did not wait for him and about lunchtime, he came, looking as lovely as he always does. He is really a surprising person! An oval face, dark short wavy hair framing his olive complexion with deep warm shadows, and smudged black eyes, in whose depth glitters the unusual fire of genius. Suddenly he smiles, with a sweetness that could subdue wild animals. He creates around him the vibrations of gaiety and devotion. At the same time he confuses the ordinary slow-going creatures like myself. Attention! What does the Mercury of Indian dancing intend to do next?

When he came to fetch me, he was only the radiant friend who tucked me into his car, delightedly telling me what a lovely time he was having and simply bubbling with appreciation of life. I was still stunned. 'You haven't arrived yet, it will take a few days before all of you comes over from Europe.' I settled down beside him while Denny the chauffeur drove us quickly out of Colombo.

That was a comfort – Colombo is blue and hard and sunny but one does not feel impressed or strange in it. The hotels and shops and white buildings are all safe, moored to a familiar world of events. You can bathe in a swimming pool and shop and chat as in London, Paris and New York, yet there are abrupt transitions into the unknown in this outpost of a world of altered values. As I found out when I returned to it.

'See, a little Ganesha!' cried Ram. I saw an elephant, a real elephant ambling along under the palms which flanked the road. Next stop was a village to buy pineapples. They seemed very large and Ram and I had to make room for them, while Denny cheerfully piled in bananas and something round and green and oval called pawpaws. We were beginning to climb and the hills were not so crowded with villages and bungalows. What a day, and fantastic of Ram to initiate me. We arrived at the Queen's Hotel, Kandy, and at once I was plunged into the film world. Here were groups of men in those absurd floral shirts, and lovely ladies drinking, smoking and shouting at one another in high American. I was introduced – 'Frieda,' said Ram casually. 'Oh yes,' echoed from various Americans and I faded into the routine of the film. 'Tomorrow eight am,' Ram told me, 'We go early to the dancers. You are in my car.'

The next morning I was on time and Ram was not. Gathered in the hall and waiting were several girls collected in Colombo who were to be taught to dance in the American film, which was being rehearsed. They greeted me although I was an outsider and a stranger. I noticed amongst them the energetic Minette de Silva, a little Sinhalese lady in a mauve and gold sari. She was a hard worker and organiser who did not deserve the intolerance that Ram meted out to her for it was her opinion that work should be danced through not strained at. Also I saw Manil who was anything but serious-minded. She was a pretty pet with small hands and fingers, always expressing her frivolous thoughts, her dear little person gesturing all the time as she gossiped. There was a lumpy Dutch girl, very young and very unsuitable. How she became a member of the troupe was never explained. She bulged in the wrong places and had the boastful idea that she was a ballet star after receiving twelve lessons in some obscure dancing class. Ram soon undeceived her. And then there was dark Theresa. Tall, slim, contemptuous and very Westernised in her fashionable black slacks, a crucifix dangling from her neck.

It was not the most appropriate costume for a girl about to be initiated into the tribal dances of Ceylon. Also in attendance was the Hawaiian-American film star, Milee. She was the darling of some producer and here she was quite inappropriately cast to play the village siren, whose blandishments and dancing were to lure the hero to his destruction. Milee was tall and giraffe-like. She was more than slender. Slapping herself, she confided in me that she had the flattest stomach in Ceylon, this in spite of the amount of jam she consumed.

'Boy, Boy!' she commanded at each meal (she sat at our table). 'Bring jam. Say, Ram, I must have jam with everything.' Ram took no notice. It was very interesting to watch the reaction of the Kandy men in the practice shed, who are real dancers and the admiration of anyone who is lucky enough to see them. They looked on astonished at Milee's gyrations and were slightly shocked when she wound her arms around everyone and hissed 'Darling' to us all. Ram worked her ceaselessly, he has the artist's passion for perfection, and again and again Milee went through her antics.

I mildly said, 'Can't you think of love, you have to seduce the hero.'

'Oh, yes,' replied Milee, pouring coconut milk down her throat, and waggling her young bottom as she screamed at Ram, 'Is that better, Darling?' Ram was silent.

All the star dancers were individuals. There was Jayana, the secretary of the dancing school, a brown beauty and the most romantic of them all. He had long black hair which he tossed back, a slight curve in his figure, so that he did not appear to reach you directly, it was a dancing approach. He adored Ram and followed him about, reminding me of a spaniel, and he inserted himself into the car in answer to one of Ram's royal gestures of invitation, snuggling himself between us with a gratified, affectionate expression. But he could dance! He is a passionate man and in the end found himself a victim of the little tinsel film star. He wooed and won her with urgent love without words, for he had no English, and so, through the vulgarity and false romanticism of the hectic American film, there loomed the dusky wooing. She, poor little cardboard thing, was completely submerged. They parted in a cheap restaurant, Milee mingling her tears with her curry. Each of the star dancers gave a separate performance and, as I attended the practice every day, I was able to study them separately. The most important of them was old Guenyar. But as much as I wanted to talk to him I could never understand his gibberish. I think he said he was sixty-five, but he was able to leap high in the air, always alighting exactly where he intended. Later on, Ram and I climbed up a very crooked path through the paddy fields to his home, where he showed us the certificates and silver medals he had won for his dancing. The cottage was a single room and in the centre of it was a sunken concrete square, which was his bath. There was only a brass bowl for water, no taps or waste and no water in it. We sat rather uncomfortably round it while Ram talked to him, treating him with the respect that was due to the great professional of Kandyan dancing. As I could not understand what they were saying I looked at the swaying palms without and the austere barrenness within, which seemed to have no relation in its primitiveness to this man's controlled intellectual dancing.

There were two others I remember most clearly. One was the brother of the drummer. Surambo always started excited drumming as he sprang into the centre of the group, and from that moment it seemed as if he had come unstuck, so quickly did he move. And last but by no means least was that terrific Gunemala – Black Lightning. This man always remained my particular delight and I think he was more than a dancer; he was the principal exponent in the ritual worship of their God. What a face, dark and brilliant and naughty and sexy! He was not so young, and he had big shoulders and what muscles! They shone and caught the light as he moved. Black lightning, that is just what he was. He leapt into the group when Surambo beat out his rhythms. He was nothing but determined movement, his hands coming towards the other dancers, who swayed and stamped with him. I had to join in. From my lazy chair on the raised platform beside Ram I found myself clapping my hands too, climbing down and standing amongst the performers, clapping and stamping, inspired and breathless. Ram too came down, laughing with pleasure, alert.

It was always the same every day. We went there torpid from the Queen's Hotel and American film gossip and after half an hour of this flashing dancing and drumming, we behaved as if we had drunk champagne and could have jumped over the moon.

There is a great difference between Indian and Kandyan dancing, both in their drumming and gestures. The Kandyans do not attempt to tell a story. They struck me as being meticulous and mathematical in their movements as a Bach Fugue is in sound, and quite as restrained. This particular tribal tradition is handed down from father to son, and taught carefully to the children. It is, doubtless, an ecstasy of nature worship in its more exalted dance movements. It was obviously very ancient and luckily unspoilt. The dancers belonged to the earth and sprang out of it. It was the first time I thought of man as a perfect animal, or imagined no barrier between the wild, beautiful tiger and elephant with the shadows of the leaves of the palms dappling them in the jungle.

Ram had to condense all this talent into the narrow confines of a film. They recognised that he was a great master and there was no envy or pettiness in their appreciation.

Yet we had fun too. Ram wanted a black magic priest to do some miracles and at last he found one. 'Come on, Frieda.'

I followed him in the sunshine to Jayana's office. There we saluted an old priest who had a coconut in front of him on the floor. He motioned Ram to climb onto it. 'I can't,' said Ram, but as he is not departed [sic] by small obstacles he did succeed at crowding himself on top. The priest spoke to the coconut and slowly it began to turn. Ram stuck to it, as it went faster and faster until, in an explosion of laughter, he flung himself on the ground. It was our only experience in the black art.

2

Soon after, one morning before practice, we were taken through the rice paddies on a very precipitous path up a hill to the temple they had prepared.

'Look at this, Frieda,' said Ram. 'It is made of bleached palm trees. It seems so innocent and fruitful.' We were given a truncated palm leaf which we planted in front of the altar. We were blessed and mantras were recited by the priest and we had scarlet signs put on our foreheads. I wanted to test our friends so I scribbled in the sand a glyph of a pentagon. They gathered round me and looked at it carefully. Yes, it was a universal language for them, they recognised and saluted it reverently.

How friendly and kind these simple people were. I was honoured and touched by them for I was the first white woman to see their ritual. Ram and I looked forward in secret to our initiation. We were not anxious to let our secular film friends know about our secret idolatory.

But before this ceremony, and to help me to understand it, I had to meet a really great Sinhalese artist, George Keyt. His paintings are easily the equal of Picasso in vigour, and much deeper in emotion.[1]

He has beaten out his own path and he can paint the poetry of the lives of the Hindu gods with unabashed feeling. How he faces up to it! We went to his house near Amunugama, where he lives with his Sinhalese wife, and his children and his many, many pictures. He has long black hair and wears a white embroidered loose coat and a spotless white dhoti. He face is hard and keen and he has large dark eyes, which burn if he detects hypocrisy.

---

1 George Keyt is one of very few Sri Lankan artists with an international reputation that survives to this day. He 'retired' to the mountains near Kandy in the 1940s, where he became increasingly involved in the life of the villagers. Influenced by Buddhist and Hindu texts, he reflected these and the vigour and colour of Kandyan life, particularly its expression in dance.

I was afraid I would be found wanting and be subjected to his sarcasm and indifference, but sheltering behind Ram's imperious indifference, I did in fact find the courage to make friends. He was waiting for us and escorted us up the steep uneven steps to his veranda. He offered us drinks, which we refused, for we were in a hurry and wanted to see all his sketches. These were in his studio through a small room in which he slept. They were crowded with pictures, lining the walls, propped up carelessly everywhere in heaps. He took down first one, then another, telling us hastily about the Hindu stories and allegories on which they were based. The outlines were black and sure and the movement dynamic. Much of his work had been burned in a warehouse fire in Bombay on the way to an exhibition but the disaster had only stimulated the intrepid artist.

Ram bought many pictures – in his imagination alas – whilst I lusted to possess them all! George has a small son who goes with him everywhere. He was often fretful with his father and looks like a little black pixie, with a crimson cap fringed with gold on his head. He peeped out at you from his father's cap and if you noticed him he escaped like a shy little animal. Behind George's house was an old, very old, temple surrounded with big green Bo-trees. Here George told us stories about the Hindu gods and Lord Buddha. We felt our way amongst the shadows at the temple and caught a glimpse of the ancient massive gates made of wood and iron and encrusted with nails. Inside in the dark shrine was calm, gigantic recumbent Buddha. I put out my hand to feel the stone. 'No,' said George quickly, 'you must not touch the holy master.'

3

Ceylon is in the East and yet it is hemmed in by Western conventions. Kandy has an English Club and tennis courts. It also has the Temple of the Tooth. Almost opposite the Queen's Hotel, which looks onto the lake and the tame tortoises, this Buddhist temple stands.

APPENDIX

I was determined to worship at the temple with the correct formula, and so I dragged myself from the hotel alone to visit it. It is raised above the road and old carved steps lead up to the shrines. From many stone arches and balconies you can look at the fountains in the lake. They are illuminated at night with coloured lights and are spectacular. Inside is the sacred tooth of Buddha. It was brought there by a woman in about 362 AD. Of course it is too holy for mortal sight and is covered by sheath upon sheath of silver for protection, assuming an enormous size. Round the temple are the trees with the temple flowers blossoming all the year and dripping with perfume. There are little stalls under the trees and here you buy, for one rupee, baskets of palm leaves. Heaped upon them lie the white, thick-petalled flowers with golden yellow centres, and they have a scent so strong that it makes the air around you hum with fragrance. You take your delicious basket and go to the foot of the steps, and after climbing a short way you are requested to remove your shoes. These are left with an unreliable-looking individual and you pad on upwards, conscious of the dust and dirtiness you are treading on. You join the pilgrims that throng the entrance twice a day, when the tooth is shown. They are there always and every day, crowding in, devout people holding their flowers in the palm of their hands over their heads, an endless procession. In the temple, before you reach the central shrine, is a round hall and, curiously enough, it has huge carved Shivas, Ganeshas, Vishnus, and Parvatis all around it. On the walls are lovely ancient paintings, illustrating the Vedas. Yet the temple is Buddhist.

A yellow robed priest with a shaven head begins to beat a large drum at regular intervals, a hollow sound amongst the arches and domes of the temple. A younger priest blows the conch, or spiral shell. It is shrill, weird, and barbaric. This is a signal that you are to go on towards the shrine in the queue and be allowed to see the tooth at a distance.

In its august presence you present your flowers to the officiating priest, bow very deeply and are dismissed to another painted chamber. Here the pilgrims sit in meditation, or bow themselves to the ground or lie prostrate for a very long time. They look very intense and holy and you are embarrassed to be observing them. So, not wishing to disturb these praying mantises, you patter out the back exit, recover your shoes and retreat to the secular existence of the hotel.

The temple is ancient and magnificent, but it chatters with formalised religion. One feels compelled to utter the conventional, 'How lovely! How strange! How rare!' when an obliging priest shows you the ancient Sanskrit books written on palm leaves, the glorious view over the lake, and the golden images and jewels of the shrine. The isolated little Ganesha Temple in the poorer streets of Kandy, crouching in the dust and covered outside and in with crowding statues of Hindu gods and godesses, has more reality. Indeed I felt as I descended from the Temple of the Tooth that I had visited the Royal apartments, but Ganesha was my home.

4

Although I was taken for a three-day drive around part of Ceylon by some English acquaintances, it has made no mark on my memory, for I was engrossed in the complications of the film arrangements and the chatter of the ladies of Ram's court. We all ate at the same table, Ram successively too late or too early for the throng. We were waited on by a large Sinhalese who looked – face, hair and hands – as if he was made of beige tow. He had drooping dundreary moustaches, which did not please Ram. 'Why not cheer up those moustaches?' he said unexpectedly to the complacent fat boy. Next meal we had a shock for, when he offered us the usual meal of pea soup and boiled mutton, he appeared with the offending whiskers sticking straight up in spikes and waxed into rigidity. He was very proud of himself. Subsequently I met him in the post office and, sadly, the spikes had drooped again alas.

APPENDIX

In the hotel and upstairs in Ram's bedroom was the usual muddle of theatrical life. There were costumes bulging in and out of the wardrobe, Ram's little images of Shiva and Ganesha peeping out from the melee, and books and books, some theatrical, some religious.

Ram had a servant named Charles, or Uncle Charles as I called him. He inspired confidence in us although he never did anything.

'Charles,' said Ram every other minute.

'Here,' he always replied.

'Prepare my bath.'

'Yes, Master.'

'Repair Lady's shoes.'

'Yes, Master.'

'Is my coat ironed?'

'Yes, Master.'

'Take Lady to the bathroom.'

'Yes, Master.'

And so on, all day. Devoted and lazy, he seemed a bulwark against all this dancing insanity. By night or day he stood just outside or inside Ram's door.

'Is Mr Ram Gopal inside his room?'

Charles would look at me solemnly and then open the door without permission, and through it I would glimpse hurried exits from other doors. Young Gopal trying to relax on one bed and Milee, chewing gum on another, the dark dancer Jayana sweeping out and bowing and Teresa and Manil wriggling in and out of brilliant heaps of saris in the hope they would wear them in the film. From the scrimmage I could distinguish Ram's gentle unhurried voice: 'Come in, Frieda.' There was also Paul, the dusky masseur in attendance. He rubbed us all indiscriminately. Early morning found him soothing Ram before and after the bath – Milee, Gopal and finally me.

'Your legs are stiff,' said Ram, 'Why not have Paul?'

I looked at Paul. After all I was English and it seemed a strange idea to let this dark strange man massage me – but after all! Paul came to my room and I have never had such a massage in my life. He was scrupulous and workmanlike. He pummelled my neck, my back, my knees, and worked the muscles scientifically all the time covering me with a blanket as if he were a Sunday School teacher. I was refreshed beyond measure and annexed Paul as part of my daily routine.

Whilst we were all doing nothing waiting for the first dress rehearsal of our film, I was introduced to our principal star, Vivien Leigh. She came occasionally into the lounge of the hotel, surrounded by admirers. Everyone who saw her said, 'How lovely she is,' and inevitably the echo, 'How sweet.' She was charming to me and invited me to join a picnic in the jungle, in company of four tea planters who had cars. She brought a large hotel hamper containing sandwiches and beer. Under her direction we drove to a clearing amongst the palms. I was sorry for her friend who staggered with the basket to the exact spot she indicated. Whilst we ate and flopped she, who never yielded to any fatigue, went to bathe in an adjacent river. Through the burning sun and sand she reappeared in her spotless white shirt and knife pleated black skirt, exactly as if she had just been unwrapped from cellophane. I looked at her with admiration as she instructed her companions the exact route by which she wished to return. Glancing at me, crumpled and in slacks, she said with a twinkle, 'I like your clothes, they are so very odd.'

One evening a party was held in honour of Vivien Leigh, Ram and the company by a rich Sinhalese. It interested me to see this house, designed by Minette de Silva, who was an architect. The house fulfilled every modish requirement. Bathrooms for each bedroom, staircases with banisters painted scarlet and decorated with delicate designs peculiar to Kandyan craftsmen. It was painted all through in restrained beige and had no extremes or Oriental splashes of splendour.

The kitchen was screened off with a long glass window and you could see the cooks in their white robes preparing the meal. There were several drawing rooms, large terraces, gardens and a suitable view over the lake and Kandy. Inside were several ultra modern pictures, but how I enjoyed the incongruity of a large fresco painted by George Keyt on the main staircase. He had depicted with gusto the pink, curved backs and fronts of numerous Hindu gods and goddesses at a voluptuous feast. My host was a little doubtful about it and asked my opinion. It certainly did not suit the house and its refined owners although it was essentially Sinhalese.

We were given a large variety of curries wrapped up hot in palm leaves. I tried most of them burning my mouth and making my mouth water. Delicious. Also I consumed as much as I could of the native sweet, jaggery. When you buy it from the little muslem sweet stalls in a round pat you want to go on scrunching it forever. It is a mixture of sugar cane and honey. Whilst everyone was discussing politics, art, religion and philosophy, in an unreal and conventional way, I searched for jaggery but found it cut into unsatisfying small and tasteless cubes. I had come there with Vivien Leigh, as I could not find Ram. Just as we left the hotel I imagined I saw him in tennis clothes drifting about the lounge so I called out to Charles to remind Ram he was expected at the reception. Yet he had not come. There were mutterings of disappointments amongst the ladies in their Paris fashions or glowing saris. We began to watch the door. The party showed signs of ending and no Ram had arrived. Minette de Silva, accustomed to his peculiarities, decided to telephone her house. Yes, he was waiting patiently there for the guests. A car was sent for him and he came in sullen obedience but I have a shrewd idea he meant to sidetrack us and have a quiet relax on his bed.

5

We were ready now for the shooting of the film. This was located, as they say in America, in the English Governor's Residence in Kandy. It is a white Regency building surrounded by flowers, and luckily it was just the moment for every flower to be in bloom. Temple trees with their white blossoms and overpowering scent and other trees blazing with scarlet and mauve blooms. Ram took to tree climbing and swarmed up one of the tallest on which there was a large pink flower nearly a foot wide, crammed with petals and dark crimson stamens. I watched him go from branch to branch that swayed perilously, but he got to the top safely and then slid down the trunk which was adorned with mauve spotted leaves in bunches. 'Here you are. For Frieda,' he said as he threw the flower to me. On the lawn which did not even look the right surrounding for our dancers, the entire film crew were in action, and made the air ring with their raucous commands. Hoot, hoot went their awful apparatus, motor vans churning up the gravel and the flower beds. They erected a platform with cameras that looked like the guns of an invading army. Striding on it was the chief producer, a huge German. In another part of the garden, on a platform of his own, was the make-up man. I suppose he was an artist, but after submitting to his ministrations Ram was unrecognisable. He had practised some of his art on himself, for, failing to grow a little pointed moustache, he had just painted one on his face, which gave him a dandified look in variance with his loose, chintz-like shirt and shorts.

It was very hot and Ram put on a large sunhat over his Shiva costume, for he was going to dance his famous Shiva impersonation with Gopal, who was disguised as the little Elephant God, Ganesha. The sunhat was grotesque, but more so when at intervals the make-up man rushed at Ram with a wet sponge and put it on his back. It was hot for all of them. The girls got blisters on their necks. For hours they stood while the producer from his platform roared: 'Ram das iss wrong – you go left okay,' which meant that Ram had to persuade his bewildered dancers to do the opposite of what they had arranged. After a week's trial the day came for the final pictures. The night before one of the producers said, 'Do try to get Ram up on time. We must begin at six.' So at about 4.30 I

APPENDIX

went along the hotel corridor to Ram's room. Charles was there. 'Mr Gopal getting up?' I inquired. 'He must go to fetch dancers.' 'Master not getting up!' Charles looked anxious. I banged on the door and finally Ram acknowledged me. I got up myself and went to the location. Everyone was there. A bus drove up and out got all the performers – except the dancers. Ram finally sauntered in about 8 am. 'Where are the Kandy dancers?' was the immediate inquiry. Ram seemed to think there was a muddle about the bus to fetch them. Charles was dispatched to find Denny the chauffeur and finally, in a leisurely manner, Ram's car appeared. By that time Ram was seriously engaged in the rehearsal and I, being superfluous, was dispatched to fetch the dancers. Denny drove frantically. I was really frightened as we dashed around narrow corners and barged into groups of pedestrians, bullock wagons and elephants. Arriving at Amunugama, there was the bus and the dancers talking in groups. 'Hurry up. Hurry up,' I said in a Western flurry and, seating themselves very quietly in the bus they drove off. We followed, racing past them in the car. I shepherded them into the garden but in their own time. Here was another difficulty. The film bosses had decided they must wear yellow dresses with red bands, not the white of their national costumes, which does not reproduce well in technicolour. This was handed out to them, each man receiving so many yards of coloured muslin. I don't think they liked it but they calmly went to the veranda of the Governor's house and with these uncut yards they constructed their garments. They folded a length around their waist and tied a piece of string very tightly. With cunning fingers they made the rest into accordion pleats and pushed them under the string quite perfectly. Then they took the yards of red material and, with help from me, they pulled it round and round their waists. I know it was tight because, when I saw what a flap the American staff were in, and the slow pace of the costume making, I had gone to help and, holding the material whilst it was being wound, I had to use all my strength to prevent it being pulled from my hand. 'Ma!' they shouted to me. (I was accepted as 'Ma' and what an honour I felt it to be.) 'Ma, please.' And a smiling face was turned to me for assistance. At last, glittering with their silver headdresses and shoulder pieces and putting on necklaces and earrings, they were ready. I felt sad. It was horrible to see them in orange and red, dancing before an audience which did not understand them. Even beautiful, tall Surambo was dwarfed by the vast film apparatus, his drum silenced by the raucous cries of the producers. But of all the sad waifs of the day the saddest were the three who came from Ganesha's Hindu Temple.

Ram and I used to escape before dinner, or during dinner (time being no object to Ram) and go to this Ganesha's Temple. It is a little one, fitting the little son of Lord Shiva, and is covered with carvings right to the top. It is dark and small inside. The first time we went there we were welcomed by a young priest who spoke English. Ram asked if I would like to have a blessing as it was the right hour when the priest was officiating in the shrine. Of course I said 'yes.' Whilst he was praying we peeped in through a dark cavern at the little Elephant God surrounded by coconut flares. The priest blessed us and we gave him flowers and had bananas and ashes presented to us. We looked at the images of Shiva and his wife Parvati, the father and mother of the Elephant God of Wisdom and at the large clay peacocks that are used to carry the god when he goes in the procession in Kandy. As we went around the shrine I saw a group of about nine gods about two feet high, blackened with oil and sacrificial flares, and was told they were the planets with the sun in the middle, but no one could explain their connection with Ganesha. Ram always coveted every form of benediction and believed in them so, when we were given a coconut and told to throw it on the ground and wish, he instantly threw his down. As I did not seem able to break mine he threw it too and got my wish. The temple drummer was called to meet Ram as an honour. He was very fat and had a big bulging stomach, long hair and a longer beard and all of him was very brown. He was a distinguished yogi, spoke no English and had a very large drum. When he struck it the sound was deep and compelling, a lovely dark brown sound like himself. A younger man played a conch, which had a high silver note, and a third musician played a slender Krishna flute. Ram saw the dramatic possibilities of these three people immediately and he demanded they come to rehearsal and be musicians for his Shiva dance in the film. 'Lovely old man,' he said, 'like the Indian Rajput pictures of a yoga. What a fine tummy!' I knew it was good theatre but I was sure they did not want to do it. I do not think they had ever been out of the Temple. Ram overcame their scruples. When they anointed us with a red sign on our foreheads and hung red and orange garlands round our necks the bargain was concluded. So here they were in the Residency gardens, more lost and unhappy than they would have been in a dense forest. And the profane filming went on. The performers got good money. The girls of Ram's court, the society girls of Colombo, pretty little creatures who were more at home in Western fashions, stood about in rigid postures, while Kandyan women swayed and clapped their hands to beat time for the male dancers. But to fit in was impossible when it was all wrong.

What were the Kandyan dancers doing on the lawn of the Residency without even a palm tree behind them? On that cultivated turf the stamp of their feet was inaudible, but the shouts of Herr Professor, Producer de Film, almost deafening. As for Ram, even his dramatic interlude, heralded by his three solitary temple musicians, seemed shrunk into mediocrity.

The ladies of Colombo, who were supposed to represent his audience, remained statuesque and indifferent. I asked Teresa, who had a college education and came from a smart home, if she realised that Ram was representing Lord Shiva and did she not think, as a great god was supposed to have appeared in the village in the film story, she should somehow express some fear and awe. She replied, fingering her little gold crucifix which dangled on her native sari, 'Who is Shiva?'

6

The next day was Sunday and we all rested. Ram, with his usual car companion Manil, and young Gopal and myself, drove to the famous Peradeniya gardens. It was early and the light was crystal. The spiral trunks of huge palm avenues looked like battalions of giant cones alongside another avenue of straight uniform palms like an army of wooden soldiers. There were dark cork trees, trees with scarlet blossoms, trees with purple leaves, huge fruits lying on the earth, and there was the Shiva lingam flower. This is called by Europeans the cannonball tree because it bears as its fruit an enormous black spherical fruit. It is very heavy and if it falls on your head, plomb, you are bombed. The flower grows without a stalk and sticks straight out of the trunk. It is one of the most beautiful flowers I have ever seen, with heavy creamy petals that shade through every colour of the spectrum. It has in the middle two folded petals like a cup, fringed with golden stamens, and inside them is a lovely little green pistil, like a lingam, the origin of its native name. This large flower does not last. It becomes quite black in a short time. As Ram put it into my hand I was overpowered by its penetrating and aromatic fragrance. We spent some time with the orchids and Ram successfully collected the most remarkable ones – green, yellow, scented and spotted. I was disappointed they were not growing wild but cultivated in a greenhouse. We returned with a car full of flowers, fading as we looked at them, their thick fleshiness forshadowing a hasty decay. One morning I went back to the garden early and saw its true tropical nature. I was almost afraid of the trees and flowers, they seemed about to be transformed into savage animals. Under the dark savage trees lurked huge creepers that descended like twisting snakes to the ground and sprang up to fling themselves over brooks. It was a speckled world of dark holes in bright sunshine. Huge flowers leered at you and trees, rushing out of the hot earth, followed the sun from morning to evening, turning their twisted trunks like dancers. At the moment I fancied I saw creeping shapes under the trees, but it was only dazzling light falling on the unknown vegetation.

As the film crew were finished on Monday the Queen's Hotel was full of portmanteaus. Ram's room echoed with 'Charles, have you packed all my things?'

'Yes, Master.'

'Then what is all this in my cupboard?'

'Yes, Master.'

'Gopal, Denny, Jayana, Milee, Charles.'

'Yes, Master.'

Ram sped to Colombo with the film artists and I went to stay with the parents of Teresa in a grand bungalow outside the main town, as there was no room in the Galle Face Hotel.

I had to wait for a friend from England who had arranged to join me and also I wanted to see Ram off. My hosts were most kind and I met the flower of Colombo society, but, being strangely allergic to social life, all I can remember about it is a lizard who, in spite of the artificial barriers of the existence I was living, made my nights musical with a muffled, whistling murmur and finally lost his balance and fell on me with an alarming soft splodge.

'Goodbye, goodbye!' We all hurried to the airport. 'Thank you, dear Ram, for all your kindness. Goodbye!'

Then, 'How do you do.' My friend arrived just as Ram left, travel stained and weary from her flight from England, but keen on seeing everything at once and very thoroughly. She is a practising Ramakrishna devotee, and a gallant woman, she was determined to cram into our short remaining stay as many Buddhas, temples and ashrams as she could find. I was delighted to see her and we annexed many of Ram's retainers – Charles, Denny and the car – and set out to do Ceylon in style.

7

Before starting on our tour of Ceylon, my friend wanted to call on the swami at the Ramakrishna Ashram in Colombo. I had heard very little about the work and influence of these ashrams, which are numerous in India and Ceylon. They are study centres for a way of life as taught by Ramakrishna and have competent masters (swamis) and disciples. It took us a long time to find the settlement. My friend had been told to bring a gift of yellow flowers with her. Yellow flowers were unobtainable that morning but she finally found a shop with some golden marigolds. I chose a sheaf of arum lilies. They looked sacerdotal to me, but they were not the right colour or symbol as homage to Ramakrishna. Armed with our bouquets we drove hither and thither in Colombo, asking the way. Denny, our chauffeur, was sceptic and disapproved of our religious paperchase. Charles, Uncle Charles, was quite useless of course, though he is a Buddhist and might have been expected to know where the ashram was. We found it at last, a modern bungalow and indistinguishable from the surrounding villas.

The front door opened on a yellow beach dotted with palms and beyond was the deep blue sea, whose colour in the morning sunshine made me think of precious stones. 'Sapphires, amethysts, beryls, emeralds,' I murmured to my friend. Shyly she asked for the head swami to whom she had an introduction.

We were admitted at once. He came to greet us in a yellow robe. His head was shaven. My friend presented her flowers and bowed very low. I copied her exactly. The swami took us into the temple, where my friend bowed again before the pictures of Rama and Buddha. I was not sure what was expected of me, so I made a few bobs around the room. As a beginner I was left to a lay brother, who was slightly bemused by my gyrations. He spoke good English, so I tried to find out what sort of religion this was. I received no coherent reply. How could he explain in a few sentences? So I asked him if he could tell me how to concentrate. 'What do you do?' he said gently.

'Paint, rather indifferently,' I replied.

'Don't you concentrate when you paint?' he asked quietly.

'Of course, I can't do it at all if I don't,' I replied.

'Well then you can concentrate. Go on painting.'

APPENDIX

This was a good commonsense answer, combined with shrewd sympathy. I wanted to ask more but my friend, who had been having a less productive interview with the head swami, called me to say goodbye to him. Our adieux were interlaced with more bows and salutations.

It was really obtuse of me not to charm the head of the ashram on the first meeting. I thought he was a disciplinarian, possibly a politician, but I was wrong. At the end of the month I decided to call on him by myself. This time he greeted me with smiles and was not at all aloof. I was hoping he would tell me the way to the shrine of Bhagavan Ramana Maharshi outside Madras. The swami, although sympathetic, was not encouraging. He said, 'Lady must not go to India alone.' I insisted, 'I must go alone, I want to see India and I have no one to go with.' He shook his head sadly, 'It is not safe.' Just then a taxi drove up and another yellow robed dignitary stepped out. He was drawn into our conversation. 'The Lady must not go alone,' he repeated. Luckily his colleague did not agree, and together they arranged for letters and telegrams to be sent all over India to ask them to look after 'Lady travelling alone.'

I was much touched by their concern for a lone female, although I was relapsing into usual dreamy state of relying on someone to look after me. I did not appreciate that for them this was a way of putting into practise Ramakrishna's teaching to show kindness and love to every creature. Not approving of our inquiries, Denny hurried us away from Colombo. We had arranged to go to a river where elephants were taking their mid-day bath. The bathing was fun with the elephants tearing up trees and using them as huge toys to play with. One of them was enticed out of the water and enticed to do circus tricks. He balanced himself halfway up a tree and then lay down when he was told, front legs first, back legs later, looking slyly at me all the time as if to say 'What awful rot!'

I was induced to climb on his back, a long way up and with nothing to cling to but his collar. He rose slowly but then mercifully decided against moving and subsided slowly, allowing me to slide off. My friend was having a debauch with her camera but because of its small size and the closeness of the elephants I am afraid none came out. Charles, who was on sentry duty, told me that one of the elephants had gone on strike a few days before. He had been given more than his share of trees to carry but had refused to be sweated. To the alarm of the villagers he stampeded. There was an old beggar sitting in the road right in the way of the huge animal's progress. The elephant seized him with his trunk and was about to trample the poor man to death. 'Allah, Brahma,' prayed the wretch in terror, picking an assortment of gods to save him. Then he screamed louder, 'Ganesha, Ganapatim, Gajananam!' The elephant released him and then rushed on, creating havoc wherever he went. We saw him later, carrying trees. Denny swerved to the side of the road to let him pass. An elephant which has stampeded is respected even by hardened chauffeurs.

8

When we reached the mountains behind Kandy, driving up very rough roads, we found the bungalow used by the film company, actually a dummy, empty inside. I knew Vivien Leigh had been riding round it on a white horse with other actors for over three weeks. I pitied her, for the ground was very rocky. A stockade was being put up, and on the ridges there were elephants everywhere. The plan was that the elephants were to stampede and destroy the bungalow, which was to be set on fire. We took up our positions well out of the way of the marauding elephants. They were quiet enough, and their legs amongst the palms looked like animated tree trunks. But their mahouts seemed a bit anxious.

The cameras were up and the familiar American voice echoed in the glen. 'Now then, we're ready.' The elephants did not move, but there was some ominous trumpeting. We retreated to a safer viewpoint. Sticks were brandished and fires lighted by the intrepid Yanks. About forty elephants advanced very cautiously, with winking eyes and waving trunks. They flapped their ears and again the earth resounded with their trumpeting. They reached the stockade and very slowly and delicately they picked it to pieces and walked calmly through. Nothing could be done. They could not be goaded into action. After a consultation, it was decided to shoot this scene at the studios in Hollywood. I was impressed by the mammoths' quiet victory over the film invasion and, after we had commiserated with our friends the photographers, we said goodbye to film life and drove on to Sigiriya. This is a hill with a black rock at the top, like a cube, and looks very ominous.

As we had had a good lunch at the hotel, I decided to lie on the grass and let my friend visit the temples and climb the rickety staircase, which is suspended almost in midair, to reach the caves at the summit.

It was peaceful there, watching the pilgrims and sightseers wind upwards on the circling paths of the rock, until Charles disturbed me. He had decided it was necessary to protect me against snakes, which was one of his useless preoccupations, but this time he found a poor little black snake and drove it into its hole with such ferocity that I had to protect it.

Down came my friend with her hands full of the lovely reproductions of the mural paintings she had seen. Then I regretted my laziness, for the paintings must have been unique. In 477 AD King Kassapa had retreated with his court to that black Sigiriya and up that rock must have climbed many artists, whose technique had the subtlety of Persian paintings combined with the sexuality of the Hindus, and on the walls of the caves they painted the ladies and courtesans of the King. They are undamaged. The portraits are of lovely women and full of tempting seductiveness.

We did not want to stay in Sigiriya long enough for me to attempt to toil up the rock. We were surrounded by guides chattering and mobbing us and we wished to avoid the polite company of the Sinhalese sightseers. So we decided to try driving up the unexplored side roads, and poor Denny lost his way. We also made Charles buy the native delicacy of cold curry wrapped in a palm leaf, and we devoured this in clearings in the jungle which were very prickly and uncomfortable, but we felt freer than at the roadhouses we passed occasionally. I don't think Charles knew what to buy for us; I had to make him get that coarse perfect jaggery, which we ate in chunks. He was distrustful of it as unsuitable for us, but when we insisted on the native intoxicant, arak, it was a very rigid Charles who had to buy it for us, and hovered near us in case we fell in a drunken heap. His religion taught him to loathe all alcoholic liquors.

But Charles was developing. I don't think he had ever minded two ladies before. Our clothes were a mystery, especially my friend, who had many boxes and was very particular. He packed and unpacked for us both, and insisted on taking everything out of our boxes whenever we stopped. My lip-salve was generally packed in one shoe, with my toothbrush in the other. He stood outside our room at attention, and was very shocked by us. He wore a soldier's white coat and he was very serious and inattentive. 'Charles, bring tea.' He would depart at once and never bring it. But he never deserted us and we trusted him, even with our money. I slapped him if he displeased me, he was such a sweet, useless old thing.

I was getting impatient. This was just like a Cook's Tour. My friend visited every famous place, read it all up in a guidebook, and often had a learned Sinhalese from the local Architectural Association to show her around. But when we went on to Polonnaruva it was worth all the effort. We arrived at the guest house to find it ramshackle but imposing. It had the largest bedrooms I had ever seen. It was like going to bed in a church with bathrooms attached and private balconies. 'Splendid,' we cried as we imagined sitting out in the moonlight and looking over the 'bund', really a reservoir, at the primeval forest on the other side.

'But you can't sit out. There are mosquitoes, and after one bite you'll be under the net.' Charles unpacked and lost our things in the colossal cupboards. We were very excited; we knew there was a famous Buddha cut out of the rock. In the midst of all these enchanting distractions, I had begun to think of embarking on my task of finding a satisfactory god. Already my appetite had been whetted by the strange rights of the Kandyan dancers, and the Ganesha temple I visited with Ram. I had seen some of these long, recumbent Buddhas outside Colombo which was so much admired by the Russian philosopher Ouspensky. He claimed that the sight of this remarkable figure had thrown him into a samadhi, or trance.

Hoping I would have the same experience I had persuaded Ram to take me to see it before he left Ceylon. It was constructed, I found, according to all the rules of Hindu proportions, painstakingly painted. The eyes, made of sapphires, were unexpectedly open. To reach it we were obliged to cross stone courtyards, hot from the burning sun. We were glad to reach the solemn shadows of the calm shrines in the temple and reach the cool sacred presence of the Buddha. I watched with envy the reverence of my companions and the attentive face of Ram Gopal and his friends, but I do not like distempered statues and no thrill overcame me.

So far the Buddhas had been a disappointment to me. But here in Polonnaruva, this Buddha was different. He was not painted but cut right out of the rock in which he lay. He is described as 'a recumbent Buddha, 44ft in length, carved on the vertical face of a rock boulder. There is also another figure, 22ft high, beside him, popularly supposed to be Ananda, the disciple sorrowing over the death of his beloved Lord, and yet another seated image, slightly smaller. A fourth Buddha is inside a Shrine and attended by various deities.' As I had enjoyed the eulogies in the book, I looked forward to seeing this Buddha.

We sauntered up the valley, and suddenly there was the great statue. A Buddha who would fructify the faith of any worshipper. It belongs to the rock; a long, long figure, grey and peaceful, so peaceful that a silence descends on those who look at him. Questions such as 'what am I looking for?' rose up in my mind, and the stillness round him left them unanswered. The sorrowing, or watching disciple, touched by Buddha with his golden fingers in the legend, breathed the same peace. Untrammelled by the world. Escaped! The shrine must have been carved by a loving believer and although as the guidebook says, 'Buddha was attended by various deities', yet the same calm aloofness was inherent in that figure too. The fourth figure, cut out of the golden rock of another cliff, is 'contemplation in beatitude.'

We sat silent for some time and would have sat longer had there not arrived a charabanc full of cheerful sightseers. They drove away the only human we had seen, a very small boy with a dirty bag of sweets, who under the loving influence of the divine statue, had offered to share them with us. We decided to come back that night, this time with Charles. He amazed me for he burst into tears. 'What is it, Charles? What's the matter?' He went on mumbling his prayers, bowing low, first to one Buddha, then to another, and finally flung himself at the feet of the recumbent one and remained prostrate. I ventured near. 'What happened, Charles?'

'Lady doesn't understand. Bad spirits here at night. And snakes,' he replied.

We looked around carefully and selected moonlit stones to sit on. Not a sound except Charles' muffled prayers and the blue trees sighing against the starry sky. At last I broke the silence. 'It's all very well, this contemplation of the mind, but how does it help you to endure the daily trials of life?'

My friend replied, 'It could teach you to extract omnipresence or the substance of mind from our trivial existence.'

The lake at Polonnaruva is quite beautiful and very large. Opposite the rest house and about two miles across the lake is the jungle, but for a long way along the edge there is a good road. The head waiter, dark faced and very learned looking, took us to see the wild birds. They were hard to see, and I missed the smaller ones, but I saw the white herons flying against the setting sun, and the kingfishers and cormorants. There was also a dark mass floating in the water.

'Crocodiles,' said our waiter.

We had arranged to go in a catamaran across to the forest, in spite of the tropical rain and the dark mass. The catamaran was a burnt out tree trunk with a balancing log attached.

Our vessel was ready at the foot of some steep stones and a boy like a bronze statue in charge. Charles was there to help. He removed my friend's shoes as she stepped into the boat and took her umbrella and placed it in a safe place onshore. Not receiving my share of attention, I tumbled into the craft with my mackintosh on and gripping my umbrella, which had become my treasure since I bought it second-hand and cheap in the bazaar at Kandy. (It was probably stolen from a monk for there is never a yellow robe without an umbrella.) The catamaran was pushed off with Charles clucking on the bank. 'Ladies never go out in catamaran', he complained, 'but of course, English Ladies…'

The bronze statue propelled the log very slowly. Luckily the 'dark mass' had disappeared. My friend was lamenting the loss of her shoes. Why had Charles taken them? To keep them dry, I suggested, for it was very wet in the log.

We reached the opposite bank and got out. The bronze statue had no English, so we could not explain ourselves. We started along the edge of the forest, but the wicked Charles had foreseen this. My friend could not totter a yard. The beach was covered with sharp stones and some kind of thistle. We tried, imagining we would see elephants, tigers and snakes in the forest – a whole zoo rampant. But we had to give in and signal to the bronze statue to return. In due course, a very long course, he understood and we pushed off. The rain began to fall and there was thunder and lightning. The log began to fill with water. It wobbled alarmingly. The bronze statue was paddling but making no progress. All my training on the Thames came into action. I seized the paddle and, standing in my cellophane mackintosh, I rowed and paddled across the lake, across the dark mass, to the far bank. 'Well rowed, Oxford,' shouted my friend who found my mackintoshed rear view, ballooning as I sweated and strained, worth the risk of crocodiles or drowning.

The bronze statue – never a word said he. And though the Sinhalese smart set leaned over their verandas to watch our ignoble arrival, swarming up the rocks, wet through and bare footed, neither they nor the bronze statue held out a helping hand. And Charles had disappeared.

It was a queer mixture, this Polonnaruva. Under the tree just outside the rest house was a dead cow, and it was hot, thundery weather. 'Why don't they bury it, or take it away?' I asked. 'Only the outcasts can touch it,' was the reply. I hope they hurry, I thought, realising it would be useless to order Danny or Charles to remove the decaying beast. They would be horrified at the contamination. By night there was a great barking and growling around the carcass, and I could see numerous dogs fighting and wolfing lumps of flesh. It was horrible. I tried never to look again, and kept a sharp lookout for bluebottles and mosquitoes.

The jungle was sometimes unpleasantly close. Sudden glimpses on the road. Large grey monkeys swinging across the path, green parakeets in hedges that looked like Surrey, jackals skulking and buffaloes in the marshes. These unexpected encounters were always a surprise. Inside the car we were guarded by our two retainers. I never found out where they slept at night, or ate or to where they disappeared. We paid the daily five rupees, about five shillings.

Danny was a cynical, atheistic mechanic, who had acquired our civilisation and was quite ruthless but cleverer than Charles, and aware of the limits of our exchequer. You couldn't trust him but he kept us out of trouble and, because he idolised Ram, he tried not to fleece us for more than was necessary for his amour-propre as a servant in the East.

9

The smell of the decaying cow followed us out of Polonnaruva and into Anuradhapura. As we reached this very ancient city we came through a park, at least it looked like a park. The large cassis and bo trees looked as if they had been planted specially to throw dark, tropical shadows on the grass.

Looking more closely, we saw they were covered with troops of monkeys. Of course we stopped and out came the camera. But you can't snap a monkey. He is in the trees before the lens can pop and he is a more distant tree, gibbering and grinning at you. In despair we drove on and in front of the hotel I was interested to see a tree that looked half-eaten by some pest. Instead of leaves, it had bunches of monkeys hanging on it – pa, ma and the baby who was carefully put by his parents on the furthest branch from the ground. We gave them some of our afternoon tea but they were shy and snatched at the fragments thrown on the ground.

The head boy told us they were going to drive them out in a few days or there would be no garden left. I don't know how they do that, but imagine a forlorn little family party swinging from tree to tree until joining the company swinging about in the park outside the city. My friend dug out an architectural intelligentsia whilst Charles and I untangled our luggage and found our rooms. We never appropriated any particular room in the hotel, the guests constantly moving from one room to another, Charles packing and unpacking and carrying clothes about on clothes hangers. It didn't matter, I found a bed and slept in it.

Among the guests at lunch was a party of noisy men and girls. The men were in shorts and those atrocious floral shirts, making them look like freshly upholstered early Victorian cretonne sofas. I noticed two of the men were identical. 'Look,' I whispered. 'Which is which?'

'I have no idea,' said my friend. Whether it was our covert staring, or that we were constantly calling for Charles, they started to take an interest in us.

'Charles,' they mimicked, 'fetch us a newspaper.'

'Yes, Master,' replied Charles automatically. But they did not know dear old Charles and of course they did not get it. At dinner we had a look at the rowdy Americans and were amazed to see the twins still dressed exactly the same, but in clerical black coats with reversed collars. My curiosity had to be satisfied. 'Gentleman American Baptist missionaries,' I was told by the hotel manager, 'They come to visit their missions and to teach us. They are twins.' There was no humorous twinkle, only resignation in his dark eyes. Poor Ceylon, twin Baptist ministers causing havoc amongst the innocent workers in the paddy fields. What do they make of total immersion? A very strange God and therefore to be worshipped along with Lord Shiva and the marvels of mechanical inventions.

When I asked Charles about religion, I found he had an objection to Roman Catholics. 'Why, Charles?' I asked.

'All tell lies,' he replied.

That was a curious complaint from any Oriental, who always lies for politeness and a sense of the poetry of living. I insisted further. 'What lies, Charles?'

He muttered fiercely, 'Take Lady mother Parvati, call her Mary, say she have son, no father. Not true!'

So he objected to the virgin birth. Deep in his blood is hidden the drumming of those Kandyan dancers. He believes lust is holy and birth is natural. Interested, I watched him serving and deceiving us, entirely without conscience, and when he insisted in washing my feet himself when I had done a barefoot circuit of the temples, he did it without self-righteousness or a sense of duty.

In the morning my friend had already visited shrines with her chosen guide, and now she fetched me. It was very hot and sunny but it was too early for the car so we walked. We saw a palace but it was, as all the palaces in Anuradhapura, a ruin. Red pieces of masonry and some broken statues.

After getting soaked in a sudden tropical downpour, we returned to the hotel to change and have breakfast before setting out again in the car. Driving through the park, we came upon an armless Buddha. He was carved with great simplicity, and his figure dominated the shadows and green light surrounding him.

We stopped to look at him, and I made a rough sketch. His proportions were quite perfect and he had a curious fleshy quality to his limbs, though he was cut roughly out of cold grey stone.

My friend examined him closely and from the few symbols she found on him, told me he was a Jain Buddha. I remembered they were opposed to decoration, and her deductions were corroborated in a few minutes by our coming across the remains of a Jain monastery. They were very faint remains, and I was not bothering with them when she called me. These Jain monks must have been humorists. There, completely intact, was their stone pissoir, just like a horrible French standing one. It was elaborately carved with semi-reliefs of all the Hindu gods and was a charming example of the transmigration of religious intolerance into a dirty joke.

We drove to the famous bo tree at Mahavihara. You approach it through a temple gate, past little shabby booths where you are pestered to buy flowers. Temple trees, with their scented white blossoms and dark green leaves are dotted about the dusty courtyard. You look into various shrines of sitting (perhaps it is more respectful to be seated) Buddhas, always with clean distemper wash over them, which makes them look tawdry.

I think it was here we saw a terrace supported by hundreds of elephants, also distempered. 'Quite modern,' we thought, but the guide corrected us. 'Two thousand years old, Ladies.' Charles paid the fee and we were admitted through an iron gate to the back of the main temple. Without our shoes we respectfully advanced towards the tree. This is the original tree they tell us, under which Lord Buddha meditated and became conscious of the reality and omnipresence of Brahma, and the uselessness of forms and rituals. Here, protected from the sun's rays by the holy tree, he taught the religion of compassion which has illuminated the world ever since. Blessed be his name.

I do not think this can be the original tree. It looks like boughs coming out of the earth. It must have been much higher. But if it is not, it is from the same stock. It has a heart-shaped leaf and is covered with floating coloured ribbons. The pilgrims leave them as tokens of their worship, and the iron palings in front are festooned in the same way. It looks as if someone was trying to frighten away marauding birds, but the ribbons embody the prayers of the faithful.

Plenty of priests in yellow robes and with black umbrellas were walking to and fro, accepting money, but, in spite of the sacred associations of the hallowed tree, I missed the pagan fleshy warmth of the idolatrous Hindu shrines.

10

I was becoming exhausted by all this endless driving about in Ceylon. It was interesting whilst I was with Ram Gopal as he made everything come alive around him, but we were degenerating into a couple of 'umph-to-umph' sightseers.

Also the modern Sinhalese society was impinging on my sacred search. I could not help feeling they were bores who had borrowed our Western estimate of right and wrong. They had copied our schools, our clothes and, alas, our food – and our negation. 'Thou shalt not.' It probably means that the Buddhist religion has declined into a ritual of laws not worship, for it is very old. But I had hoped to meet contemplative monks and holy fakirs. Possibly they did exist, but drive where we might in Ceylon, we did not meet them. I must not include the Ramakrishna Ashrams, about whose activities and sanctities I was totally ignorant. Still, I found this wholesale transplantation of the standards of Bath and Brighton rather shameful and disfiguring to this wonderful island.

The awful decency of suburban living will eventually choke these dear people, strip off their beautiful clothes, drive out the Kandyan dancers and the life of men who illogically worship their gods with gaiety and licence and smile with friendliness and joy. I fear they will be submerged, rationed and educated until, like us, poor idiots, they will spend their lives filling up forms and have no sense of delight and ecstasy.

The Buddhists do not drink, so perhaps they may manage to remain beautiful for a few more generations, but already they are sure that they know what is wrong with their limiting narrowness.

And, if those magnificent flowers and trees on the island are infected with the same restrictions, I will not be able to sense a mysterious hidden presence in the jungle. The boisterous flowers will no longer flame on the top of tall, dark trees and the temple flowers will stop filling the air with fragrance all the year. They will be boxed in a greenhouse or in conventional gardens, to be visited on bank holidays or Sundays by a crowd of picnickers.

However it was with real reluctance that we eventually left Anuradhapura and beautiful Mihintale with its perched temples and terraces and mountains covered with yellow and pink flowering trees.

We needed a rest and decided to stay with Ram's friends, Minette de Silva and her mother. So it was time to part with Denny and dear old Uncle Charles, for we could not take our Sinhalese servants to India with us. It was a wrench to our pockets and our affections and I have missed them both, particularly Uncle Charles, who was indispensable to me as an amusing nuisance.

11

The de Silvas lived at the top of a very steep hill in Kandy. The drive winds round and round and at night it is too dark and is insurmountable except by the fleetest of cars. I tried walking out at night but it was dangerous.

The bungalow has a terrace with a garden, and inside there are many bedrooms, a very large kitchen, an architect's office for Minette, and weaving looms for making native materials – mats, etc. for the de Silvas are ardent believers in keeping the home fires burning, so they support Sinhalese homespuns and homemade sweets.

Minette is very busy and goes all day to Colombo about the houses she is designing. In fact she is very capable and superior in her wonderful saris. She told me she possesses forty-two saris, all different. I saw them flaming with every colour, in rich profusion in her wardrobe.

In the house are books on Picasso and Corbusier, under whom she has studied, but happily there also peep from the walls crude, bold pictures by George Keyt, that explode the convention of fashionable French art. Mrs de Silva is a complete individual. Her husband was a distinguished politician but, since his death, she has removed herself from the local wrangles and does exactly what she likes and knows exactly what she wants. She is a marvellous cook and many a stomach-ache I got while staying with her, for we had curry for breakfast, lunch and dinner, and always a different one.

And I am greedy and decided to perish rather than miss one of her tasty meals. But as usual it is the servants or the animals that interest me most in a strange land. The animals were a biting dog which had a good nip at my surprised friend, who believes dogs like her, and mosquitoes. These were very busy. At night I was plastered with every antidote and cowered under the only net in the house. But they were there and my friend, who thought she was immune, had several rude awakenings and sleepless nights. It was getting very hot and the windows were covered with creepers. I don't think the poor insects ever got out. There was also a drought in Kandy, and although there were majestic guests' bathrooms, we had to be content with a brass bowl of hot water which we had to pour over ourselves native fashion. I never managed it, but my friend was adept.

I found the cabinet a bit difficult. It had two doors and a window. The doors were never both locked, so it acted as a passage or a cul-de-sac, and from the rustlings in the creepers that festooned the windows, I discovered the gardener or the chauffeur was always looking in. One morning I heard Mrs de Silva calling for help. She was in the garden and had seen a very large green snake. Large and beautiful, but not poisonous. Out ran the maid. She was old, but I shall never forget her. Her hair was grey and very smooth, her thin body was yellow-brown. She wore a dark blue sari with heavy gold necklaces, enormous gold earrings and a nose ornament, and a red caste mark on her brow. How beautiful she was. She carried the trunk of a large palm and moved swiftly on the snake, banging the palm on the ground. The snake escaped and Mrs de Silva returned to her meditation on the veranda.

At night, one was aroused by the watchman. He walked around the house all night and occasionally fired off his gun. They were afraid of burglars or brigands on their lonely hill.

I saw him once, a little meek man with a great curiosity about my nocturnal movements. Several nights when I was up late because of the mosquitoes or writing letters, he quickly opened the door and turned off the light. I had no Tamil, so I could not explain, but when, fumbling, I turned it on again, in he popped and out went the light. This became a bewildering game in which I unwillingly participated.

The de Silvas were more than kind to strangers. But, as my urge for India was insistent and I could not move my friend (she wanted to shop) I decided to go on alone.

So I said goodbye to all my kind friends, took the wonderful train journey through the mountains to Colombo, intent on my tickets, my money and my departure. The polite society of the Sinhalese and my English mania for sanitation and cleanliness had frightened me away from many adventures. I still regret the bungalow George Keyt offered me in the palm trees and jungle of Amunugama, which was full of books, mosquitoes and rascally retainers, but its rudimentary drainage alarmed me.

I might have learned to paint better watching George, the primitive rice pickers and the Kandyan dancers. But in spite of these lost opportunities, I did have my quota of fun beyond my wildest imagination.

And now for India and my search in the temples for a god.

Bibliography

Author unknown, *Waimahoe: The Old House,* The Turnbull Library NL Elder, New Zealand, 1910

Harris, Sir Jack *Memoirs of a Century,* Steele Roberts, Wellington, 2007

Harris, Sir Percy *Forty Years in and out of Parliament,* Andrew Melrose Ltd, London, 1947

King, Michael *The Penguin History of New Zealand,* Penguin Books, Rosedale, New Zealand, 2003

Nathan, Lawrence D *As Old as Auckland,* LD Nathan Group of Companies, Auckland, 1984

Symonds, John *The King of the Shadow Realm,* Gerald Duckworth & Co, London, 1989